Platonopolis

Platonopolis

Platonic Political Philosophy in Late Antiquity

Dominic J. O'Meara

CLARENDON PRESS · OXFORD

*This book has been printed digitally and produced in a standard specification
in order to ensure its continuing availability*

OXFORD
UNIVERSITY PRESS

Great Clarendon Street, Oxford OX2 6DP

Oxford University Press is a department of the University of Oxford.
It furthers the University's objective of excellence in research, scholarship,
and education by publishing worldwide in

Oxford New York

Auckland Cape Town Dar es Salaam Hong Kong Karachi
Kuala Lumpur Madrid Melbourne Mexico City Nairobi
New Delhi Shanghai Taipei Toronto
With offices in
Argentina Austria Brazil Chile Czech Republic France Greece
Guatemala Hungary Italy Japan South Korea Poland Portugal
Singapore Switzerland Thailand Turkey Ukraine Vietnam

Oxford is a registered trade mark of Oxford University Press
in the UK and in certain other countries

Published in the United States
by Oxford University Press Inc., New York

Oxford is a registered trade mark of Oxford University Press
in the UK and in certain other countries

Published in the United States
by Oxford University Press Inc., New York

ISBN 0-19-925758-2

for Alix

Preface

In an earlier book (*Pythagoras Revived*, 1989), I proposed taking a theme in the legend of Pythagoras, Pythagoras as a mathematizing philosopher, as a way of examining the development of Platonic philosophy in the late Roman Empire, between the third and the sixth centuries AD. The late antique philosopher was also aware of another theme in the Pythagoras legend, Pythagoras as political thinker, as legislator and reformer of cities. In the present work, a sister to the earlier book, this second theme is taken up (indeed the two themes, mathematical and political, are linked, as it will turn out), in the context of an attempt to reconstruct the political philosophy of the late antique Platonist.

For reasons which will be discussed below in Chapter 1, this is the first reconstruction of this kind to be undertaken. My purpose in consequence has been to make a sketch of the main contours of the subject. I have adopted for this purpose a thematic approach, dealing with a range of subjects in political philosophy, rather than a chronological method which would have attempted to track in detail the evolution of ideas throughout the period. However, within the thematic framework I have tried to note some major developments in the history of the ideas which I explore. It is my hope that the book might serve as a provisional chart of a largely unexplored field of research, an outline to be filled and corrected by further detailed investigation.

The ambition of this book is limited furthermore in that it is concerned with the reconstruction of philosophical *theories*; in general no attempt is made to demonstrate that these theories did or did not influence historical events. Whether or not one believes that philosophical ideas actually matter in the course of human history, it is at least necessary to be reasonably clear first about these ideas, before the question of their historical impact can be examined.

The matter presented here was first proposed in a lecture course at the Université de Fribourg, in a seminar at the École Normale Supérieure (Paris) and in various lectures given in Washington, D.C., Dublin, Liverpool, Oxford, Paris, Lausanne, Neuchâtel, Pavia, Thessaloniki, and Würzburg, which produced generous suggestions and criticisms which have been of great assistance. I am also very grateful to John J. O'Meara, Henri-Dominique Saffrey, Ilsetraut and Pierre Hadot, and Oxford University Press's readers for detailed criticism. Completion of the book was made possible by a sabbatical leave from the Université de Fribourg, with the support of the Prince Franz Joseph II of Lichtenstein Prize and with help provided by Valérie Cordonier and Marlis Colloud-Streit.

D.J.O'M.

Fribourg, Switzerland
May 2002

Contents

Contents

Abbreviations

ANRW *Aufstieg und Niedergang der römischen Welt*, ed. W. Haase and
H. Temporini (Berlin, 1972—)

CAG *Commentaria in Aristotelem Graeca* (Berlin, 1870—)

DPA *Dictionnaire des philosophes antiques*, ed. R. Goulet (Paris, 1989—)

PLRE A. Jones, J. Martindale, J. Morris, *The Prosopography of the Later
Roman Empire*, i: AD 260–395; ii: AD 395–527 (Cambridge, 1971–80)

PR D. O'Meara, *Pythagoras Revived. Mathematics and Philosophy in Late
Antiquity* (Oxford, 1989)

PT H. Thesleff, *The Pythagorean Texts of the Hellenistic Period* (Åbo, 1965)

RE Pauly, Wissowa, Kroll, *Realencyclopädie der klassischen Altertum-
swissenschaft*

SVF *Stoicorum Veterum Fragmenta*, ed. H. von Arnim (Leipzig, 1905–24)

Ancient authors are usually cited by book, chapter, and/or section number, as given in the editions listed in the first part of the Bibliography. In cases where I give the volume, page, and line number of the edition, this is indicated by a reference to 'p.' (e.g. Proclus, *In Remp.* I, p. 110, 1 = vol. I, page 110, line 1 of Kroll's edition; but Proclus, *Theol. Plat.* I, 4 = book I, chapter 4 of the *Theol. Plat.*). The authors of published translations which I quote (and sometimes slightly modify) are named only in the first quotation and can be found in the Bibliography (first or second part). Other translations are mine.

Introduction

The Two Functions of Political Philosophy

1

1. The Conventional View

It is the conventional view that the Platonist philosophers of Late Antiquity had no political philosophy. It is believed that this is so because these philosophers[1] appear to have taken little interest in the affairs of this world, in practical life, in social questions. On the contrary, their interest lies elsewhere, in another world, an immaterial world outside time and space which, in their view, is our true 'homeland', where we can at last attain the good that we desire. For these philosophers, 'we' are our soul, not the entity arising from the relation between soul and body. The relation to body is, if anything, a handicap, an obstacle, a danger to the soul in her search for a life that will really satisfy her. Implication, therefore, in the affairs of the body—and this means implication in social and political life to the extent that this life is connected to the necessities of the body—is to be minimized and transcended as far as possible. It is philosophy's task to liberate the soul, to provide her with the means for reaching a higher plane of existence where she will find the perfection of life that she seeks. Since this perfection of life can be described as 'divine', 'godlike', the purpose of philosophy can be defined as the divinization of man, the 'assimilation of man to god as far as possible'—words of Plato's *Theaetetus* (176b) which the Neoplatonists made their motto. In this connection, an interest in political questions can only be a distraction. The very purpose and spirit of Neoplatonic philosophy therefore appear to exclude political thought: there is no Neoplatonic political philosophy because there *can* be none.

---

[1] Known in modern studies as 'Neoplatonists', i.e. Platonists inspired by Plotinus (205–70), as distinguished from the members of Plato's own school and from Platonists of the Roman imperial period preceding Plotinus ('Middle Platonists'). These modern classifications are not entirely satisfactory, breaking as they do the strong continuity linking 'Middle Platonism' and 'Neoplatonism'. Historically speaking, it would be better to refer simply to 'Platonists'. For purposes of convenience, however, I will refer to 'Neoplatonists'.

The belief that the goal of Neoplatonic philosophy *in principle* excludes interest in political philosophy is confirmed, it would appear, by various facts. In particular we are told that Plotinus encouraged friends and pupils to withhold themselves from political life:

> Another of his [Plotinus'] companions was Zethus, an Arab by race. . . a close friend of Plotinus, a politician with political leanings whom Plotinus would try to curb.[2]

Perhaps a clearer example is that of

> Rogatianus, a senator, who advanced so far in renunciation of this life that he gave up all his property, dismissed all his servants, and resigned his rank. When he was on the point of appearing in public as praetor and the lictors were already there, he refused to appear or have anything to do with the office. . . Plotinus regarded him with great favour and praised him highly, and frequently held him up as an example to all who practised philosophy.[3]

Indeed Plotinus in his works recommends that the sage put aside political ambitions.[4]

To these instances of withdrawal from political affairs can be added the further point that the Neoplatonists seem not to have produced works of political philosophy comparable to the *Republic* and *Laws* of Plato and the *Politics* of Aristotle, a further confirmation, it seems, of the opinion that the otherworldly goal of Neoplatonism is such as to exclude any interest in political philosophy. In short, one could describe not only Plotinus, but also Neoplatonism in general, as 'Plato by half', that is a 'Plato without politics', a 'Plato without Socrates'.[5]

A consequence of the conventional view that I have just summarized is that no systematic study of Neoplatonic political philosophy has been attempted.[6] Nor does Neoplatonism appear in any significant way in the standard histories of political philosophy. If we are to believe these histories, Neoplatonic philosophy is largely silent: the monarchic ideologies of the Hellenistic and Roman periods are followed by the theocratic and

---

[2] Porphyry, *Vit. Plot.* 7, 17–21 (trans. Armstrong modified). We notice a little later in Porphyry's report that there is no suggestion that Zethus actually gave up his political career (7, 28–9).

[3] Porphyry, *Vit. Plot.* 7, 31–46.

[4] *Enn.* I 4, 14, 20: he will 'put away authority and office'.

[5] W. Theiler coined the phrase 'Plato dimidiatus' (1960: 67); cf. Bröcker (1966), Hathaway (1969a).

[6] There have been some dissident voices and suggestions to the contrary, but no comprehensive theoretical enquiry; cf., for example, Jerphagnon (1981). Schall (1985), while accepting the conventional view, finds Plotinus relevant for political philosophy, basing this claim however on very vague and misleading generalizations about Plotinus. Ehrhardt (1953) is perhaps the most important dissident voice: he collects useful material and makes some important points to which I will refer later in this book.

anti-theocratic programmes of Christian theologians (Eusebius of Caesarea and Augustine) and by the monarchic ideas of some late antique pagans, one of them, Themistius, not belonging it seems to mainstream Neoplatonism, another, Julian, an emperor, not a professional philosopher.[7] This silence of the Neoplatonic philosophers is only really broken by their immediate heirs in the early Islamic world, where, unexpectedly, Plato's political works and Platonic political philosophy assume considerable importance.

It is the purpose of this book to argue against the conventional view. The theoretical principle that the goal of Neoplatonism, the divinization[8] of man, necessarily excludes political philosophy will be examined more closely. It will be shown that the process of divinization, as the Neoplatonists understood it, far from excluding political life, actually includes it. Reflection on the function of political life in the divinization of man inspired a political theory the main lines of which I will attempt to trace. What is involved is the recovery of philosophical theory, the 'reconstruction' of a theoretical structure which, because of the conventional view, has remained largely invisible to the modern reader.

Once the relationship between divinization and political life is more adequately understood, a more appropriate context becomes available for the interpretation of relevant facts, such as the instances of withdrawal from political life mentioned above. In particular, this context will permit the assembly of a considerable library of Neoplatonic political philosophy. Although this library is for the most part lost, some of its contents has survived: these works are there, if we know how to recognize and read them.

2. Preliminary Definition of 'Political Philosophy'

Late antique philosophers who withdrew from political involvement could appeal to illustrious predecessors. There is above all the example of Socrates, who explains as follows (in Plato's account) his idiosyncratic behaviour to the court that was to condemn him:

[7] Cf. for example Sinclair (1951), Dvornik (1966). This is not to say that much useful information cannot be gleaned from these works, in particular from Dvornik. Dvornik summarizes the political thought, for example, of Julian, Synesius, and the anonymous dialogue *On Political Science*, without however taking their Neoplatonism seriously. On Themistius see App. I below.

[8] I will use the term 'divinization' as shorthand for 'the assimilation of man to god'; it will be seen below that there can be various kinds, or rather degrees, of assimilation to the divine.

It began in my early childhood—a sort of voice which comes to me. . . It is this that debars me from entering public life, and a very good thing too, in my opinion; because you may be quite sure, gentlemen, that if I had tried long ago to engage in politics, I should long ago have lost my life, without doing any good either to you or to myself. . . No man on earth who conscientiously opposes either you or any other organized democracy, and flatly prevents a great many wrongs and illegalities from taking place in the state to which he belongs, can possibly escape with his life. The true champion of justice, if he intends to survive even for a short time, must necessarily confine himself to private life and leave politics alone.[9]

It is difficult not to read this passage without mixed feelings. Even if he did not actually seek out political responsibilities, Socrates was nonetheless very active at the centre of Athenian life—indeed he must have been difficult to avoid!—working at his self-appointed mission to reform the morals of his city. And his withdrawal from politics did not prevent his execution in 399 BC, although it may have put it off for a while.

Some thirty years after his mentor's death, Plato still reflected on the problem of withdrawal:

Those who have become philosophers and have tasted how sweet and blessed a possession philosophy is, when they have fully realized also the madness of the majority, that practically never does anyone act sanely in public affairs, that there is no ally with whom one might go to the help of justice and live—then, like a man who has fallen among wild beasts, being unwilling to join in wrongdoing and not being strong enough to oppose the general savagery alone, for he would perish, useless both to himself and to others, before he could benefit either his country or his friends, of no use to himself or anyone else; taking all this into account he keeps quiet and minds his own business. Like a man who takes refuge under a small wall from a storm of dust or hail driven by the wind, and seeing other men filled with lawlessness, the philosopher is satisfied if he can somehow live his present life free from injustice and impious deeds, and depart from it with a beautiful hope, blameless and content.[10]

Plato himself had withdrawn from the centre of Athens to the periphery, to the moral and intellectual shelter of the Academy.

Two other interpretations of Socratic withdrawal might also be recalled. The obvious case is that of Epicurus who, well hidden in his garden, tells us that 'we must liberate ourselves from the prison of routine business and politics', and that the sage 'will not engage in politics'.[11] Another heir to Socratic withdrawal is the Stoic sage, who retreats into the inner citadel of

---

[9] Plato, *Apology* 31d–32a (trans. Tredennick).
[10] Plato, *Republic* 496c–e (trans. Grube).
[11] Epicurus, *Vatican Sayings* 58 (trans. Long and Sedley); Diogenes Laertius X, 119.

his freedom of judgement, indifferent to and above the vicissitudes of politics, even if he be, like Marcus Aurelius, emperor.[12]

If so many philosophers advocated some form of withdrawal from politics, it does not follow that they necessarily refused political responsibilities, as can be seen in the case of Marcus Aurelius, or took no interest in the elaboration of a political philosophy, as seems to be the case for Plato. Yet it has also been claimed that Plato is a non- or even anti-political thinker and that he has no political philosophy.[13] As the problem is one of definition of terms, it will be as well to indicate on this occasion what will be meant in the following pages by 'political philosophy'.

Leys can say that Plato has no interest in 'politics' because he stipulates what he takes to be a modern meaning of the term 'politics': 'politics' has to do with the treatment of irreducible disagreements and conflicts over 'goals and policies' within a community. Conflicts between organized groups or factions are a given of politics, which has to do with the disposition of such conflicts, if the groups are to continue to relate to each other in a community.[14] To the extent that Plato does not recognize this 'given' of politics and has no theory of conflict management, he is no political philosopher.

We are also free to stipulate another meaning for 'political', which we can declare to be ancient and/or modern as we like, but which comes nearer to what Aristotle, for example, means by 'political science'[15] and which seems to be of most interest to Plato in the *Republic* and in the *Laws*. Let us say that the philosopher may wish to subject the diverging 'goals and policies' of groups or individuals to scrutiny, in an attempt to determine more clearly what the best, most desirable, satisfactory, fulfilled life for humans might be: their ultimate goal or 'good'. On the assumption and to the degree that human groupings, forms of social organization, are essential to attaining this goal, this will be a 'political' enquiry. 'Political philosophy' will then have to do with the study of social structures, the principles of human social organization, and their realization (in constitutional order, legislation, and jurisdiction) to the extent required for achieving, in part at least, the human good. In this sense, Plato is as much a political philosopher as Aristotle, and it is in this sense that I will speak in the following chapters of the 'political philosophy' of Neoplatonism.

[12] Marcus Aurelius VIII, 48.
[13] Leys (1971); cf. F. Sparshott's reply and Leys's 'Afterthought' in the same volume. Cf. also Trampedach (1994: 279).
[14] Leys (1971: 167–9).
[15] *Nicomachean Ethics* I, 2, 1094^{a}22–1094^{b}11; I, 13, 1102^{a}5–25.

3. Divinization and Politics: Two Functions

On the conventional view, the goal of Neoplatonism, the divinization of man, in principle excludes interest in political philosophy. The discussion of this view will require a closer look at what divinization actually involved for the Neoplatonic philosopher (below Chapter 3). However a start might already be made here, as a way of indicating the lines which will be followed in this book. In particular two directions to the enquiry into the relation between divinization and political life are suggested in the opening chapters of a text Plotinus wrote in Rome in the early 260s, the treatise *On Virtues (Enn.* I 2).

Plotinus begins the treatise by quoting the 'assimilation to god' passage of Plato's *Theaetetus,* where this assimilation is linked to the endemic presence of evils 'in this place' and the need for 'escape' from these.[16] This assimilation, as 'escape', does not entail going to *another place*, as Plotinus stresses in the same connection in another treatise.[17] Rather, the 'escape', the divinization, means becoming virtuous, becoming 'just and pious with wisdom', again in the words of the *Theaetetus* (I 2, 1, 4–5).

However, a problem immediately arises. Plotinus, following Plato, has suggested that becoming godlike means becoming virtuous. Yet how could this be? The virtues involved are human; it would hardly be right to attribute them to what is superior, the divine (1, 10 ff.). How then can the virtues make us godlike if the gods are above human virtue?[18]

This difficulty in Plato's text is resolved by Plotinus in the following way. The virtues which we are to cultivate are, in the first instance, the four cardinal virtues defined by Plato in the *Republic*: wisdom, courage, moderation and justice.[19] These virtues, described as 'political' by Plotinus,[20] have to do

---

[16] I 2, 1, 1–4 (Plato, *Theaetetus* 176a–b).

[17] I 8, 6, 9–13; 7, 11–13.

[18] On the history of this problem see below Ch. 4, n. 5.

[19] The definitions (*Rep.* 442c–443b) are summarized by Plotinus at 1, 17–21.

[20] 1, 16–17; the expression 'political virtue' (πολιτικὴ ἀρετή) is found in Plato's *Phaedo* 82a 12–b 1. The translation of it as 'civic virtue' (Armstrong's trans., for example) seems to go back to Augustine, *Contra Acad.* III, 17, 37. Jackson et al. (1998) translate πολιτικός as 'constitutional' (in soul and state), considering the translation 'civic' or 'political' as misleading, since the word may not have anything to do with politics or community life (cf. 30–1). However they are not able to stick to this policy consistently (cf. 278 and n. 832, for example) and must go so far as to translate the knowledge which includes legislation and judicial art as 'constitutional craft' (e.g. at 124). At any rate 'political' covers a range of relations for Plotinus and other Neoplatonists, going from the internal 'affairs' of the soul in its relation to body (as in the present text of Plotinus) to matters of social organization (below, Ch. 5) and it would be misleading to exclude the latter aspect. In what follows I will use the term 'political', with quotation marks, to refer to its extended sense in

with the correct functioning of the different parts of the soul and in particular with the ruling function that reason should exercise in relation to the irrational parts of the soul. The latter are connected to the relation soul has with body. Thus the 'political' virtues have to do with soul in its relation to the body and require essentially the rule of reason in this relation, as opposed to a life subject to the irrational, chaotic and unlimited drives of material desire. This is why the gods are above such virtues: in their serene sovereignty, they are not affected by the psychic disorder and turmoil that is human vice. Yet, Plotinus insists (1, 23–26), by cultivating the 'political' virtues we can be said to be godlike: they constitute a first level in a scale of divinization which ranges beyond them to a higher moral level, that of the 'purificatory' virtues, which emancipate soul from her preoccupation with the body and bring her nearer to the perfection of divine life.[21] Plotinus therefore points to the idea of a hierarchy of moral excellence, a scale of virtues, of which the first level, that of the 'political' virtues, is presupposed by higher moral states, those brought by the 'purificatory' virtues which constitute a greater degree of approximation to divine life (cf. 7, 10–12). We can conclude from this that the practice of the 'political' virtues is a first step on the path of divinization, of which the more advanced stages are hardly accessible without the preliminary acquisition of these virtues.

The resolution of the problem of how the virtues can make us godlike, if the gods are above virtue, does not consist in saying that the acquisition of the 'political' virtues is an arbitrary precondition for becoming godlike, as if these virtues had no particular relation to the life of the gods, as if, for example, we were to decide on the ability to wiggle one's ears as a precondition for obtaining a driving licence. In fact Plotinus sees a connection between a life expressing the 'political' virtues and a divine life in that the former is an image expressing the latter as its model:[22] if the 'political' virtues do not characterize the gods, they nevertheless resemble, or approximate to, the life of the gods. Plotinus distinguishes between two kinds of 'assimilation': a reciprocal assimilation or resemblance in which two things resemble each other, are identical, by reason of the common source of their resemblance; and a non-reciprocal relation of resemblance of one thing to this source, in which the resemblance involves, not identity, but difference between the

---

Neoplatonism (covering also the internal affairs of the soul and of the household), and write political, with no quotation marks, when indicating the more restricted sense defined above at the end of s. 2.

[21] I 2, 3. The 'purificatory' virtues also come from the *Phaedo* (69c 1–3).

[22] 1, 15 and 46–52; 2, 1–4 and 19–20; 6, 16–18.

thing and its source (2, 4–10). This second kind of assimilation, that of an image to its model, expresses the continuity and difference between a life of 'political' virtue and divine life. The former can be a first approximation to the latter precisely because it images the divine. We can indeed conclude that what makes the virtuousness of a 'political' life is the extent to which it expresses the divine in the context of the relation between soul and body.

From these ideas of Plotinus it will be convenient to abstract two ways of identifying the function of political philosophy in the divinization of man: (1) as concerning the first stage in a *progressive* divinization of soul, a process that goes above and beyond the political level; and (2) as dealing with the imaging forth of divine life, its transposition down to the level of the political. For the purpose of analysis it will be convenient to distinguish these two functions, even if they are closely related, in Plotinus' treatise for example.

The two functions might be compared furthermore to two movements which govern the allegory of the cave that Plato develops in the centre of the *Republic* (514a–517d): (1) the ascending movement whereby a prisoner is freed from the darkness of ignorance and opinion and brought up, out of the cave, into the light of knowledge, knowledge in particular of the Good; and (2) the descending movement whereby the liberated prisoner, the philosopher, must return into the cave to put the newly acquired knowledge in the service of fellow-prisoners.

Many Neoplatonic echoes of Plato's image of the cave will be encountered below. Its double movement expresses well the complexity of the relation between political philosophy and the goal of divinization in Neoplatonism: if political philosophy has a function in relation to the first stage of divinization, it must be surpassed, transcended, if the process of divinization is to continue; yet it returns again in connection with the divinization of political life, the transformation of soul's life in relation to the body into something better, something more godlike.

4. Plan of the Work

The two movements, of ascent and descent, as expressions of the double function of political life in the divinization of man, will serve below in Chapters 3–11 as paths for the argument against the conventional view and for the purpose of reconstructing Neoplatonic political philosophy. In Chapters 3–6, the theme of ascent will be developed by further analysis of what divinization, as the goal of Neoplatonism, involves and how it is to be achieved (Ch. 3). The theory of the scale of virtues will be discussed with particular reference to the 'political' virtues (Ch. 4). The virtues were cultivated in the Neoplatonic schools by study of a corresponding scale of sciences (practical sciences such as ethics and politics leading up to the higher virtues and their corresponding sciences, the theoretical sciences). This scale of sciences (Ch. 5) was in turn expressed in a curriculum drawn primarily from Plato's dialogues, where the scales of virtues and sciences were thought to be exemplified (Ch. 6). This curricular theory will permit identification of the works that the Neoplatonists used as relevant to political philosophy.

In Chapters 7–11, the reverse movement, that of descent, will be followed. The motivation of the political philosopher will be examined: why should the Neoplatonist philosopher 'descend'? What motivates the philosopher-king? How does descent affect his happiness? And what of Plato's philosopher-queens (Ch. 7)? What relations are there between the theory of the ideal state and realistic political reform? What principles guide the political philosopher? How can these principles be expressed in political constitutions, in legislation (Ch. 8) and in judicial art (Ch. 9)? What is the function of religion in the state (Ch. 10)? What are the limits to political action (Ch. 11)? On all of these questions it will be found that the Neoplatonists have much to say.

Chapters 3–11 will introduce evidence drawn from a range of Neoplatonist philosophers, going from Plotinus and his school in Rome in the third century AD to the last members of the Alexandrian and Athenian schools in the sixth century, a wide variety therefore of personalities living in different parts and at different periods of the late Roman Empire, reflecting different stages in the evolution of Neoplatonic philosophy. It may be of use to have at first some general view of this variety. This is the purpose of Chapter 2, which is limited to situating briefly in time and place the philosophers mentioned in later chapters, while indicating at the same time the connections these philosophers often had with centres of Roman power.[23]

Chapters 3–11, it must be emphasized, concern the reconstruction of Neoplatonic political theory in its main structural articulation. No attempt is made to assess the historical impact of this theory. However, in Chapters 12–14 of the book, I discuss some Christian and Islamic thinkers of the late

---

[23] The reader familiar with the history of the Neoplatonic schools of Late Antiquity might prefer to skip this chapter.

antique and early medieval period, with the purpose of showing that the political theory reconstructed in Chapters 3–11 may throw some new light on the origins of political thought in the Christian and Islamic worlds. I will begin (Ch. 12) with the theocratic programme recommended to Constantine by Eusebius and with Augustine's anti-Eusebian epic of two cities, moving then to the Justinianic period (Ch. 13), to the ecclesiology formulated by the Pseudo-Dionysius and the political project of an anonymous dialogue *On Political Science*. The final chapter will evoke the importance of Platonic political philosophy in early Islamic thought and will attempt to show in particular that al-Farabi's 'perfect state' is an Islamic version of the ideal city of the late antique Neoplatonist, an Islamic 'Platonopolis' of which some more recent examples will be mentioned in the Conclusion.

Neoplatonist Philosophers in Time, Place, and Social Context

2

The purpose of this chapter is to introduce briefly the philosophers to whom reference will be made in the following chapters. These philosophers represent many different periods and places in the late Roman Empire, as well as relating to different phases in the evolution of ideas. So great in fact is the number and variety of Neoplatonist philosophers that it will hardly be possible here to go much beyond a brief mention of those in particular whose ideas will be considered later in this book (their names are printed here in bold type). I will indicate briefly the period, school affiliations, social status, and political connections of these philosophers: here also it will not be possible to do more than note some of the more significant facts.[1]

For the purpose of convenience I have grouped the information in four sections: (1) the circle of Plotinus in Rome in the mid-third century, (2) the Iamblichean schools in Syria and Asia Minor in the fourth century, (3) the Athenian school in the fifth and early sixth centuries, and (4) the Alexandrian school in Egypt in the fifth and sixth centuries.

1. Plotinus' Circle in Rome

Plotinus was born in 205, perhaps in Egypt.[2] At any rate it was in Egypt that he studied philosophy, in Alexandria in the 230s under the direction of

---

[1] References to fuller sources of information will be given at the beginning of each of the following sections. Cf. Blumenthal's survey (1996: ch. 4), which concentrates on Neoplatonist commentators on Aristotle.

[2] The information in this section derives largely from Porphyry's *Vit. Plot.*, for which an indispensable companion is Brisson et al. (1982–92), which contains much useful matter.

Ammonius Sakkas. In 243 Plotinus joined a military expedition, under the youthful emperor Gordian III (238–44), against Persia. Whether or not Plotinus was in search of Persian and Indian philosophy, as Porphyry alleges (*Vit. Plot.* 3, 15–17), his place in the expedition is likely to have been that of a philosopher such as those who sometimes formed part of a Roman imperial entourage.[3] This in turn suggests that he already had access to the influential circles in which he was to move later in Rome.[4] The expedition failed and the emperor was killed (244). Plotinus escaped to Antioch in Syria and went thence to Rome.

In Rome Plotinus was received in the household of a certain Gemina. It has been suggested that his hostess was Gemina, the wife of the emperor Trebonianus Gallus (251–3), a woman of senatorial class.[5] Even if this suggestion has been shown to be untenable,[6] it does appear to be the case that Gemina's household was such as to favour Plotinus' contacts with influential members of Roman society. In Gemina's house Plotinus created an unofficial philosophical circle or school. Of the fourteen regular and dedicated members of this circle mentioned by Porphyry, three were women (Gemina, her daughter, and Amphiclea), most came from the eastern part of the Empire, five were politicians (three of them senators), three were doctors, and two literary men.[7] Of the three senators, Orontius, Sabinillus, Rogatianus, the last might be identified with the military prefect (241) and proconsul of Asia (254) of the same name[8]—we have seen above (p. 4) how great an impression he made in renouncing high office—whereas Sabinillus was consul in 266 with the emperor Gallienus (253–68). Of the other two politicians, Zethus had political ambitions which Plotinus sought to limit (above p. 4) and a property in Campania where Plotinus retired. Castricius, the fifth politician, also owned a property in Campania. Zethus was a doctor, as were Eustochius, who attended Plotinus on his death, and Paulinus.

Plotinus' philosophical circle, informal and open to visitors and other less regular members, was organized along lines characteristic of a late antique philosophical school: texts of Plato were read out and explained, publications were prepared, and Plotinus was assisted in this work by two close and devoted pupils, Amelius and Porphyry. **Amelius**, from Etruria, was Plotinus' pupil and assistent in Rome from 246 to 269, when he left to live in Apamea in Syria where he continued to promote the works of his

---

[3] Rawson (1989: 233–57).   [4] Cf. Harder (1960: 280–2).
[5] Saffrey (1992: 32).   [6] Cf. P. Hadot (1997: 85 n. 1).
[7] Brisson et al. (1982–92: i. 55–6).   [8] Ibid. i. 109.

teacher. **Porphyry** joined the circle much later, in 263. He was born in 234 in Tyre (Phoenicia) to a noble family:[9] his Phoenician name Malkos was translated by Amelius as 'king' and his Greek name given him by his former teacher in Athens, Longinus,[10] has the same connotation. Intensely involved in the work of the school, he went through a crisis and was advised by Plotinus to leave Rome and rest in Sicily (268), where he was still living when Plotinus died two years later. Little is certain about Porphyry's subsequent life. He married Marcella, the wife of a deceased friend, and, at the beginning of the fourth century, published his biography and edition (the *Enneads*) of Plotinus. Whether or not he returned to Rome and taught there is uncertain. He may have had pupils at some time, but this is not clearly established.[11] His publications were of considerable importance to Latin-speaking thinkers of the later fourth and early fifth centuries such as the Christian bishop **Augustine** in Africa (below, Ch. 12) and the pagan **Macrobius**, senator and, in 430, praetorian prefect of Italy.

Aside from exercising an educational and deeply edificatory influence on members of his circle, Plotinus also acted as guardian of the financial interests of the children of deceased nobles left in his care, whom he received in his household and to whose education he saw. Plotinus thus assumed the role, Porphyry suggests, of a 'divine' protector and patron.

> Yet, though he shielded so many from the worries and cares of ordinary life, he never, while awake, relaxed his intent concentration upon Intellect.[12]

To this philanthropic work Plotinus added the activity of unofficial arbiter and judge of disputes, apparently to the satisfaction of the judicial authorities.[13] We might feel that Porphyry is exaggerating the scope of these activities. He is, however, recommending to our attention a model of practical virtue, benevolent and selfless stewardship, and fair arbitration, exercised in conjunction with contemplation of transcendent principles.

Something more ambitious seems to have been intended in the project with which Plotinus approached the emperor Gallienus, who, with his wife Salonina, held the philosopher in high esteem. Plotinus proposed to revive a 'city of philosophers' that long lay in ruins in Campania, which, if the

---

[9] According to Eunapius, *Vit. philos.* 455.

[10] Again according to Eunapius, *Vit. philos.* 456.

[11] Bidez (1913: 104–5), for a list of these pupils and Saffrey (1992: 39–40) for a critique of this list.

[12] *Vit. Plot.* 9, 16–18: Intellect is a transcendent hypostasis second to the supreme metaphysical principle, according to Plotinus, the 'One'.

[13] Porphyry, *Vit. Plot.* 9, with the helpful comments in Brisson et al. (1982–92: ii. 243–6).

emperor granted the surrounding land, would be colonized (Plotinus would join, with his companions) and run according to Plato's laws and would be called 'Platonopolis'. Opposition in the court however blocked the project.[14]

What and where was this ruined city of philosophers? A Pythagorean or Neopythagorean community of the kind that once existed in southern Italy? Or perhaps Cicero's 'Academy', now a dilapidated estate near Cumae?[15] What sort of city did Plotinus wish to establish? A kind of pagan monastic community of otherworldly philosophical ascetics? Such an answer is required by the conventional view of the Neoplatonist attitude to politics.[16] Or did Plotinus intend to realize in some way the utopia of Plato's *Republic* or rather, as the reference to Plato's laws suggests, the city projected in Plato's *Laws*?[17] These questions must remain unanswered as long as we are unclear about Plotinus' theoretical position on the relation between philosophy and political life.

For whatever reason, the project was not carried out. However, Plotinus remained active, in his philosophical circle in Gemina's household, composing his treatises until, in 268–9, his circle began to disperse, sickness driving him to retirement on Zethus' property, where he continued to write and where he died in 270.

2. The Iamblichean Schools in Syria and Asia Minor

Amphiclea, one of the women in Plotinus' circle, married the son of a certain Iamblichus, who might well be the **Iamblichus** of Chalcis who founded an important philosophical school in Apamea (in Syria) where Amelius had retired. Iamblichus seems to have been born *c.*245 into a Syrian royal family which had ruled Emesa.[18] He himself was a wealthy landowner.[19] He is described by Eunapius as having studied philosophy with Porphyry,[20]

---

[14] *Vit. Plot.* 12.

[15] For these hypotheses cf. Brisson et al. (1982–92: ii. 258–60).

[16] Cf. Edwards (1994), for example.

[17] Cf. Jerphagnon (1981), who prefers the latter view; Rist (1964: 171–3).

[18] Our major source for the Iamblichean schools is Eunapius, *Vit. philos.*, who is not always reliable and is quite inadequate as regards the serious philosophical work of these schools. There are valuable studies by Fowden (1979), (1982), and Penella (1990). On Iamblichus' biography cf. Dillon in *ANRW* ii. 36.2, 863–78.

[19] Fowden (1979: 195); (1982: 494).

[20] Eunapius, *Vit. philos.* 458, on which cf. Penella (1990: 39 n. 1).

a relationship made likely by the possible connection with Amphiclea and by Iamblichus' extensive knowledge and constant criticism of the work of Plotinus and of Porphyry. At any rate Iamblichus became a famous philosopher and successful teacher in the Greek-speaking prosperous urban world of the eastern Roman Empire. Along with considerable effort devoted to the explanation of the works of Aristotle and of Plato,[21] Iamblichus took a strong interest in what he considered to be more ancient forms of wisdom, Greek (Pythagoreanism, Orphism) as well as barbarian (Chaldaean and Egyptian), which he sought to harmonize in a synthesis whose essential structure derived from a development of the metaphysics of Plato, Aristotle, and Plotinus. Iamblichus appears to have died c.325.

Among the more important of Iamblichus' pupils were Sopatros, Aedesius, **Theodore of Asine** (who had also studied with Porphyry), Eustathius, and Dexippus. Of these Sopatros appears to have been pre-eminent.[22] On Iamblichus' death, Sopatros joined the court of Constantine (306–37) where, as a close and influential adviser of the Christian emperor, he sought to 'control and reform through reason (λόγῳ) the purpose and impulsiveness' of Constantine.[23] That, at least, was the Iamblichean school's view, as passed down to Eunapius, of Sopatros' aim. In 330 Sopatros conducted ceremonies relating to the foundation of Constantinople.[24] At some time between 330 and 337, Sopatros fell victim to court intrigue and was executed. A philosopher who had come too near to power? Eunapius compares Sopatros' fate, in the court of a Christian monarchy, with that of Socrates in the Athenian democracy.[25] Another pupil of Iamblichus, Eustathius, became less compromised, although he went in 358 to the Persian court as an ambassador for Constantius II (337–61), son of Constantine, where, according to Eunapius, his impact on Sapor was such that the Persian king was almost ready to exchange his regalia for the philosopher's cloak.[26] Aedesius seems to have taken over the leadership of the Iamblichean school on Sopatros' departure for the court, but it was in Pergamum in Asia Minor that he established his own school, where, in 351, now old, he was visited by the young **Julian** in search of philosophical instruction: Aedesius referred the future emperor (361–3) to

---

[21] On the curriculum designed by Iamblichus, cf. below, Ch. 6.

[22] See Penella (1990: 49–50), who provides a useful critical discussion of the evidence concerning Iamblichus' pupils (and their pupils).

[23] Eunapius, *Vit. philos.* 462; cf. Penella (1990: 51).

[24] John Lydus, *De mens.*, pp. 65, 21–66, 1.

[25] *Vit. philos.* 462.

[26] *Vit. philos.* 465–6.

some of his pupils.[27] Of Iamblichus' other pupils, Theodore of Asine and Dexippus also seem to have established their own schools.

Before coming to the second generation of Iamblichean philosophers, we should note that some excerpts surviving from Iamblichus' correspondence are taken from letters addressed, not only to close pupils such as Sopatros, Eustathius, and Dexippus, but also to others (perhaps former pupils) who are likely to have been high-ranking and influential, such as Arete, perhaps the woman whose interests were defended by Julian,[28] Dyscolius, and Agrippa, to whom Iamblichus wrote concerning the correct use of power and the importance of law.[29]

Among the second generation of Iamblichean philosophers we might include Sopatros' son, also called **Sopatros** (Sopatros 2), decurion at Apamea, who addressed a letter on good rulership to his brother Himerius on the occasion of the latter's taking up an important office[30] and whose own son was called Iamblichus (Iamblichus 2). As for Eustathius, he is not reported as having had pupils. However his wife Sosipatra taught at Pergamum where she moved on her husband's death and lived under Aedesius' care.[31] Where she received her philosophical training is something of a mystery. At any rate Eunapius' report suggests that her teaching was not only accepted, but very much admired by Aedesius and his pupils. The latter included Chrysanthius (a member of a senatorial family of Sardis in Lydia and Eunapius' philosophical mentor),[32] Eusebius of Myndus, Maximus of Ephesus, all of whom were frequented by Julian—Chrysanthius and Eusebius in Pergamum, Maximus in Ephesus—and whom he called to his court, along with another pupil of Aedesius, Priscus, when he became Emperor (361). At his court they would assist him in the effort to overthrow the power of the Christians and restore the ancestral religion as formalized by Iamblichean philosophy. Chrysanthius preferred to abstain, and indeed, when appointed high priest of Lydia by Julian, showed moderation and prudence in carrying out his task.[33] As for the others, who accepted the invitation, Maximus, the most radical of them, survived

---

[27] On Aedesius cf. *DPA* i. 626–31.

[28] Julian, *Or. VI*, 6, 259d. Cf. Bidez (1919: 39).

[29] These letters are discussed below, Ch. 8, 1 and 4. On the circulation of Iamblichus' correspondence in the Neoplatonic schools, cf. below Ch. 9, n. 6. Dyscolius may have been praetorian prefect of the East (317–24); cf. *DPA* ii. 915.

[30] On this letter cf. below Ch. 9.

[31] On Sosipatra cf. Penella (1990: 58–63), who compares her with another woman-philosopher, Hypatia (below p. 24).

[32] *DPA* ii. 320–3.

[33] Eunapius, *Vit. philos.* 501.

the fall of Julian (363), but was later arrested, then freed, arrested again in connection with a conspiracy involving divination and executed (371), whereas Priscus was arrested, but later allowed to move to Athens.

There was thus a third generation of Iamblichean philosophers: 'Iamblichus 2' (to whom I return, below); Sosipatra's pupils and her son Antoninus, who set up as a philosopher in Egypt; the pupils of Maximus, including Julian and his friends, in particular **Sallustius,** an adviser of Julian and prefect of the East;[34] and the pupils of Chrysanthius in Sardis, including Eunapius.

3. The Athenian School

The presence at Athens towards the end of the fourth century of Priscus and of 'Iamblichus 2' is likely to have contributed to the development of an important Neoplatonic school at Athens in the fifth and early sixth centuries.[35] 'Iamblichus 2' was recognized by the city, not only for his public benefactions, but also for his wisdom derived, according to Libanius, from Pythagoras, Plato, Aristotle, and the 'divine Iamblichus'.[36] The first important member, perhaps the founder of the Neoplatonic school of Athens, Plutarch of Athens, may have known Priscus or 'Iamblichus 2', and his school—not to be identified as an institution with Plato's Academy, which had long ago disappeared[37]—traced its intellectual ancestry back to Iamblichus.

Plutarch's pupils included Domninus, Odainathus (probably a descendant of the third-century king of Palmyra of the same name), **Syrianus,** and Hierocles (on whom see below section 4). On Plutarch's death in 432 Syrianus succeeded as head of the school and was succeeded in turn by the

---

[34] For this identification of Sallustius, author of *On Gods and the World*, with critical review of the evidence, see Clarke (1998: 347–50).

[35] On the earlier stages of the development of the Athenian school cf. Proclus, *Theol. Plat.* I, ix–liv (introduction by Saffrey and Westerink), for which our major sources are Marinus, *Vit. Procl.* and Damascius, *Vit. Is.*, which also concerns the later stages of the Athenian and Alexandrian schools and which, although clearly a fascinating document, has survived only in fragments that are difficult to coordinate and use, a situation much alleviated now by Athanassiadi's (1999) translation and notes.

[36] Proclus, *Theol. Plat.* i. xlv–xlvi.

[37] Cf. Glucker (1978: 248–55, 322–9); *DPA* ii. 548–55 (an important review by Hoffmann of the archaeological evidence concerning the Neoplatonic school at Athens, its location, and its considerable wealth).

most important philosopher of the Athenian school, **Proclus**. Proclus was born in 412 in Constantinople and educated at first in the profession of his father, law, in Alexandria. There he also began the study of philosophy, moving to Athens (430/1), where he was trained by Plutarch and by Syrianus, whom he succeeded in c.437. Throughout his long career (he died in 485) he proved to be a very industrious and influential teacher and writer. He followed in general the Iamblichean curriculum (reading Aristotle and Plato, integrating the ancient wisdom of the Greeks and barbarians) and the commentaries and treatises he wrote in connection with this teaching came to constitute the canon of late antique Neoplatonism, in Athens and in Alexandria, supplanting the works of Porphyry and of Iamblichus.

Before coming to Proclus' many pupils, we might take note of some of his public activities as recorded in the encomium written shortly after his death by his successor **Marinus**.[38] In his praise of Proclus, Marinus shows how, throughout his life, Proclus ascended the scale of virtues, starting with the ethical and 'political' virtues (*Vit. Procl.* 14–17). Not only did Proclus, according to Marinus, acquire these virtues by study (see below Ch. 6), he also practised them in ways that Marinus proceeds to describe. Being precluded from political action through his occupation with 'greater things', Proclus urged his close companion Archiadas, grandson of Plutarch of Athens and 'beloved of the gods', in this direction,

Teaching him and training him in political virtues and methods, and, as one encourages people in a race, exhorting him to be at the very head of public affairs in his own city, and to be a private benefactor to everyone according to every species of virtue, but especially in justice. (*Vit. Procl.* 14, trans. Edwards)

Proclus inspired Archiadas[39] by the example of political largesse that he himself practised[40] in relation both to Athens and his native home in Lydia, as well as by the benefaction of friends, relations, pupils, and foreigners. He also wrote to 'the powers' for the benefit of various cities. In Athens he took part sometimes in political assemblies, offering 'wise advice' (γνώμας ἐμφρόνως), intervening also with the authorities on judicial matters, using his philosopher's freedom of speech to see that each received his just due (*Vit. Procl.* 15). To this example of wisdom and justice Proclus, for the

[38] On this subject, somewhat neglected in Saffrey and Westerink's introduction to Proclus, *Theol. Plat.* I, see Blumenthal (1984: 487–8).

[39] Theagenes, a child in Archiadas' household, became ruler of Athens; cf. Proclus, *Theol. Plat.* I, xxxii–xxxiii.

[40] On this political virtue see below Ch. 7, 1.

emulation of his pupils, added that of the moderation of his life and the courage of Heracles, as Marinus puts it, in a period of turmoil and danger which forced him into temporary exile from Athens. On the domestic level Proclus showed (*Vit. Procl.* 17) the same virtues of benevolent stewardship, as tutor, educator, and arbiter, as those Porphyry found in Plotinus.[41] Proclus' philanthropy in the case of Archiadas deepened into a friendship of equals.

Among Proclus' many pupils[42] we might consider first the closest, those who often went on to teach philosophy themselves: Marinus (Proclus' successor), Isidore (Marinus' successor), Zenodotus (perhaps Isidore's successor), Ammonius and his brother Heliodorus (see below, section 4), Asclepiodotus (son-in-law of an illustrious citizen of Aphrodisias),[43] and Agapius of Athens, teacher of John Lydus.

Of the others who attended Proclus' school we might note the following men of distinction: Rufinus, described as a high-ranking Athenian official (Marinus, *Vit. Procl.* 23); Severianus, who, seeking a political career, became a provincial governor, but showed excessive judicial severity and inflexibility as regards his superiors, turning to teaching and refusing the emperor Zeno's offer of an important post;[44] Pamprepius, who went to Constantinople in 476, impressed Zeno's *magister officiorum* Illus with a lecture on the soul, became a prominent pagan leader in Illus' revolt, and was executed for treason in 484;[45] Marcellinus, who became *magister militum*, patrician, and ruler of Dalmatia;[46] Anthemius, consul in 455 and emperor in the West (467–72);[47] Flavius Illustrius Pusaeus, praetorian prefect of the East (465) and consul (467);[48] Flavius Messius Phoebus Severus, consul in 470, prefect of Rome and patrician.[49]

This list, a veritable Gotha of aristocrats and high government officials of the period, makes plausible Marinus' claim that Proclus could exert influence in the highest political spheres (*Vit. Procl.* 15). It is also a list of prominent pagans, some, such as Pamprepius, clearly involved in pagan revolt. Proclus himself, although suffering morally from the domination of

---

[41] This comparison is made by Blumenthal (1984: 488). Cf. also Damascius, *Vit. Is.*, frs. 50 (Isidore), 124 (Aedesia).

[42] On this see Proclus, *Theol. Plat.* I. xlix–liv.   [43] Cf. *DPA* i, 626–31.

[44] Damascius, *Vit. Is.* fr. 278; *PLRE* ii. 998–9. On Severianus' poor use of power see below, Ch. 9.

[45] Cf. *PLRE* ii. 825–8.

[46] Cf. *PLRE* ii. 708–10. Marcellinus, as well as Severianus and Pamprepius, are discussed by Chuvin (1990: 99–103, 124).

[47] *PLRE* ii. 96–8.   [48] *PLRE* ii. 1005–6.

[49] *PLRE* ii. 930.

Christianity, which he seems to have thought temporary,[50] appears to have been protected by his prestige and by the conservatism of Athens.[51] At any rate his relations with Christians cannot always have been poor: a Christian, Christodorus, wrote a book not long after Proclus' death *On the Pupils of the Great Proclus*, and another Christian, the anonymous author whom today we call 'Pseudo-Dionysius' (below, Ch. 13), knew Proclus' work so well that he may possibly even have been his pupil.

The last head of the Athenian school appears to have been **Damascius**, who was born early in the second half of the fifth century in Damascus.[52] In Alexandria he studied rhetoric and (under Ammonius and Isidore) philosophy, moving then to Athens (*c.*492), where he studied with Marinus and Zenodotus. When Damascius took over the leadership of the Athenian school he seems to have sought to reinvigorate it; he was certainly of the philosophical calibre of Proclus. Among his pupils in Athens, but possibly already in Alexandria, were **Simplicius**[53] and Theodora, perhaps a descendant of Iamblichus' family and also a pupil of Isidore, to whom Damascius dedicated his *Life of Isidore*.

Damascius' activity in Athens was cut short as a consequence of anti-pagan legislation introduced in 529 by the emperor Justinian (527–65).[54] Yet Justinian had in his court a high official, the anonymous author of a dialogue *On Political Science* which is inspired by Neoplatonic philosophy and to which we will return (below Ch. 13). His peer in the court of Theoderic in the West, the aristocrat and Christian **Boethius**, was also very well trained in Neoplatonic philosophy, perhaps in Athens or in Alexandria, and, in his distinguished career (he became consul in 510), attempted to live Plato's hope that the philosopher become king or the king philosopher.[55] He became involved in an intrigue and was executed in 524.

Prevented from teaching, Damascius left Athens for the Persian Empire, together with Simplicius, Priscian of Lydia, another Neoplatonist, and four other distinguished philosophers.

[50] Cf. Saffrey (1975).

[51] This point is made by Fowden (1982: 45–6). A good review of the gradual suppression of paganism in the Christianized Roman Empire, from Constantine's toleration, through Julian's revolt, to Theodosius' outlawing of pagan rituals (392) and Justinian's outlawing of pagans (527), is provided by Chuvin (1990: chs. 3–8).

[52] On Damascius there is a very thorough study in *DPA* ii. 541–93 by Hoffmann, who reviews the various scholarly controversies surrounding the last years of the Athenian school. Cf. also Athanassiadi (1999: 19–57).

[53] On Simplicius' biography, cf. I. Hadot (1978: 20–32); (1987: 3–21).

[54] On the closing of the school at Athens see the critical review in Thiel (1999).

[55] Plato, *Rep.* 473c–d. See below p. 80.

Because they did not share the view of God prevailing among the Romans and thought that the Persian state was far better—they were persuaded by the very widespread tale that the Persian government was supremely just, the union of philosophy and kingship as in the writing of Plato, and the people disciplined and orderly, that there are no thieves or robbers among them, nor do they practise any other sort of crime, and that even if some precious object is left in a lonely place, no one who comes by will steal it, so that it remains safe, even if it is unguarded, for the man who left it there to return. So, therefore, they thought that this was true and were inspired by it, and besides, they had been forbidden by law to live here in security, since they did not subscribe to the existing order, so they left forthwith for a foreign and wholly alien people, meaning to live there for the rest of their lives.[56]

The philosophers were disappointed in Persia. They found self-glorification, inhumanity, and cruelty among the rulers, as well as theft, injustice, and other forms of immorality; the king himself had philosophical pretensions, but was no true philosopher, or so, at least, our Christian report has it. Yet Chosroes was certainly a patron of philosophy and solicited from Priscian of Lydia answers to a series of questions about the soul. The philosophers nevertheless returned from Persia, protected in their lives and liberty of thought by an article in a treaty signed in 532 between the Persian king and the Roman emperor.

Where the philosophers settled in the Roman Empire is not known. Did some return to Athens or to Alexandria? Did they settle in the border town of Harran, where they could continue to benefit from the protection of Chosroes?[57] At any rate it seems that Damascius was still alive, in Syria, in 538.

4. The Alexandrian School

As can be seen from the above, the distinction between the Athenian and Alexandrian schools of Neoplatonic philosophy is somewhat artificial: the Alexandrians were often trained in Athens and the Athenians often studied in Alexandria. The close links between the two groups were reinforced by the family ties that did much for the perenniality of these intellectual dynasties.[58]

---

[56] Agathias II, 30 (trans. Cameron); a commentary on this text is given by Cameron (1969–70). For this idealization of the Persian Empire (as a just state), see also the anonymous dialogue *On Political Science*, pp. 11, 25–13, 4.

[57] Cf. Thiel (1999) and Luna (2001), who has effectively disproved this supposition.

[58] For the importance of family relationships, cf. Proclus, *Theol. Plat.* I, xxvi–xxxv.

The Alexandrian school's history is less clearly established than that of Athens. The first recognizably Neoplatonist philosopher of Alexandria was a woman, Hypatia, daughter of the mathematician Theon and roughly a contemporary of the third generation of Iamblichean philosophers. While some traces of her mathematical work survive, nothing is left of her philosophical teaching apart from its expression in the writings of her pupil Synesius.[59] Hypatia's impact in Alexandria must have been very great. Almost a century after her death Damascius had only the highest praise for her in his *Life of Isidore*:[60] she excelled at all levels of virtue and of philosophy; she was superior to her father in natural talent and intellectual achievement; to her physical beauty she added logical acumen; she reached the summit of 'practical' virtue—just, moderate, and pure, she was wise (ἔμφρονα) in her acts and 'political' (πολιτικήν). So highly was she regarded in her city that the local officials, on assuming their office, would pay her their respects (as they would later in Athens in the case of Proclus). She taught in public, mainly explaining the works of Aristotle and Plato, and her lectures were attended by distinguished citizens, notably by the prefect of Egypt.[61] Such success, Damascius tells us, provoked the fury of Cyril, bishop of Alexandria, who arranged for her assassination in 415, the work of impious, savage and vicious men, the greatest of shames inflicted on her city, a shame, Damascius prompts us to think, such as that inflicted on Athens by the death of Socrates.[62]

One of Hypatia's most distinguished and dedicated pupils was **Synesius** of Cyrene, a rich landowner who went to the imperial court in Constantinople in 397–400 as ambassador for the purpose of obtaining tax relief for his city; his work *On Rulership*, addressed to the emperor during this period, will concern us later. The political skills he demonstrated no doubt explain his election as bishop of Ptolemais (Libya) in 410, a post he accepted despite reservations about some Christian doctrines.

The next prominent Neoplatonist of Alexandria was **Hierocles**, whom we have met in Athens as a pupil of Plutarch and a contemporary of Syrianus, who took up teaching philosophy in Alexandria some twenty years after Hypatia's death.[63] Hierocles dedicated his work *On Providence* to one Olympiodorus, an ambassador-philosopher who possessed 'political

---

[59] On Hypatia, see Beretta (1993), Dzielska (1995).   [60] *Vit. Is.*, fr. 102.

[61] Cf. Socrates, *Hist. eccles.* VII, 15.

[62] I summarize here Damascius' version of things. For a historical account of the circumstances surrounding Hypatia's murder see Chuvin (1990: 90–4).

[63] On Hierocles' biography, cf. I. Hadot (1978: 17–20); Schibli (2002: ch. 1).

wisdom',[64] perhaps the Olympiodorus who was an Egyptian historian and ambassador to the Huns in 412.[65] In his teaching, Hierocles commented on the Pythagorean *Golden Verses* and on Plato's *Gorgias* which, much to the astonishment of his pupil Theosebius who took notes, he explained on two different occasions without repeating himself in any way. The *Golden Verses* and the *Gorgias*, as will be seen (below, Ch. 6) were considered as relating to the first stages of the philosophical curriculum, the *Gorgias* having to do in particular with 'political' virtue. Indeed it is on this level of excellence that Damascius situates Hierocles.[66] If Hierocles demonstrated courage and greatness of spirit when he was arrested, beaten, and exiled by the authorities in Constantinople, he was lacking, Damascius found, as regards the higher levels of philosophical excellence.

It is also on the level of practical virtue that Damascius places Theosebius:[67] Theosebius excelled in moral instruction, a veritable Epictetus of his time, but a Platonic, not a Stoic Epictetus, Damascius hastens to add. Indeed Epictetus was used as a manual of propaedeutic moral instruction in the Neoplatonic schools (below, Ch. 6). Theosebius also commented on Plato's *Republic* and concentrated on ethical questions, living accordingly; if not politically active in the ordinary way, he set in order his own 'interior republic' (τὴν ἑαυτοῦ καὶ ἐν ἑαυτῷ πολιτείαν), as did Socrates and Epictetus, thus being able to relate to others for the best (πρὸς τὸ βέλτιστον).[68]

A contemporary of Theosebius and a fellow-student of Proclus under Syrianus in Athens was **Hermias**, whose notes of Syrianus' lectures on Plato's *Phaedrus* survive.[69] Hermias married Aedesia, a relative of Syrianus, and taught philosophy in Alexandria. Damascius, in emphasizing his ethical qualities, places him also on the lower levels of philosophical excellence.[70] His sons Ammonius and Heliodorus went to train under Proclus in Athens and then returned to teach philosophy in Alexandria. **Ammonius** was born in 435/45 and seems to have died between 517 and 526. At some point he reached an agreement, or compromise, with the patriarch of Alexandria, Athanasius II (c.489–96), but the details of this are unclear. His

---

[64] Photius, *Bibl.* cod. 214, 171b.
[65] On this Olympiodorus see Chuvin (1990: 97–9).
[66] As noted by I. Hadot (1978: 18).
[67] *Vit. Is.*, fr. 109.
[68] I summarize here *Vit. Is.*, fr. 109.
[69] On the school of Alexandria from Hermias on, see Westerink (1990).
[70] *Vit. Is.*, fr. 120.

pupils included Asclepius, the Christian John **Philoponus**, **Olympiodorus**—all of whom transcribed his lectures—Damascius, and Simplicius. Olympiodorus himself taught in Alexandria up to and beyond 565.[71] Related to the teaching of Neoplatonic philosophy in Alexandria in the middle and late sixth century are the anonymous *Prolegomena to Platonic Philosophy* and the commentaries going under the names of **Elias** and **David**. These works, like those of Olympiodorus, give a vivid and detailed impression of the lecture room of the Alexandrian Neoplatonist in the sixth century, as he followed the curriculum traced by Iamblichus and formalized by Proclus a century before. This teaching may even have persisted up to the Arab conquest of Egypt in 642.

This brief survey of the Neoplatonic schools between the third and sixth centuries has shown that many of the members of these schools belonged to, or had close relations with, the highest circles of society and power in the late Roman Empire. We might take this simply as meaning that philosophy was an activity characteristic of a cultural and educational elite and thus to be expected in such circles. This would not in any way prevent the philosophers themselves from turning away and turning others away from the political affairs of their time. Perhaps comparable to the Christian ascetics of Late Antiquity, they could give voice to social forces in preaching a rejection of the world.[72]

However, we have also seen that political action and sometimes even political projects are not uncommon in the lives of the Neoplatonist philosophers and that Plato's call in the *Republic* for the union of philosophy and political power was far from forgotten. What we need to establish is the way in which the Neoplatonists *themselves* understood the relationship between their philosophy and political action. What is their *theory* of political action and how does it fit into their overall view of the philosophical life?

---

[71] On Olympiodorus' relations with Christians, see Westerink (1990: 331–6).
[72] See Brown (1978).

Part 1
Neoplatonic Political Theory
Reconstructed:
The Divinization of Soul

Part 1 Synopsis

It has been suggested in Chapter 1, on the basis of ideas found in Plotinus' treatise *On Virtues* (*Enn.* I 2), that the question of the relation between political philosophy and the goal of Neoplatonism, the divinization of man, can be approached in two ways: (1) 'political' virtue can serve as a first, preparatory stage in the 'ascent' of the soul to higher levels of divine life, and (2) since 'political' virtue itself images divine life, the philosopher can 'descend' so as to bring this divine life to expression on the political level. In Chapters 3–6 the first approach will be examined in more detail, leaving matters concerning the second approach to Chapters 7–11. This division of the subject is to some extent artificial: it is the same virtues that are stages 'upwards' towards and expressions 'downwards' of divine life, and in general, in Neoplatonic metaphysics, ascent and descent are merely two aspects of one process. However, from the pedagogic point of view, that of the student in a Neoplatonic school, the two paths can be distinguished, as they can, for our purposes, for expository convenience.

To explore the function of 'political' virtue as a preparatory stage in the divinization of man, it will be necessary to discuss in more detail what 'divinization' as a goal actually means, not only as regards Neoplatonism, but also in relation to Plato and to other philosophical movements in Antiquity (Ch. 3). The complexity of divinization, as understood by the Neoplatonists, calls for a correspondingly complex variety of methods of divinization, a scale of types of virtue including 'political' virtue (Ch. 4). This scale corresponds to a scale of philosophical sciences which includes, on the level of 'political' virtue, political philosophy (Ch. 5). Matched in turn to these scales of virtues and sciences is the curriculum taught in the Neoplatonic schools of Late Antiquity, a curriculum which specifies the textbooks to be used in the teaching of each level of virtue and of science (Ch. 6). Thus, having examined divinization as a goal, I will discuss the path leading to this goal: the scale of virtues and of sciences, and their curricular application.

Divinization in Greek Philosophy   3

The term 'divinization' (θέωσις) was made current especially by two
Christian theologians, by Pseudo-Dionysius towards the beginning of the
sixth century and by Maximus the Confessor in the seventh.[1] Pseudo-
Dionysius, to whom we will return below in Chapter 13, who is very much
indebted to Proclus, defines divinization thus: 'divinization is the assimilation (ἀφομοίωσις) and unification, as far as possible, to god'.[2] The term thus
serves to express the notion of 'assimilation to god as far as possible' that
the Neoplatonists took from Plato's *Theaetetus* (176b) and used to define the
goal of their philosophy.

What does 'divinization' mean? Whatever 'god' means and however
'assimilation' or 'unification' to god is conceived. As regards Greek philosophy, we must at the outset put aside an exclusivist, monotheist notion of
'God' and remember the generous Greek sphere of the divine, which
includes many different types and ranks of gods. We should ask in particular what, for a Greek philosopher, do 'god/s', or 'the divine' in fact represent. 'Assimilation' can also have a wide range of possible meanings, going
from actually 'becoming a god' (deification) to imitating some form of
divine life (*imitatio dei*), in one way or another. This range of possibilities
must also be kept in mind.

Well before Plotinus, Platonists of the first and second centuries AD such as
Alcinous had already found in the phrase of Plato's *Theaetetus* an expression

---

[1] See Lot-Borodine (1970); Beierwaltes (1979: 385–90); Larchet (1996: 21–59); de Andia
(1996: 288–300) for a survey of the theme of divinization in Patristic literature. The language used
by Neoplatonists to express 'divinization' includes not only the term θέωσις (cf. Damascius, *Princ.*
III, p. 64, 14), but also such expressions as θεοποιεῖν, θεὸς γίγνεσθαι, θεουργία (on this last term,
cf. below p. 129). Augustine, translating Porphyry, uses 'deificari' (*City of God* XIX, 23) and
Boethius writes 'deos fieri' (*Cons.* IV, 3).

[2] *EH*, I, 3, 376A.

31

of the goal of their philosophy.[3] Some attributed the notion of assimilation to god not only to Plato, but also to Pythagoras before him, associating with it the Pythagorean precept 'follow god' (ἕπου θεῷ).[4] If we may have doubts about whether in fact the theme of assimilation to god made such an early appearance in Greek philosophy, we can recognize its presence in Plato and indeed in the work of many other Greek philosophers, Aristotle, Epicurus, and the Stoics in particular. To reach some idea of the pervasiveness and significance of the theme throughout Greek philosophy, it may be useful to consider briefly the latter philosophers before returning to the texts in Plato that were especially decisive for Neoplatonism.[5]

1. Aristotle, Epicurus, and Stoics

At the end of the *Nicomachean Ethics* (X, 7–8), Aristotle describes the most desirable of lives, the final object of human aspiration, the human good, as the 'life of knowledge' (βίος θεωρητικός), a life in which is fully realized the activity of the highest of human faculties, the intellect, in relation to the highest of objects, the immaterial and immutable first principles of reality.[6] This is the best of lives because it satisfies most the criteria for such a life: continuity, pleasure, independence, leisure. It is also the kind of life that we must suppose the gods to lead (for we assume that they enjoy felicity): it would be unworthy for them to be engaged in the inferior practical activities that we perform (making contracts, for example). Indeed Aristotle elsewhere describes the life of his 'divine' first principle(s) of the world, the unmoved mover(s), as the life of pure intellect, pure knowing (*Metaphysics* XII, 7 and 9). The best life for man, then, is a divine life. Aristotle insists on this at the end of the *Nicomachean Ethics*, in reaction to the objection that we

---

[3] Cf. Merki (1952: 1–2); Dörrie and Baltes (1993–6: iv. 234); Annas (1999: ch. 3).

[4] Merki (1952), 1. Merki also quotes (pp. 34–5) a much later text, Boethius' *Cons.* I, 4, where the Pythagorean dictum 'follow god' is again associated with assimilation to god ('*consimilem deo*'). Cf. Damascius, *Vit. Is.*, fr. 24.

[5] Annas (1999: 65–6), points out that modern discussion has in general been blind to this theme in Plato; to some recent exceptions she mentions one might add the studies listed in Squilloni (1991: 63 n. 1) and Alekniene (1999). Rist (1964) is largely concerned with the theme of divinization, from Plato to Plotinus.

[6] My rendering 'life of knowledge' may be desperate, but not perhaps as misleading as some other translations of βίος θεωρητικός, such as 'contemplative' life (too mystical), 'theoretical' life (too abstract), 'speculative' life (too vague). Later, however, I will be obliged to have recourse to 'theoretical' to render θεωρητικός, for want of a better adjective.

are mere mortals: we should, he says, 'be immortal (ἀθανατίζειν), as far as possible and do all to live in accord with the highest' in us, the divine in man, intellect (1177ᵇ31–4). This divine life, which is not easily or often attained (we are mortals after all), is not conceived by Aristotle as solitary: it is better if shared with others (1177ᵃ34) and is made possible when appropriate conditions are supplied by the political context.

The divine life for man presupposes then a favourable social/political context: human nature is not simply that of the divine in man, intellect, but also that of an organic unity of soul and body. Excellence achieved on this lower level, that of a life of ethical/political action (βίος πρακτικός), a life marked by moral virtues (as distinguished from the intellectual or scientific excellence of the βίος θεωρητικός), is ranked as a secondary good (X, 8). It is not the highest good, the divine life that humans seek and sometimes attain, but a secondary good subordinate to this divine life.[7]

In the context of a completely different approach, Epicurus also sees the goal of human nature as a divine life: if one follows his ethical precepts, one will live 'as a god among men. For he who lives among immortal goods will be like no mortal animal' (*Letter to Menoikeus* 135). In what is probably a fragment from a letter sent by the young Epicurus to his mother, he tells her:

For not small. . . are these gains for us which make our disposition godlike and show that not even our mortality makes us inferior to the imperishable and blessed nature; for when we are alive, we are as joyful as the gods.[8]

A correct conception of the gods' felicity frees them from all disturbance, trouble, and care, in particular providential care for a world such as ours: the human good is such a life, freed from mental anguish, undisturbed as far as possible by physical pain. Epicurus himself, who lived this life, was regarded by his school as a god ('a god he was, a god!', Lucretius V, 8).

This life of the gods was cultivated in a community, at first in the small community sheltered in Epicurus' garden from the disturbances of the outside world. Were Epicurus' philosophy ever to prevail in the future, such protective isolation from others would no longer be required. A fragment from the work of a second century AD Epicurean allows us to imagine this Epicurean utopia:

---

[7] The Aristotelian passages I have noted have become an exegetical minefield, object of a veritable academic industry (for a broad approach, cf. Kraut 1989). The points I have summarized are likely to have been of interest to the Neoplatonist reader of Aristotle. They are emphasized by Sedley (2000: 806–8), who points to the sources in Plato of Aristotelian divinization.

[8] Diogenes of Oinoanda, fr. 125 III–IV (trans. Smith).

But if we assume it to be possible, then truly the life of the gods will pass to men. For everything will be full of justice and mutual love, and there will come to be no need of fortifications or laws. . . and such activities [i.e. agricultural activities]. . . will interrupt the continuity of the [shared] study of philosophy, for the farming operations [will provide what our] nature wants.[9]

Divinization can also be seen as the goal of Stoic philosophy. Very briefly,[10] we can say that, in Stoicism, if the best life for humans is a life according to nature, according, that is, to human nature and to the nature of the universe, then this means living the life of the divine *logos* in man, that is reason, in conformity with a universe determined by a cosmic divine *logos*. The Stoic ideal, the sage, is then a godlike figure, as invincible, as infallible, as perfect as the cosmic god. So extreme is this ideal of divinization that it was a moot point whether there had ever existed or would ever exist a Stoic sage, even though the divine exemplar was not some remote transcendent principle, but an immanent cosmic force. As in the cases of Aristotle and Epicurus, the life of the Stoic divine man, the sage, was not conceived as solitary: the sage would constitute, with other sages and the god(s) of the universe, a cosmic community (*cosmopolis*) of friendship and mutual understanding.[11]

Anticipating then our account of Plato, we may conclude that divinization describes the goal of the major philosophical schools of the Classical and Hellenistic periods. In this respect Neoplatonism is no exception. Of course the divine is conceived in various ways in the different schools and the methods and degrees of assimilation to the divine vary correspondingly. The limits imposed by our human mortal nature on our sharing in divine life are also stressed to varying degrees. It is noteworthy that divinization is not understood in these schools as a solitary affair: it has, in one way or another, a political dimension. It is this dimension that we need to determine in the case of Neoplatonic divinization. But first some attention must be given to some passages in Plato's dialogues which were to be of primary importance for Neoplatonists.

---

[9] Diogenes of Oinoanda, fr. 56.

[10] See Merki (1952: 8–17), for a quite full discussion, unfortunately concentrating too much on attributing material to Posidonius; Rist (1964: 160–4).

[11] On this see Schofield (1991).

2. Plato

In the *Theaetetus* passage, Plato links assimilation to god to an 'escape' from this world: this escape is not, as Plotinus points out,[12] a change of place, but a change of life, an effort to live in justice and wisdom (176b). For the divine is what is most just, and to be *just* is to resemble the divine (176b8–176c2; cf. *Republic* 613a8–b1). Sharing in the virtue of *wisdom* also makes us resemble the divine and even take part in immortality (*Timaeus* 90b–c6), as Aristotle was to propose. *Moderation* is another virtue the practice of which makes us resemble god, the true 'measure' of our moral lives, whom we should 'follow'.[13]

The idea that a life led virtuously is a life that is divine-like is strengthened by the suggestion that this resemblance results from a striving to imitate, or model oneself, as far as possible, after the divine (*Republic* 500c2–d1). The wonderful chariot myth of the *Phaedrus* gives poetic expression to this: the souls of mortals who struggle to follow the souls of the gods on their heavenly round, but fail and fall to varying degrees to earth, try to imitate their god as far as possible (248a, 252d–253c). As there are different gods with different characteristics, so there are different images of them in human souls.

This imitation is not purely self-directed: Plato is describing the power of love. Thus the souls of lovers also try to make their beloved into an image, a statue (ἄγαλμα), as it were, representing their god (cf. 252d7, 253a4–b7). The idea of the divinization of others goes beyond the interpersonal relationship of lover and beloved to include the relation between the ideal philosopher and the state of which he becomes king in the *Republic*.

So the philosopher, who consorts with what is divine and ordered, himself becomes godlike and ordered as far as man can. . . And if it becomes necessary for him to put into practice the things he sees yonder by applying them to the characters of men both in private and in public life instead of only moulding his own, do you think he will be a poor craftsman of moderation and justice. . . the city will never find happiness unless the painters [i.e. the philosopher-kings] who use the divine model sketch its outline. . . They would take the city and men's characters as a draughting board, and first of all they would clean it. . . then, as they work, they would keep looking back and forth, to [the Forms of] justice, beauty, moderation, and all such things. . . and they would compose human life with reference to these, mixing and mingling the human likeness from various pursuits, basing their judgement on what Homer [*Iliad* I, 131] too called the divine and godlike (θεοείκελον) existing in man.[14]

---

12 Above Ch. 1, n. 17; cf. Plato, *Phaedo* 107d1–2.
13 *Laws* 716c; compare the Pythagorean precept quoted above at n. 4.   14 *Rep.* 500c9–501b7.

The city of the philosopher-kings in the *Republic* is thus a divinized city, almost, or very like, the city of gods or children of gods that Plato describes in the *Laws* (739c–d). The latter city is described as the model of the city for humans to be founded in the *Laws* (739e), a city, however, which falls short of the city of the *Republic*.[15]

In summarizing the political theory of the *Republic* at the beginning of the *Timaeus*, Plato suggests a cosmic background to the divinized state: as the philosopher-king orders a city after the divine pattern of the Forms, so, on a larger scale, does the divine craftsman (the 'demiurge') of the world put it into order after the pattern of the Forms. The world is chaos brought into order, divinized. The divine is manifest in particular in the orderly motions of the heavens, which can inspire order in our souls.[16]

The divinization of man in Plato is not simply an *imitatio dei*. The suggestion is also made that there is a divine element in man (cf. *Timaeus* 90a2–b1), the highest aspect of soul, which has an affinity with the transcendent Forms (*Phaedo* 79d1–4) and which, on separation from the body, may join the company of the gods (82b10–c1). This, however, can only be achieved through the practice, here below, of the highest degree of *imitatio dei*, of moral assimilation to the gods.[17]

3. Neoplatonism

Various aspects of the theme of divinization as sketched briefly above in reference to Plato, Aristotle, Epicurus, and the Stoics reappear in Neoplatonic divinization: Plato's association of the 'divine' with the transcendent Forms and Aristotle's identification of the divine as transcendent intellect; Aristotle's claim that the divine life for humans is the life of intellect; Plato's suggestion of a life in the company of the gods; the Stoic ideal of the supreme sovereignty of the sage; the insistence in general on the necessity of a life of moral virtue as a condition for attaining the divine life. However,

---

[15] On the relation between the cities of the *Republic* and the *Laws*, see below Ch. 8, s. 2.

[16] *Tim.* 90d. On divine assimilation as a bringing into order of a complex of parts (in soul, in the state, in the cosmos), see Alekniene (1999).

[17] Annas (1999: 63–65, 70–1) finds the two aspects of divinization, assimilation by virtuous living and assimilation by separation from the body, to be two different conceptions confused by Plato and later Platonists. However she notes that this confusion is felt by modern readers and is not apparent as such to Plato and ancient Platonists. Sedley (2000) argues for a more coherent position in Plato, interpreted correctly, he feels, by Plotinus.

in order to explore Neoplatonic divinization further, it is necessary first to indicate briefly what is meant by the 'divine' in Neoplatonism and then to show in more detail, in the next chapters, how the divine life is to be attained.

In Plotinus the 'divine' ranges from the ultimate and ineffable source of all reality, the 'One', through a transcendent Intellect (which Plotinus identifies with Plato's Forms), down to soul.[18] The One (which can also be described as 'the Good', as a perfection of existence to which all reality aspires) gives rise, outside time and space, to an articulated knowable manifestation or expression of itself, Intellect, which, in an orientation to the One, knows the One as the multiple and determinate content of its own thought, the Forms. From this divine Intellect in turn arises soul, itself a further expression of Intellect.

As regards these three hypostases, or levels of divinity (Plotinus sometimes associates them with the Greek gods Ouranos, Kronos, Zeus),[19] we should note the following points. (1) The three hypostases constitute a dynamic structure: the lower levels derive from, and exist in orientation towards, the higher. Indeed this tensional relationship of 'arising out of' and 'turning back towards' is constitutive of reality in general. Thus lower levels of divinity (Intellect, Soul) are divine in relation to the higher and in particular to the highest, the 'first', the One.[20] (2) The dynamic structure is hierarchical: there are various levels or degrees of divinity, various levels of perfection of existence. Where the divine ceases is where evil makes itself felt, in the material world.[21] Evil arises from the indeterminate, irrational substrate of the material world, matter. However not all in the material world is evil: in the heavenly bodies, the 'visible gods', matter is entirely mastered and there is no evil there. Soul, too, can be present to the material world, where its function is to bring order and form to matter, without losing its orientation to divine Intellect and the One, therefore without succumbing to vice.[22]

Human nature, in this context, is, at its root, soul and therefore divine, and is dynamically linked to divine Intellect and to the One. This means that the divine, at all levels, is always present to us and available to us, whatever

---

[18] See *Enn.* V 1, 7, 49. See also Porphyry, fr. 221F. A brief account of Plotinus' metaphysics can be found in O'Meara (1993a).

[19] Cf. *Enn.* V 8, 12–13; Hadot (1981).

[20] See Rist (1962).

[21] The absence of evil is an important mark of the divine in Plato (*Theaetetus* 176a7, *Phaedrus* 246a7–b1), as in Plotinus (*Enn.* I 8, 2, 25–7).

[22] On these themes cf. *Enn.* I 8 (with commentary in O'Meara 1999a).

our aberrational preoccupation with material things and forgetfulness of our essential nature and divine 'homeland'.[23] We are therefore anchored in divine Intellect and a part of us always remains 'there' (*Enn.* IV 8, 8, 1–6), an idea for which Plotinus was notorious among his Neoplatonist successors. The human self is mobile: we can live our lives at different levels, depending where we place our interests and activities. We can live the life of beasts, or the life of gods. Indeed we can become a god, or rather come back to live the life of the god that we essentially are.[24]

Neoplatonic philosophy evolved after Plotinus in the direction of ever increasing metaphysical sophistication. This meant that the range of the divine (the 'gods') became more and more differentiated. If soul remained the lower limit of the divine,[25] many new levels of the divine divided Plotinus' hierarchy of three hypostases: a level of 'henads' intervened between the One and divine Intellect/the Forms, the latter breaking up into various levels (the intelligible, the intellectual, and combinations of them), other levels intervening again or dividing up soul. Iamblichus, in particular, seems responsible for this proliferating metaphysical universe and his successors added further distinctions and refinements.[26]

Iamblichus also seems to have played an important part in the associations later Neoplatonists made between the many levels and members of their metaphysical universe and the gods of traditional religion, not only those of the classic Greek pantheon already associated with metaphysical first principles in Plotinus, but also the divinities of other religious traditions thought to be expressive of an ancient wisdom, in particular the gods of the Egyptians and of the Chaldaeans.[27]

A consequence of the greater complexity of the later Neoplatonist metaphysical universe was a greater range in what divinization as a philosophical goal could mean: many more levels of the divine meant many more degrees of divinization. This could suggest greater continuity in the process of divinization, to the extent that the divine appears as a more graduated structure in which levels are linked by means of more intermediate terms. However the multiplication of levels also has the effect of making the

---

[23] *Enn.* V 1, 1, 1–5 with I 6, 8, 16–21.

[24] Cf. *Enn.* I 2, 6, 2–3; 7, 25–7; I 6, 9, 33–4; Merki (1952: 20).

[25] Cf. Proclus, *Plat. Theol.* I, 26, pp. 114, 23–116, 3, where different degrees of the divine are distinguished with references to passages in Plato.

[26] For a classic presentation cf. Proclus' *El. Theol.* which ranges from the One down to soul.

[27] Cf. Brisson (2000) for tables of correspondence between Neoplatonic metaphysical principles and Chaldaean divinities.

higher levels of the divine, in particular the highest principle, source of the divinity of all else, more remote, more difficult of access.

A further development in later Neoplatonism which tended to reinforce the difficulty in divinization was the general rejection of Plotinus' thesis that part of the human soul remains present in the divine: for most later Neoplatonists, *all* of human soul has descended to body.[28] Furthermore, the scale of degrees to which the human soul has fallen in the material world was formalized and in particular soul's relation to its material condition, to body, was given much more importance. Human soul, alienated from its divine origins, finds its identity in its relation to body.[29] As a consequence, the material, bodily aspects of the human condition were to be of much greater relevance for the divinization of soul in later Neoplatonism than in Plotinus.

A result both of the increasing remoteness of the higher levels of the divine and of the greater importance of the bodily condition for the human soul was a less ambitious view than that of Plotinus as to the level of divine life attainable by the human soul. Thus Hierocles identifies the god which is the object of assimilation as the demiurge of the universe, a relatively low-ranking divinity in the late Neoplatonic divine hierarchy.[30] Hierocles, however, is writing for the beginning student of philosophy, whereas Proclus suggests the possibility of higher levels of divinization for the advanced soul.[31]

The question of higher degrees of divinization will not be developed further in what follows, which relates to the primary concern of our investigation, the function of 'political' virtue and political philosophy as a first stage in divinization. The political bearing that the increasing importance of bodily aspects of the human condition in later Neoplatonism had will become clear in the following chapters, where the result of these various developments in later Neoplatonism—an elaborate theory of the variety of methods required for divinization over a wide range of degrees—will be compared with the relatively simple form divinization takes in its beginnings in Plotinus.

---

[28] Cf. Steel (1978: Part i); Iamblichus seems mainly responsible for imposing this anti-Plotinian claim in later Neoplatonism.

[29] This is again an anti-Plotinian position forcefully taken by Iamblichus; cf. Finamore (1985); Shaw (1995: ch. 2).

[30] Hierocles, *In Carm. aur.*, pp. 120, 27–121, 11; cf. Schibli (2002: 125–8); below Ch. 8, 3.

[31] See Beierwaltes (1979), 294–305 for a full and important discussion; also Psellus, *Omn. doct.* 71, 74 (on Psellus' Neoplatonic sources, cf. below Ch. 4, n. 21).

The Scale of Virtues 4

The Plotinian treatise *On Virtues* (*Enn.* I 2) suggests, as we have seen (above, Ch. 1), the idea of a scale of virtues representing different stages in a progressive divinization of the human soul, a scale beginning with the 'political' virtues and leading up to the 'purificatory' virtues. This scale was formalized and developed by Plotinus' pupil Porphyry, in particular in chapter 32 of his manual of Plotinian philosophy, the *Sentences*. Porphyry's version was in turn expanded by Iamblichus in a work, now lost, *On Virtues* which seems to have established the version of the scale of virtues that was to become common (with some variations) in later Neoplatonism. The main stages in the evolution of this theory of a scale of virtues will be traced in what follows, with reference in particular to what is of most interest in this investigation, the initial level of the scale, that of 'political' virtue.[1]

1. Plotinus, *Ennead* I 2

Plotinus finds his conception of 'political' virtue in Plato's *Republic*, in a passage (441d1–443b2) where the four cardinal virtues are defined and which Plotinus summarizes as follows:

> . . . *practical wisdom* (φρόνησις). . . has to do with discursive reason, *courage*. . . has to do with emotions, *moderation*. . . consists in a sort of agreement and harmony of desire and reason, *justice*. . . makes each of these parts [of the soul] agree in fulfilling their proper function where ruling and being ruled are concerned.[2]

---

[1] For general surveys of the Neoplatonic scale of virtues, see Westerink's note in Olympiodorus, *In Phaed.*, pp. 116–18; Lieshout (1926), a little superficial; Schissel (1928), much fuller, but severely criticized by Theiler (1929); the introduction (pp. lxix–c) by Saffrey and Segonds to Marinus, *Vit. Procl.* (very useful and rich); Vorwerk (2001). Plotinus' doctrine in *Enn.* I 2 and some possible antecedents are discussed by Dillon (1983).

[2] *Enn.* I 2, 1, 17–21 (Armstrong trans.).

Plato's four cardinal virtues are taken here by Plotinus as describing the proper functioning of the various parts of the soul (Plato had also used these virtues to describe the proper functioning of the various parts of the city), such that reason governs the other parts, exercising wisdom,[3] desire is in harmony with reason (moderation), spirit manifests courage, and justice is the exercise by each part of the soul of the function appropriate to it.

Such virtues, however, may hardly be ascribed to the divine,[4] which can have no need of courage and moderation (cf. 1, 10–16): Plotinus follows here Aristotle's exclusion of moral virtue from the sphere of the divine, whereas Plato seems, as we have seen (Ch. 3, 2), to attribute virtues to the divine.[5] But how then can Plotinus maintain that these virtues assimilate us to the divine?

Another description of the 'political' virtues, given later in the treatise, makes the connection between these virtues and divinization clearer:

[These virtues] do genuinely set us in order and make us better by giving limit and measure to our desires, and putting measure into all our experience; and they abolish false opinions, by what is altogether better and by the fact of limitation, and by the exclusion of the unlimited and indefinite and the existence of the measured; and they are themselves limited and clearly defined. And so far as they are a measure which forms the matter of the soul, they are made like the measure There (τῷ ἐκεῖ μέτρῳ) and have a trace in them of the best There.   (2, 13–20)

The soul is then a sort of matter, as it were, that is formed, put in order in its desires and opinions, by a measure,[6] by an order which derives from the divine (i.e. Intellect) and which is transmitted, we may assume, by practical wisdom (φρόνησις) in soul. We appear as divine when divine order is brought to our opinions and desires. Yet the divine differs from that which results from this imposition of order (2, 22–6).

If divinization initially involves the 'political' virtues, these virtues are instrumental and subordinate to 'higher' virtues (1, 22 and 26; 3, 2) which bring the soul nearer to a true resemblance to the divine. These higher virtues are those that bring about the 'purification' of the soul, that is, its

---

[3] Plato uses the term σοφός (441e4), whereas Plotinus speaks of φρόνησις, perhaps because he wishes to reserve the term σοφία for a higher theoretical wisdom related to, or enjoyed by, divine Intellect (cf. 6, 12–15; 7, 4 and 7).

[4] The 'divine' is understood at this point in *Enn.* I 2 as referring to the world-soul and its intellect (1, 6–9), but is later extended upwards to refer to the higher hypostases of Intellect and the One (3, 19–31).

[5] For a useful survey of the philosophical debate over the attribution of virtues to the gods, see Westerink's note in Damascius, *In Phaed.*, pp. 90–1.

[6] Cf. the divine as measure in Plato's *Laws* (above p. 35).

independence from the opinions and desires that arise in its relation to the body:

> Since the soul is evil when it is thoroughly mixed with the body and shares its experiences and has all the same opinions, it will be good and will possess virtue when it no longer has the same opinions but acts alone—this is intelligence and wisdom—and does not share the body's experiences—this is moderation—and is not afraid of departing from the body—this is courage—and is ruled by reason and intellect, without opposition—and this is justice. One would not be wrong in calling this state of the soul likeness to god, in which its activity is intellectual, and it is free in this way from bodily affections.[7]

At this new stage, the four cardinal virtues describe a reorientation of the soul, away from the preoccupations of a life related to body, towards the divine life above soul, the life of the hypostases of Intellect and of the One (cf. 3, 22–31; 6, 23–7).

Within these 'purificatory' virtues Plotinus distinguishes what relates to the process of purification from that which relates to the state soul achieves as a result of this process (4, 1–5). We may thus distinguish between the purifying virtues and those virtues that characterize the purified soul. While Plotinus continues to resist the attribution of virtues to the divine (3, 31), he also allows that this divine life, the life of Intellect, contains the paradigms, or Forms, of the virtues; the virtues are what these paradigms give to another, what exists in another, in soul (6, 14–19).

We may be tempted to compare Plotinus' scale of virtues to Aristotle's distinction between moral and intellectual virtues. However, in Aristotle, the two kinds of virtue relate to different aspects of human nature, to the desires and emotions guided by practical reason (moral virtue) and to reason, the divine in man, taken as active in itself (intellectual virtue). But in Plotinus the two kinds of virtues correspond to opposing orientations of the soul, towards the body ('political' virtues) or towards Intellect and the One (purificatory virtues). This opposing orientation means that the scale of virtues is both continuous (the soul moves from one orientation to its opposite) and discontinuous: the 'political' virtues do not provide a resemblance to divinity such as is reached through the purificatory virtues,[8] and this even if they divinize the life of the soul in its relation to the body, imposing on it a divine order, divine measure, and preparing the access of soul to the higher virtues.[9] It is the latter virtues that, properly speaking, divinize

---

[7] 3, 11–21.　　　　　　　　　　　　　　　　　　　　　[8] Cf. above, p. 9.

[9] It is in this way that Plotinus takes notice of and seeks to resolve the tension between concepts of divinization noted by Annas (above Ch. 3, n. 17). Sedley (2000), 804 depreciates too strongly, I believe, the value of 'political' virtue in Plotinus, as does Zintzen (1969).

the soul. Having become purified, soul can ascend even higher, becoming divine Intellect, sharing in its life, an experience which Plotinus describes, for example, in *Enn.* IV 8, 1. But this is no longer a life of virtue; virtue remains in *Enn.* I 2 a means of attaining the Good, not the Good itself.

It follows from the theory of the scale of virtues, not only that it is necessary to achieve the lower types of virtue, in particular 'political' virtue, in order to be in a position to reach the higher, purificatory virtues, but also that having lower types of virtues does not necessarily mean that one has achieved the higher types, whereas having the higher means that one already has the lower:

> Whoever has the greater virtues must necessarily have the lesser ones potentially (δυνάμει), but the possessor of the lesser virtues does not necessarily have the greater ones. (7, 10–12)

As if feeling the need to specify what 'potential' possession of lower virtues means for those having reached higher types of virtue, Plotinus asks if the lower are possessed 'in act' (ἐνεργείᾳ) or in some other way.[10] He briefly responds:

> Perhaps the possessor of the [lower] virtues will know them, and how much he can get from them, and will act according to some of them as circumstances require. But reaching higher principles and different measures he will act according to these. . . [he] will altogether separate himself, as far as possible, from his lower nature and will not live the life of the good man which 'political' virtue requires. He will leave that behind, and choose another, the life of the gods: for it is to them, not to good men, that we are to be made like. (7, 19–28)

It is important to notice that Plotinus is speaking of the *ascent* of the soul to higher forms of life, an ascent in which lower activities are left aside in favour of the higher. In this context, the soul will use 'political' virtue as a stage to be reached and surpassed. However, having reached divine life, soul may wish to 'descend', to return to the exercise of 'political' virtue. These two movements, that of ascent described in our passage of I 2 and that of descent, to be examined in Chapters 7–8 below, imply two distinct attitudes to 'political' virtue, one using it as a way of getting beyond it as

---

[10] 7, 13–14. We might compare the scale of faculties of the soul in Aristotle's *De anima*, where a similar system of non-reciprocal inclusion (of the lower in the higher) obtains and where the status of faculties possessed but not functioning leads to the distinction between a 'first' and 'second' act (412a22–8).

much as possible, the other practising it as a way of communicating divine life, divine order.[11]

2. Porphyry, *Sentences*, ch. 32

Plotinus' treatise *On Virtues* was extensively used by Porphyry in his *Sentences* (ch. 32) and it is also cited by later Neoplatonists, for example by Macrobius, Marinus, and Olympiodorus.[12] Porphyry formalizes Plotinus' scale of virtues as a scale of four levels: (1) 'political', (2) purificatory, (3) theoretical, and (4) paradigmatic virtues.[13] The 'political' virtues (1) are defined in Plotinus' words, following Plato's example in the *Republic*. However Porphyry adds just beforehand:

> The virtues of the political [man], lying in moderation of the passions (μετριοπάθεια), consist in following and accompanying reasoning as to what is appropriate in the realm of actions (πράξεις). These virtues are called political, because they look to the community, free of harm, of those who are neighbours through constituting groups and communities. (*Sent.* 32, p. 23, 4–8)

The political dimension receives an emphasis here which is missing in Plotinus' treatise. Plotinus is concerned with good order in the inner life of the soul, as defined in the *Republic*, neglecting, however, the outer order between citizens that Plato also describes in the *Republic* in terms of the cardinal virtues.

The political aspect of the first level of virtues is stressed even more by Macrobius:

> The political [virtues] are of man, in as much as man is a social animal. By these virtues good men look after the state, protect cities; by these, they revere parents, love children, and cherish those close to them; by these, they guide the welfare of the citizens. . .[14]

[11] This distinction is generally ignored in accounts of Plotinus' ethics, which thus tend to be one-sided; cf. e.g. Dillon (1996).

[12] Macrobius, *Somn.* I, 8, 5–13; Marinus, *Vit. Procl.* 18; Olympiodorus, *In Phaed.* 8, 2, p. 119. Plotinus' treatise is also cited in a Neoplatonic ethical work (attributed to a certain Nicolaus) which has survived only in an Arabic version (Lyons 1960–1: 37, 4–5). Cf. also the *Virtues of Soul*, a lost Greek text cited in Arabic by Miskawayh (Pines 1986: 8–13).

[13] In general cf. I. Hadot (1978: 152–8); the extent to which Porphyry departs from Plotinus here is a matter of dispute (see also Festugière 1969: 548; Dillon 1983: 100). Macrobius also finds four levels in Plotinus (*Somn.* I, 8, 5): *virtutes politicae, purgatoriae, animi iam purgati, exemplares*.

[14] *Somn.* I, 8, 6. Cf. the Arabic version of Nicolaus (above n. 12): 'His [Plotinus'] view is that there are four types of virtue. . . One of these belongs to man in that he is a social being' (Lyons 1960–1: 45).

There follows a long list of virtues, the four cardinal virtues (*prudentia, fortitudo, temperantia, iustitia*), each accompanied by a host of minor or derivative virtues, which concern both the inner state of the soul and attitudes and behaviour in relation to others. Macrobius concludes:

Through these virtues the good man is made ruler first of himself and thence (*inde*) of the state, ruling justly and with foresight, not deserting human affairs.[15]

Macrobius suggests that 'political' virtue should first be cultivated within the individual, as good order in the soul, and thence in relation to others, including in the political sphere. The suggestion is that the inner ordering of the soul is the precondition of outer ordering, in social and political affairs.[16] Macrobius also indicates that the 'political' virtues are human virtues, a point also stressed by Porphyry: they govern a life according to *human* nature, whereas the higher virtues, relating to intellect, represent assimilation to the divine (*Sent.*, pp. 22, 1–23, 3; 25, 6–9).

If Porphyry expresses in this way the distance Plotinus sets between 'political' virtues and higher virtues, he also brings out clearly the importance of the 'political' virtues as precursors (πρόδρομοι), as preparatory to the higher virtues: if the goals of the 'political' and the purificatory virtues are different, the former imposing measure on the passions associated with the activities of human nature, the latter seeking detachment from these passions, the latter cannot be reached without the former.[17]

The higher virtues in Porphyry include (2) the purificatory virtues defined, as in Plotinus, as a reorientation away from bodily concerns and towards Intellect; (3) the theoretical virtues (virtues corresponding to Plotinus' state of the purified soul), and (4) the paradigmatic virtues, the paradigms of soul's virtues, an idea more systematically worked out here in Porphyry's *Sentences* than in Plotinus' treatise.

In general, then, Porphyry provides a more formalized and systematic scheme of the scale of virtues than that in Plotinus. He reminds the reader of the social and political dimension of the 'political' virtues, and brings out

---

[15] *Somn.* I, 8, 8. see Zintzen (1969) and Flamant (1977: 599–614) for a discussion of Macrobius' use of Plotinus and Porphyry. Zintzen explains Macrobius' emphasis on the political as due to a Roman approach. He notes some of the Greek texts mentioned in this and in the next section, but seeks to limit their importance by assigning them to 'Neopythagorean' influence.

[16] See also Proclus, *In Remp.* I, pp. 210, 21–211, 3; 217, 6–15; Olympiodorus, *In Gorg.*, p. 204, 11–14; Damascius, *Vit. Is.*, fr. 109: Theosebius ordered 'his republic within. This was his first concern, and then to deal with every one else in turn with the aim of their improvement' (Athanassiadi trans.). The latter activity did not extend, however, to political affairs in the case of Theosebius.

[17] *Sent.*, pp. 24, 6–9; 30, 5–31, 1.

very clearly the function of the 'political' virtues as a preparatory stage presupposed by the higher virtues which bring about a closer assimilation of man to the divine.

3. Iamblichus and Later Neoplatonism

Porphyry's chapter on the virtues was also read by later Neoplatonists, by Synesius, by Marinus, perhaps by Macrobius,[18] and very probably by Porphyry's own pupil Iamblichus, who may have had Porphyry specifically in mind when he composed his own work *On Virtues*.[19] This work no longer survives,[20] but it was probably still available to the eleventh-century Byzantine Neoplatonist Michael Psellus, who attributes to Iamblichus a more elaborate list of the virtues than that to be found in Porphyry's *Sentences*.[21] It seems indeed that Iamblichus was the source of a further differentiation of the scale of virtues that is common in later Neoplatonism.[22]

The scale of virtues was extended both downwards and upwards. It was extended downwards so as to include, as the lowest level of the scale, the 'natural' virtues, that is, natural qualities of the soul in relation to particular bodily constitutions: lions, for example, are 'constitutionally courageous. . . all cattle are moderate, all storks just, all cranes clever'.[23] The notion of natural virtue is of Aristotelian origin and can be found in Iamblichus.[24]

Furthermore, a level of 'ethical' virtues was inserted above the lowest type of virtue (natural virtue) and below the 'political' virtues. The 'ethical' virtues are inferior to 'political' virtues because they concern children and certain animals and are acquired by habituation (ἐθισμός) and by correct opinion (ὀρθοδοξία) under the guidance of parents or teachers (or trainers). These virtues exist without the activity of reason in the animal or child, whereas 'political' virtue requires precisely the activity of reason, ruling the other parts of the soul.

---

[18] Cf. the apparatus of Porphyry's *Sent.* (Lamberz).

[19] Iamblichus often wrote in opposition to Porphyry. The most well-known case is Iamblichus' *De mysteriis*. For other examples cf. Taormina (1999) and the references in O'Meara (1990: 412).

[20] It is referred to in Damascius, *In Phaed.* I, 143.

[21] Psellus, *Philos. Min.* II, p. 111, 18–19. Psellus may have used Iamblichus' work in writing some of the chapters (66–81) on the virtues in his *Omn. Doct.*, as is suggested by Saffrey (1971: 237 n. 42).

[22] For comprehensive accounts see Olympiodorus, *In Phaed.* 8, 2; Damascius, *In Phaed.* I, 138–44; Philoponus, *In Cat.*, pp. 141, 25–142, 3; Proclus, *In Alcib.* 96; Marinus, *Vit. Procl.*, ch. 3.

[23] Olympiodorus, *In Phaed.* 8, 2, p. 119, 6–7 (trans. Westerink).

[24] See *PR*, 73; Blumenthal (1984: 480, 482); Westerink's note in Olympiodorus, *In Phaed.*, p. 117. 'Natural' virtues are mentioned in Plotinus, *Enn.* I 3, 6, 18.

The notion and terminology of 'ethical' virtue reminds us, distantly, of the habituation that is so important in Aristotle's theory of moral virtue. However, moral virtue in Aristotle involves practical reason. Closer are Plato's accounts of the moral upbringing of children[25] and of virtue that is acquired 'by habit (ἔθος) and practice, without philosophy and reason'.[26] Iamblichus, again, is likely to be the source of the introduction of the level of 'ethical' virtue in the Plotinian–Porphyrian scale. In a letter to Sopatros, he offers advice on the education of children in ethical virtue, as a moral upbringing through habituation, prior to the stage when children reach an understanding of virtue,[27] i.e. before they reach the level of rational virtue represented by 'political' virtue.

The transition from 'ethical' to 'political' virtue is described in the preface of an ethical treatise that an otherwise unknown Neoplatonist, Nicolaus, wrote for his daughter:

A long time ago, my little daughter, when you were a very small girl indeed, I was in the habit of drawing you on by stages that might be useful to you in the development of your life. . . I wanted to make sure that you had all those necessary qualities which are formed by keeping to orderly habits, so that this might serve to introduce you to the moral life in its highest possible aspect. But now God and Time have brought you to an age at which you can conceive of true discipline. So I have formed the purpose of writing for you this tract, which contains an introduction to the art of ethics, so that theory backed by proof may follow on the habits which you have already acquired in your life's course.[28]

In moving from the level of good habits and correct opinions inculcated by her father, Nicolaus' daughter reaches a moral life guided by her own reason, 'political' virtue, the first level of the Plotinian–Porphyrian scale.[29]

'Political' virtues, requiring the activity and rule of reason in the soul, are

---

[25] Cf. *Rep.* 337b, *Laws* 788a.

[26] *Phaedo* 82b2–3. Plato's description of this type of virtue (82a12) as 'popular' (δημοτική) and 'political' (πολιτική) must be problematic, however, for the later Neoplatonist who would distinguish between it and 'political' virtue.

[27] In Stobaeus, *Anth.* II, 31, pp. 233, 19–235, 22 (esp. p. 234, 11–13).

[28] Lyons (1960–1: 35); cf. above n. 12.

[29] There is another, but related, way of distinguishing between ethical and 'political' virtue: the 'political' virtues entail each other, whereas ethical virtues do not have this strong unity, yet are not mutually incompatible as natural virtues can often be: Damascius, *In Phaed.* I, 138–40; cf. Festugière (1969: 542–3). Plotinus (I 2, 7, 1–3) and Porphyry (*Sent.* 32, p. 28, 4–5) describe the virtues higher than 'political' virtues as mutually entailing. Cf. Annas (1999: 121–2), for earlier Platonic sources. Different virtues also characterize or predominate in the different types of virtue, moderation in ethical virtue, justice in 'political' virtue ('in view of commercial relations'), etc. Cf. Proclus, *In Remp.* I, pp. 12, 26–13, 6; Olympiodorus, *In Phaed.* 3, 8–10 (with Westerink's note) and Saffrey and Segond's introduction to Marinus, *Vit. Procl.* LXIII n. 2.

the first really human virtues, corresponding as they do to the definition of man as a 'rational soul using body as an instrument' that the Neoplatonists found in Plato's *Alcibiades*.[30] The political dimension of this definition was stressed by Damascius in his argument that the goal of the *Alcibiades* is political self-knowledge, a claim he proved

from the definition in the dialogue of man as a rational soul using body as an instrument: only the political man uses body as an instrument, sometimes needing spirit, on behalf of his homeland, but also desire for citizens to fare well.[31]

Although, as we have seen, 'political' virtue can be practised within the soul and without, in a limited social sphere, Damascius advocates strongly a wider application:

The virtue which engages in the midst of public life through political activity and discourse fortifies the soul and strengthens through exercise what is healthy and perfect, while the impure and false element that lurks in human lives is fully exposed and more easily set on the road to improvement. And indeed politics offers great possibilities for doing what is good and useful, also for courage and firmness.[32]

In the first part of this passage, the practice of 'political' virtue in political action is regarded as morally beneficial to the soul in its progress to perfection. The second part mentions benefit for others, the communication of good to others that will be examined below in Chapter 7 in the context of the descent of soul from divine life to political action.

Moving from the 'political' virtues to the higher levels of virtue, soul begins her true assimilation to the divine. Here again Iamblichus seems to have extended the scale, this time upwards: to the purificatory, theoretical and paradigmatic virtues of Porphyry's scheme he appears to have added a level of 'theurgic' virtues uniting soul to the highest levels of reality.[33] One can imagine, on Marinus' suggestion (*Vit. Procl.*, ch. 3), yet higher levels of virtue required by the ever-increasing number of intermediate steps separating soul from the ultimate principles of reality.

If, under Iamblichus' influence, the Plotinian–Porphyrian scale of virtues became more complex, involving new degrees or levels of virtue and thus stages of divinization, this multiplication of degrees did not weaken

---

[30] *Alcib.* 129e–130c; cf. Simplicius, *In Epict.*, Praefatio 61–89.

[31] In Olympiodorus, *In Alcib.* 4, 15–21; cf. 177, 14–15. Cf. Olympiodorus, *In Phaed.* 3, 6, 7–8.

[32] *Vit. Is.*, fr. 324. Cf. Boethius, *Cons.* II, Prose 7, 1.

[33] Cf. Westerink's note in Olympiodorus, *In Phaed.*, pp. 117–18 (where difficulties as to the precise place of these theurgic virtues are discussed; cf. also Festugière 1969: 549–50). Levels of divinization and the scale of virtues are succinctly coordinated in Psellus, *Omn. doct.* 71.

the continuity whereby lower levels of virtue were seen as preparing the ground for access to higher levels. The Iamblichean scale of virtues remains a method of progressive divinization, a process of a complexity worthy of the metaphysical world-view of the later Neoplatonist. The continuity linking 'political' virtues to the higher virtues is expressed concisely by Hierocles as follows:

For we must first put in order the irrationality and slackness in us, and then in this way look to the knowledge of more divine things. For as an eye that is bleary and impure is not able to see things that are very bright, so it is not possible for a soul that has not attained virtue to contemplate the beauty of truth. . . First one should become a man, and then a god. The 'political' virtues make a good man, the sciences that lead up to divine virtue make man a god.[34]

The late Neoplatonic scale of virtues was used by Marinus and by Damascius as a method of biographical edification. Thus Marinus, in his life of Proclus, follows the career of his teacher through the ascending scale of the virtues.[35] Damascius, in his life of Isidore, applies the scale as a way of articulating and evaluating the lives of his peers and predecessors. Some of them, for example Theosebius, are pegged at the level of 'political' virtue, not having gone much higher,[36] whereas others reach the highest levels. Among the latter is Hypatia: not only did she have a nobler *nature* (φύσις) than her father Theon, according to Damascius, but she also demonstrated the highest practical virtue, the 'political' virtues of justice and moderation, and, on the theoretical level, corresponding to higher virtues, surpassed the achievement of her mathematician father.[37]

[34] *In Carm.*, p. 6, 5–10 and 19–21; cf. p. 5, 5–7. Hierocles' good man (ἀγαθός) who has 'political' virtue (cf. Plotinus, *Enn.* I 2, 7, 25) is referred to as σπουδαῖος in Psellus, *Omn. doct.* 74; cf. Porphyry, *Sent.* 32, p. 31, 5.
[35] This has been examined by Blumenthal (1984).
[36] Damascius, *Vit. Is.*, fr. 109; compare fr. 106 (Hierocles).
[37] Damascius, *Vit. Is.*, fr. 102.

The Scale of Sciences 5

If the scale of virtues constitutes a kind of ladder whereby human nature can be divinized progressively, assimilated to higher levels of divine life, the question arises as to where and how these virtues are to be acquired. A question of this kind is already posed in Plato's *Republic*: if society has a decisive function in moral education, and if society is corrupt, then it is difficult to see how a young person can escape this corrupting influence and develop the appropriate moral character (cf. 491d–492d). For a Platonist, then, it would in principle be far from clear that, given society as it is, adequate moral education and thus divinization is possible. In practice, by the end of the fourth century, as the pagan philosophers became more and more objects of suspicion and persecution, more and more isolated in an overwhelmingly Christian world, the impression of an all-encompassing moral perversity in society must have been at least as strong in them as that conveyed in Plato.

1. Science as the School of Virtue

A context, however, in which divinization might still have seemed possible, a context in which corrupting influences could be excluded and the means for divinization found, was provided by the philosophical school. The school could be much more than a teaching institution: it could constitute, and sometimes did in Late Antiquity, a community of life and moral education.[1] Indeed the curriculum of the Neoplatonic schools was so designed as to lead the pupil to live a different and higher life, a life as divine as possible, and the books used in the curriculum were assigned an appropriate

---

[1] See P. Hadot (1995: 237–59). This might be said not only of Plotinus' school in Rome in the third century (cf. M. Goulet-Cazé 1982: 254–6) and of other Neoplatonist circles, but also earlier, in the second century, of Epictetus' Stoic school, or of the Epicurean groups of which Diogenes of Oinoanda was a member.

50

edificatory function: these books were to be studied, not simply as sources of information, but especially as instruments for the formation of the soul, as pagan 'spiritual exercises', so to speak,[2] leading the pupil to higher modes of life.

It is difficult to determine from Porphyry's biography of Plotinus if the school of Plotinus in Rome followed a specific curriculum[3] and how this curriculum might have been used for the purpose of education in the virtues. We can say at most that texts of Plato and Aristotle were read, accompanied by the work of more recent commentators, Platonist and Aristotelian. However, to the extent that Plotinus' treatises originated in his teaching and that the edificatory purpose and tone of a number of these treatises is unmistakable,[4] we can take it that Plotinus' teaching also sought to provide moral education.

In his treatises he sometimes reflects, as we have seen, on the methods and stages whereby the soul may reach higher forms of life.[5] However, relatively little in the *Enneads* appears to be directed to promoting the first stage that he identifies, that of 'political' virtue, as compared to the higher stage of purification, to which much of Plotinus' philosophical effort seems to be directed: his demonstrations, which are a 'leading up' (ἀναγωγή) of the soul (I 3, 1, 6), seek to show the original nature of soul and its roots in the transcendent Intellect and the One. Such teaching can show and explain the way to divine life. However, the pupil must also live accordingly:

Therefore analogies teach, as do negations and knowledge of what comes from it [the One], and certain steps upwards. But what conveys us are purifications, virtues, and setting in order, and approaches to the intelligible, establishing ourselves there, and feasting on what is there.[6]

When, at the beginning of the fourth century, Porphyry published his edition of Plotinus' treatises, he arranged them as far as he could in an order that would serve to lead the reader from the material world to the highest levels of reality, the divine Intellect and the One. His edition can thus be described as a philosophical curriculum aiming at the divinization of the soul. As he describes the edition, Porphyry saw this curricular progression as structured according to a division of sciences. Thus *Ennead* I, the first

---

[2] The expression is that of P. Hadot (1987b); cf. also I. Hadot, in Simplicius, *In Epict.*, pp. 51–60.

[3] On this question, cf. M. Goulet-Cazé (1982: 269).

[4] See for example *Enn.* VI 9.

[5] In the treatise *On Virtues* (I 2), discussed above in Ch. 4; see also *Enn.* I 3, 1, 1–6, for example.

[6] VI 7, 36, 6–10 ('setting in order', κοσμήσεις, may refer to the 'political' virtues; P. Hadot (1987a: 349) takes the expression as referring to theoretical virtues).

stage, contains matters which are 'more ethical',[7] whereas the following *Enneads* group treatises relating to physics[8] (II and III), to the soul (IV), to Intellect and the One (V and VI). It has been shown that Porphyry applies here a tripartite division of the sciences (ethics, physics, and 'theology', i.e. the science of the divine) and that this sequence of sciences represents a progression from lower to higher levels of virtue corresponding to the scale of virtues systematized by Porphyry.[9]

The notion that a scale of sciences corresponds to a scale of virtues and that progression in the former brings progression in the latter may seem strange, if we think of scientific training as unrelated to the moral life. However, it may be of help in reaching the point of view of a Neoplatonist in Late Antiquity to recall, for example, that the division between practical and theoretical sciences in Aristotle corresponds to a division between moral and intellectual virtues, and that excellence in theoretical science represents the highest human virtue, a divine-like life. For the Neoplatonist too, theoretical knowledge at its best constitutes a perfection of human life at its highest level, that of intellect.[10] Moral virtue, in Aristotle, also involves a form of intellectual excellence, practical wisdom, an aspect stressed also, we have seen (above, Ch. 4, 3), in the later Neoplatonic distinction between 'ethical' and 'political' virtue.

An edificatory purpose and curricular progression through the sciences comparable to those of Porphyry's edition of Plotinus inspired the composition of Iamblichus' large work *On Pythagoreanism*, whose successive books were organized so as to lead the reader up from preliminary moral commonplaces towards the higher reaches of Pythagoreanism (with which Iamblichus identified Platonism), through physics and ethics towards the highest theoretical knowledge, 'theology' (metaphysics).[11] The scale of virtues is ascended, here too, through a scale of sciences. However, the connection between the scale of virtues and a scale of sciences is established most clearly and most importantly in the curriculum of Platonic dialogues

---

[7] Porphyry, *Vit. Plot.* 24, 36 (ἠθικωτέρας ὑποθέσεις). [8] 24, 37–8 and 59–60.

[9] P. Hadot (1979: 219–20). Porphyry thus considered the treatises he grouped in *Ennead* I as relating to 'political' virtue. It is possible that Porphyry had a more specifically Aristotelian division of the sciences in mind, in which practical sciences (including ethics) are subordinated to theoretical sciences, which themselves constitute a scale (physics, mathematics, theology), soul and mathematics being seen as equivalent in level (cf. *PR* 45).

[10] See above, Ch. 4, 1.

[11] Cf. *PR* 32–5. I have suggested (*PR* 214–15) that *On Pythagoreanism* was designed to outclass (through the venerable authority of Pythagoras) Porphyry's Plotinian curriculum as represented by the *Enneads*. Saffrey has suggested that Porphyry published the *Enneads* as part of a reaction to Iamblichus (1992: 55).

that Iamblichus introduced and that was generally followed later in the Neoplatonic schools of Athens and of Alexandria. Before looking more closely at Iamblichus' curriculum (below, Ch. 6), it is necessary first to examine in more detail the later Neoplatonic theory of a scale or hierarchy of sciences, since it was in effect through this scale that the successive levels of virtues were to be acquired.

2. The Scale of Sciences in Iamblichus

Philosophy, in the later Neoplatonic schools, was generally divided into a number of sciences constituting a hierarchy of lower and higher forms of knowledge. Both this division of the sciences and their gradation are ultimately of Aristotelian inspiration. A primary division, corresponding to the distinction between practical and theoretical reasoning, was subdivided so as to constitute the following hierarchy.[12]

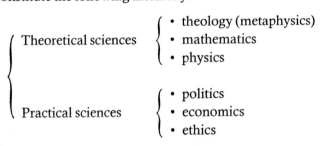

Theoretical sciences
- theology (metaphysics)
- mathematics
- physics

Practical sciences
- politics
- economics
- ethics

The Aristotelian division of the sciences had already been adopted by Platonists in the first and second centuries AD. A well-examined example is found in the *Handbook* of Alcinous, who, in presenting (ch. 3) the theoretical and practical sciences, describes the latter as concerned with 'the care of morals' (ethics), with 'the administration of the household' (economics), and with 'the state (πόλις) and its preservation' (politics). However, to the two (Aristotelian) branches of the sciences, Alcinous adds yet a third branch, 'dialectic' (including logic), under the influence of another very widespread Hellenistic division of philosophy into physics, ethics, and logic (or 'dialectic').[13]

---

[12] For the Aristotelian source cf. Aristotle, *Met.* VI, 1 and, for the notion of gradation, I, 1. For the tripartition of the practical sciences, cf. Moraux (1984: 452).

[13] See Dörrie and Baltes (1993–6: iv. 214–16). Cf. Whittaker's notes *ad loc.* and Dillon (1993: 57–8), whose translation I quote. More generally on the divisions of philosophy in Late Antiquity, see P. Hadot (1979) and, on the problem posed by logic, considered as a branch, or simply as an instrument of the sciences, P. Hadot in I. Hadot et al. (1990: i. 183–8).

53

The reappearance of the Aristotelian division of the sciences in the Neoplatonic schools might be regarded as evidence of the conservatism of scholastic practice. However, the division makes itself most felt first with Iamblichus,[14] who not only uses it to articulate his curriculum of Platonic dialogues, as will be shown below (Ch. 6), but also follows it in his work *On Pythagoreanism*, in which separate volumes are given to physics (vol. V), ethics (vol. VI), and theology (vol. VII).[15]

The division of philosophy is already present in volume III of *On Pythagoreanism* (*De communi mathematica scientia*). Iamblichus wishes to show here (ch. 15) the importance of mathematics for other sciences. He does this first as regards the two other theoretical sciences, theology and physics (pp. 55, 8–56, 4), and then as regards the practical sciences, politics and ethics (p. 56, 4–18). What he says about the contribution of mathematics to politics is somewhat vague: mathematics 'leads the ordered movements of actions (πράξεις) . . . brings equality to all and appropriate agreement' (ὁμολογία). On ethics Iamblichus is a little clearer: mathematics reveals to ethics the principles of the virtues and the paradigms of friendship, of happiness, and of other goods. These are themes which Iamblichus develops later in volume VI, *On Arithmetic in Ethical Matters*.[16]

Later in volume III of *On Pythagoreanism*, in chapter 30, Iamblichus comes back to the division of philosophy into theoretical and practical sciences. Here he tells us, on the subject of politics and ethics, that mathematics reaches down to the subjects of these practical sciences, constitutions and moral order. It finds the appropriate measures in relation to rectitude of mode of life, of households and of cities, using these measures for the best, for moral improvement, for education, and for other such benefits (pp. 91, 27–92, 12). Again the language is somewhat vague, but it is at least clear that Iamblichus accepts the (Aristotelian) division of the theoretical and practical sciences, which means that ethics and politics must, in his view, have a place in philosophy and are subordinate to higher theoretical sciences, in particular mathematics, which appears to provide paradigms, in politics, for political constitutions, equality, harmony, moral improvement, and the good of citizens in general.

[14] Plotinus gives passing mention to a division of sciences (*Enn.* I 3, 6; V 9, 11, 21–6), a matter which, however, seems not of central concern to him. Porphyry seems to have given greater attention to a scholastic organization of philosophy through a division of the sciences (cf. above n. 9), in relation perhaps to his efforts to integrate Aristotelian texts in the Platonic curriculum (cf. Dörrie and Baltes 1993–6: iv. 224).

[15] See *PR* 32–5.

[16] See *PR* 70–76 for an attempt to reconstruct the contents of vol. VI.

The mathematical paradigms to be used in political science will be explored in more detail below in Chapter 8. For the moment it may suffice to add some indications Proclus provides in revising Iamblichus' text in his *Commentary on Euclid*.[17] Iamblichus' vague reference in chapter 15 to 'ordered movements of actions' is taken by Proclus as having to do with the measures of the appropriate moments (καιρούς) for actions, the measures of cosmic cycles, the numbers appropriate for procreation and harmonious life (pp. 23, 12–24, 20). What is involved is the mathematical and, more particularly, astronomical knowledge that the ruler of a state must have in administering the affairs of the citizens, as required in Plato's *Republic*.[18]

Iamblichus' indications as to the content of political science (actions, equality, agreement, constitutions, the moral good of citizens) might be compared with a more formal account of political science given later by an Alexandrian Neoplatonist. Olympiodorus describes (1) the matter of political science as actions, 'what is to be done' (τὰ πρακτά) in general for the better (πρὸς τὸ ἄμεινον), guiding and making use of particular arts and skills; (2) the form of political science as that of ruling, a ruling of humans (not of irrational animals ruled by blows (Plato, *Critias* 109c1)), humans who share with each other in mutual agreements; (3) the efficient cause of political science as practical wisdom (φρόνησις), not theoretical wisdom (σοφία); and (4) the goal of this science as like-mindedness (ὁμόνοια) and love (στοργή) in which the citizens live as if members of one family, all elders being fathers, all the younger being children, all of like age being siblings for each other.[19]

3. Some Difficulties

After Iamblichus the hierarchy of practical and theoretical sciences becomes very common in Neoplatonism. It appears, for example, in the work of Julian the Emperor, who, as regards the practical sciences, repeats the distinction between ethics (relating to the individual), economics (concerning the household), and politics (concerning the city).[20] The Athenian

---

[17] See *PR* 157–65.

[18] See below, Ch. 8.

[19] Olympiodorus, *In Alcib.* 178, 2–180, 10; for the city as a family, see Plato, *Rep.* 461d; Proclus, *In Remp.* II, p. 365, 16–20. Parts of Olympiodorus' account of political science can already be found in Proclus, *In Alcib.* 202, 4–203, 16.

[20] Julian, *Or.* VII, 215d; cf. Bouffartigue (1992: 555–9).

Neoplatonists often refer to the hierarchy of sciences, as do the Alexandrian Neoplatonists,[21] not however without mentioning some difficulties, two of which are of particular interest to us here, concerning as they do the nature of political philosophy and its function in the scale of sciences.

(i) The first difficulty has to do with the tripartition of practical philosophy into ethics, economics, and politics. Some unidentified Platonists, it appears, rejected this tripartition on the grounds that it is based on an improper use of the logic of division. The argument is subtle, but we might summarize an important point that is made as follows: a true division distinguishes between species in a genus, that is, it makes distinctions in *kind*, whereas the tripartition of practical philosophy is merely a distinction in *number* (individual, household, city). A purely quantitative difference will not yield genuinely different practical sciences, but merely a difference in the extent of application of one science. The critics therefore propose to replace the tripartition of practical philosophy (ethics, economics, politics) with a division of practical philosophy into two sciences that are genuinely different, legislative and judicial knowledge, a division to be found in Plato.[22]

Although this critique of the tripartition of practical philosophy, as reported by the Alexandrian Neoplatonists, receives a technical formulation inspired by the competence in Aristotelian logic provided by the later Neoplatonic schools, in substance it can be derived from some passages in Plato. In the *Statesman* (259c) Plato speaks of one science concerning both the household and the state.[23] Reference could also be made to the *Alcibiades* (126d9–10), where one skill (τέχνη) provides concord (ὁμόνοια) to the individual and the city, to the self and to others,[24] and to the *Republic* (368d–e), where it is the same justice that obtains within the soul and

---

[21] See Dörrie and Baltes (1993–6: iv. 215 n. 8, 216 n. 1, 224), who give many references, including examples in the Latin West provided by Calcidius and Boethius.

[22] Elias, *Prol.*, p. 32, 1–30; Pseudo-Elias, *In Is.* 22, 12–21; David, *Prol.*, pp. 75, 3–76, 17. Shortened version in Ammonius, *In Is.*, p. 15, 6–8; Olympiodorus, *In Alcib.* 186, 20–187, 1. Staab (2002: 383) points out that the bipartite division of political science already occurs in Iamblichus, *Vit. Pyth.* 172, p. 96, 15–20. For the division legislative/judicial knowledge cf. Plato, *Gorgias* 464b7–8, where the later Neoplatonists read δικαστικήν, modern Plato editions preferring the reading δικαιοσύνην. The variant δικαστικήν certainly seems supported by *Gorgias* 520b3 and Dodds hesitates (1959: 227–8) in keeping δικαιοσύνην at 464b8. Cf. also Lisi (1985: 95–8).

[23] The difference is merely quantitative (259b9–10). Cf. Aristotle, *Politics* I, 1, who makes explicit the distinction, used by the later Neoplatonic critics, between number and kind. Aristotle does not agree with Plato and distinguishes between different kinds of rule (political, domestic).

[24] Cf. Elias, *Prol.*, p. 33, 20–2 (referring in error, it seems, to the *Gorgias*).

among the citizens of the state.[25] Thus Proclus considers that political science is one, whether it concerns in its activity the internal order of the soul or the external order between citizens.[26] It seems, then, that for the later Neoplatonist, the Aristotelian tripartition of practical philosophy (ethics, economics, politics) represents one form of knowledge, applied on different scales (within the soul, between members of a household, between citizens), which may be more appropriately divided into legislative and judicial branches.

The Alexandrian Neoplatonists who inform us about the critique of the Aristotelian tripartition of practical philosophy explain the tripartition in the following ways. Ammonius notes that the political man can order the state (politics), while neglecting his inner order (ethics).[27] He refers clearly to what (often) *is* the case, not to what *ought to be* the case, where political action must be linked to, and presupposes, the inner order of the soul (above Ch. 4, 2). The Aristotelian distinction between ethics and politics (in particular) is explained as a description of actual practice. However, practical philosophy, as moral education, should deal, we may infer, with what ought to be our practice. Ammonius also claims that the Platonic bipartition (legislative/judicial) articulates each member of the Aristotelian tripartition.[28] It seems thus that he accepts the Platonic division as fundamental.

A more elaborate explanation of the Aristotelian tripartition can be read in Elias, who accounts for the tripartition as corresponding to the literary organization of Aristotle's work (the *Ethics, Economics, Politics*),[29] whereas the bipartite division (legislative, judicial) articulates Plato's dialogues (legislative in the *Laws*, judicial in the eschatological myths of the *Gorgias, Phaedo*, and *Republic*). However, this is a literary and not a systematic division of practical philosophy. In fact Elias accepts that the important systematic articulation of practical philosophy is that into the legislative and judicial, two branches that he finds in Aristotle and even in the Pseudo-Pythagorean *Golden Verses*.[30]

---

[25] Elias, *Prol.*, p. 33, 32–3.

[26] Proclus, *In Remp.* I, pp. 210, 26–211, 3. Cf. I, pp. 11, 25–13, 23.

[27] Ammonius, *In Is.*, p. 15, 9–10.

[28] Ammonius, *In Is.*, pp. 15, 11–16, 4: the purpose no doubt is to reconcile Aristotle with Plato. Correspondingly, Olympiodorus finds the Aristotelian tripartition already in Plato (*In Gorg.*, p. 226, 18–26).

[29] Cf. I. Hadot's explanation and correction (in Hadot et al. 1990: i. 85) of a similar list of works in Olympiodorus, *Prol.*, pp. 7, 35–8, 3.

[30] Elias, *Prol.*, pp. 32, 31–34, 25. The ideas presented in Elias are unlikely to be new or peculiar

The Platonic division of practical philosophy into legislative and judicial branches seems not, however, to be a true division of a genus into two coordinate species. It is noted that the legislative is prior to the judicial, since judging conformity to law presupposes that law is already established.[31] The judicial branch has to do with restoring an order formed by legislation. However, if it is the case that, of the two branches distinguished in Plato's *Gorgias*,[32] the judicial is subordinate to the legislative, in Plato's *Statesman* (305b–c) it seems that the judicial is not even part of political science, but joins the auxiliary arts and skills (such as rhetoric and military art) directed by political science.[33] Later Neoplatonists, however, do not seem in general to have gone this far, retaining, as we have seen above, the bipartition into two (unequal) branches presented in the *Gorgias*.[34]

Furthermore, another subordination might also be claimed as obtaining within practical philosophy to the extent that external order (domestic, political) presupposes internal order in the soul and may even be seen as a projection of this internal order.[35]

Putting these two factors of subordination together, we may conclude that practical philosophy consists primarily of laws productive of order and secondarily of judgement restoring conformity to these laws. The order in question is at first the internal order of the rational soul in its relation to body and then as applied to relationships with others, in the domestic and political spheres.[36] The purpose of this order, as corresponding to 'political' virtue, is to provide conditions allowing the transition of the soul to higher levels of virtue and divinization.

(ii) A second difficulty debated by the later Neoplatonists might be considered more briefly, as it has already been well examined, and is of less

to Elias: comparison of the propaedeutic works of Ammonius, Philoponus, Olympiodorus, Elias, and David shows that they share a common stock of scholastic materials, presented in versions of varying length and detail, which seems to go back to Proclus. Cf. I. Hadot et al. (1990: i. 169–77; iii. 127–46), and Hoffmann et al. (2001: 864–7).

[31] David, *Prol.*, p. 76, 17–24. Cf. Plato, *Statesman* 305b–c. The Neoplatonists also found in Plato, *Laws* 716a2–3 a subordination of the judicial branch to legislation (Proclus, *In Alcib.* 220, 5–12). See Dillon (2001: 247).

[32] See above, n. 22.

[33] See Sopatros, *Prol.*, p. 128, 1–2 (on this author cf. below, Appendix II); Alcinous, *Didaskalikos* 34, 5.

[34] Thus Proclus does not include judicial knowledge in the list of sciences subordinate to political science (*In Remp.* I, pp. 54, 28–55, 16; 67, 28–69, 9).

[35] Above Ch. 4, 2; Proclus, *In Remp.* I, p. 210, 4–30. Cf. Abbate (1999: 209–13).

[36] The account given (above s. 2) of political science can thus be seen as the extension in the political sphere of practical philosophy as concerning the internal order of the soul and domestic order.

importance to our present enquiry.[37] This difficulty concerns the starting-point of the ascent of the pupil through the scale of sciences. Since this scale represents a gradation going from the (lower) practical sciences to the (higher) theoretical sciences (of which theology is the highest), where is one to start? With logic, if logic is considered to be an instrument of intellectual discipline presupposed by the sciences? Or with ethics, if the pupil's exercise of reason presupposes an appropriately conditioned moral state?

If in general the later Neoplatonists opt for a preparatory study of logic as the instrument of the sciences, followed by a study of ethics which prepares the moral ground for access to the higher, theoretical sciences,[38] they allow that a preliminary moral conditioning might appropriately precede the study of logic. This preliminary conditioning would not presuppose logic, in the way, for example, that reading Aristotle's ethics does, but would be based on the non-technical moral edification to be drawn from such works as the *Golden Verses* or Epictetus' *Manual*. Logic would then be taken up, to be followed by the practical sciences (which presuppose logic and are found in the works of Aristotle and Plato) and by the higher theoretical sciences.[39]

The moral conditioning acquired at the very beginning of the ascent through the scale of sciences corresponds to the level of 'ethical' virtue in the post-Iamblichean scale of virtues (above, Ch. 4, 3), since what is involved is the inculcation of 'correct opinion' (ὀρθοδοξία) rather than access to scientific understanding.[40] Having then studied logic, the pupil is prepared for this access, moving up to the practical sciences, which correspond to the level of 'political' virtues and which prepare the way in turn for the transition to the higher levels of divinization attained through the higher (theoretical) sciences and their corresponding virtues.

The acquisition of 'political' virtue through education in the practical sciences cannot have been a purely intellectual matter. Plotinus refers several

---

[37] See I. Hadot et al. (1990: i. 94–6).

[38] Ammonius, *In Cat.*, pp. 5, 31–6, 8; Olympiodorus, *Prol.*, pp. 8, 29–9, 11; 9, 31–10, 2.

[39] Philoponus, *In Cat.*, p. 5, 15–33; Simplicius, *In Cat.*, pp. 5, 3–6, 5. Other starting-points that are discussed are mathematics and physics. The latter position is ascribed to Aristotelians, the former to certain Platonists (see I. Hadot et al. 1990: i. 96; Saffrey 1968: 81–4). However, since physics and mathematics both belong to the theoretical sciences and relate thus to higher degrees of virtue, they are preceded by the practical sciences which relate to the lower level of 'political' virtue. Of course *within* the theoretical sciences, physics and mathematics precede and lead up to the highest level of science and theoretical virtue represented by theology (metaphysics).

[40] See Philoponus, *In Cat.*, p. 5, 29–33 (ὀρθοδοξαστικῶς εἰδέναι contrasted with ἀποδεικτικῶς); Simplicius, *In Cat.*, pp. 5, 21–6, 5 (same contrast).

times to a phrase in Plato's *Republic* (518e1–2) as indicating the need for 'habituation and practice' (ἔθεσι καὶ ἀσκήσεσι) as regards the virtues of the soul in relation to the body, i.e. 'political' virtues.[41] The belief in the importance of habituation and practice can only have increased as later Neoplatonists had greater recourse to Aristotle's ethics in their curriculum,[42] an ethics which, as regards moral virtue, stresses the need of habituation through action. In the context of the pupil's aim of ascending through 'political' virtue to higher virtues, a sufficient practice could no doubt be cultivated within the philosophical school. A wider field of practice, that of political action, does not seem to be indispensable, although a text of Damascius recommends this.[43] For a philosopher who would have already 'ascended' and reached higher virtues, the 'descent' to 'political' virtue in action would have responded to other needs, as will be seen below (Ch. 7): the need to communicate the good, acting as a moral paradigm in the philosophical school or perhaps as part of a larger political sphere.

In discussing how the scale of sciences serves to divinize the human soul by providing an ascent through the corresponding scale of virtues, as this ascent was aimed at in the life of the Neoplatonic schools of Late Antiquity, it has been necessary to mention already some of the texts which were considered in these schools as relating to the various levels of science and virtue and which were used for the ascent through those levels. These texts included not only, of course, dialogues of Plato, but also other works, (Pseudo-) Pythagorean, Aristotelian, and Stoic. In the next chapter, the curriculum for divinization of the Neoplatonic schools will be discussed with respect to the specific texts used in this curriculum. This will allow us to identify in particular what might be described as the library of Neoplatonic political philosophy.

---

[41] See *Enn.* VI 8, 6, 25; I 1, 10, 13–14; I 3, 6, 6–7; II 9, 15, 14–17 and the passage from VI 7, 36, 6–10 quoted above (p. 51).

[42] See below, Ch. 6.

[43] Damascius, *Vit. Is.*, fr. 324 (quoted above p. 48).

The Curriculum 6

If divinization is to be achieved in a progression through the scale of virtues, and if this progression may be brought about in the privileged milieu of the philosophical school through a community of life and through initiation into a hierarchy of sciences corresponding to the hierarchy of virtues, this hierarchy of sciences can be ascended, under the guidance of a teacher, through the study of an appropriate curriculum of canonical texts corresponding to each of the sciences of the hierarchy. It remains then for us to examine the curriculum of the Neoplatonic schools, with particular reference, here also, to 'political' virtues and political philosophy as a preparatory stage of divinization.

The curriculum of the later Neoplatonic school, as it will be described below, may seem to us extremely elaborate and ambitious, and it is not necessarily the case that those who attended such a school actually went through the complete course of studies. On the other hand, in the case of particularly committed and promising students such as Proclus, the course represented a core that was extended to include further studies. I will briefly sketch the basic curriculum that was proposed, but not always realized, and indicate the further elements that could be added by the most diligent students.[1]

1. 'Minor Mysteries'

If Plato's dialogues provided the primary canonic texts for the Neoplatonic curriculum, the study of these would be preceded by propaedeutic studies, first sometimes by the simplified non-scientific moral instruction (in 'ethical' virtue) to be derived from Epictetus'

---

[1] On the Neoplatonic curriculum in general, see Festugière (1969); Goulet-Cazé (1982: 277–80); Anon., *Prol.*, Introduction, LXVIII–LXVIII.

Manual or from the (Pseudo-Pythagorean) *Golden Verses*,[2] and then by a study of Aristotle's works considered as preparatory to the study of Plato:

In less than two complete years he [Syrianus] read with him [Proclus] all of Aristotle's works, on logic, ethics, politics, physics, and, above these, on theological science. Having sufficiently brought him through these, as if through . . . minor mysteries, he led him to Plato's mystic initiation, in the right order.[3]

Aristotle and the Aristotelian commentators had already been part of the curriculum of Plotinus' school in Rome, and the integration of Aristotle in Neoplatonic teaching became more systematic with Porphyry and Iamblichus. By Proclus' time, the Aristotelian corpus was assumed to be a propaedeutic to Plato. The corpus, in the Aristotelian schools, had long before been organized so as to correspond to the Aristotelian division and hierarchy of sciences, and, prefaced by Porphyry's introduction to the *Categories* (the *Isagoge*), it was read by later Neoplatonists in an order corresponding to a gradation going from the lower practical sciences (ethics, politics) up to the highest theoretical science, theology.[4] Thus the works of Aristotle, so organized, were assumed to have the same finality as that of Plato's dialogues, the divinization of man, achieved through the same scale of virtues and sciences.[5]

2. Iamblichus' Platonic Curriculum

Having gone through Aristotle's works and reached the summit of the theoretical sciences represented in the *Metaphysics*, the student could move on to the 'major mysteries', i.e. a course of selected dialogues of Plato first instituted by Iamblichus and then widely followed in the Neoplatonic schools. This course consisted of two cycles, a first cycle of ten dialogues and a second cycle made up of two. The first cycle took the student up,

[2] See I. Hadot (1978: 160–4) or her introduction to Simplicius, *Commentaire* (2001: xcii–xcvii).

[3] Marinus, *Vit. Procl.* 13. For the Platonic image of philosophy as an initiation to mysteries, cf. Plato, *Symposium* 210d–e, *Phaedrus* 249c–250b, Riedweg (1987).

[4] See I. Hadot et al. (1990: i. 64–5, 84–92).

[5] Ammonius, *In Cat.*, p. 6, 9–20; Philoponus, *In Cat.*, pp. 5, 34–6, 2; Olympiodorus, *Prol.*, p. 9, 14–30; Simplicius, *In Cat.*, p. 6, 6–15; cf. I. Hadot et al. (1990: i. 97–103). The case of Aristotle's *Metaphysics* is revealing: this work corresponded to the highest theoretical science, theology, but was limited in its usefulness, since it attacked Plato on major questions. Syrianus could then put the work to curricular use, but was obliged at the same time to alert the student and respond to Aristotle's criticisms of Plato (see *PR* 120–1).

through the scale of virtues and of sciences, to the highest level, theoretical virtue and science; the second cycle concerned only the highest levels, the theoretical sciences of physics and especially theology. The two cycles[6] can be represented as shown in Table 1.

This curriculum calls for some comment. It may seem to us very construed and artificial: each of the chosen dialogues of Plato must serve the purpose assigned to it by its place in the curriculum, but it is far from obvious how, for example, the *Sophist*, can be made to yield a physics.[7] A measure of the artificiality can be seen in the arithmetical scheme that inspires it, the decade (the complete series of ten numbers) and the dyad (the first two numbers which potentially contain the following members of the series

Table 1. *Iamblichus' Platonic curriculum*

Cycle	Virtues	Sciences	Texts
First Cycle	political	practical[a]	1. *Alcibiades*
			2. *Gorgias*
	purificatory		3. *Phaedo*
	theoretical	theoretical	
		(i) in words	4. *Cratylus*
		(ii) in concepts	5. *Theaetetus*
		(iii) in things:[b]	
		(α) physics	6. *Sophist*
			7. *Statesman*
		(β) theology	8. *Phaedrus*
			9. *Symposium*
			10. *Philebus*
Second Cycle	theoretical	physics	1. *Timaeus*
		theology	2. *Parmenides*

[a] I have not subdivided practical science in view of the difficulty over the tripartition (ethics, economics, politics) or bipartition (legislative/judicial) of practical science (above Ch. 5, 3).

[b] The series words–concepts–things expresses the idea that the objects of knowledge, things (i.e. physical or metaphysical realities), are signified by words through the mediation of concepts (on this idea and its background in Iamblichus, cf. Anon., *Prol.* LXXII and O'Meara 2001).

[6] As reconstructed by Westerink; cf. Anon., *Prol.* LXVIII–LXXIII and ch. 26, 16–44; Festugière (1969).

[7] For an explanation cf. Anon., *Prol.* LXIX. It is also surprising, for example, that the *Statesman* is taken as representing physics, rather than politics. Iamblichus' theory that each Platonic dialogue must have a single purpose (σκοπός) facilitated its integration in the curricular scheme.

of numbers). Iamblichus' Pythagorizing tendencies are no doubt here at work.[8] We notice also that the second theoretical science, mathematics, is missing.[9] Finally, the parallelism between the scale of virtues and the scale of sciences is not absolute, since the 'purificatory' virtues fit neither into practical philosophy (ethics and politics, to which 'political' virtue corresponds), nor into the theoretical sciences. They should probably be considered as essentially transitional, bridging the divide between practical and theoretical science.

There seems to have been some disagreement as regards the bearing of the first dialogue of the first cycle, the *Alcibiades*. Proclus saw the dialogue as concerning self-knowledge, as the beginning of *all* philosophy. It thus anticipates and pre-contains the variety of sciences covered in the dialogues of the curriculum that follow.[10] However, Damascius related the *Alcibiades* more specifically to the level of 'political' virtue:

He proves this from the definition in the dialogue [*Alcib.* 129e] of man as a rational soul using body as an instrument. Only the political [man] uses body as an instrument, sometimes needing spirit, on behalf of his homeland, but also desire for citizens to fare well. But neither the purificatory nor the theoretical [man] needs the body.[11]

Thus, in Damascius' view, the *Alcibiades* should be added to the *Gorgias* as relating to 'political' virtue and science. A more extensive training might lead to reading what, for us, would be the more obvious texts in this regard, Plato's *Republic* and *Laws*, as was the case in Proclus' education in 'political' virtue.[12]

But why did Iamblichus choose the *Gorgias*, and not the *Republic* or perhaps the *Laws*, as the dialogue corresponding in this curriculum to 'political' virtue and science? A report in a late Neoplatonic Alexandrian source suggests that Proclus excluded (ἐκβάλλειν) the *Republic* and *Laws* as being too long.[13] This exclusion must have had to do with curricular considerations,

---

[8] *PR* 97–8, with comparison to Porphyry's division of Plotinus' works into 54 (9×6) treatises, for comparable numerical reasons. Fifty-four dialogues of Plato could also be counted by the later Neoplatonist (Anon., *Prol.* 26, 13)!

[9] The gap could be filled by the study of Nicomachus and Euclid, considered as Platonists, and by Iamblichus' work *On Pythagoreanism*.

[10] Proclus, *In Alcib.* 11, 1–17.

[11] Olympiodorus, *In Alcib.* 4, 15–5, 1; cf. 177, 8; 177, 12–178, 2; Olympiodorus, *In Phaed.* 3, 6; compare Olympiodorus, *In Gorg.* 6, p. 6, 1–6, a compromise position, it seems, in which the *Alcibiades* introduces the *Gorgias* ('political' virtues) and *Phaedo* (purificatory virtues).

[12] Marinus, *Vit. Procl.* 14; cf. Anon., *Prol.* 26, 45–58. There is a suggestion in Olympiodorus, *In Phaed.* 8, 18, that the *Apology* relates to the 'political' as the *Phaedo* relates to the 'purificatory'.

[13] See Anon., *Prol.* 26, 7–12 (the Greek text is somewhat garbled; for its interpretation, see the Introduction, LXVII–LXVIII).

since it is clear that Proclus himself studied, used and discussed these texts in detail. It is likely then that Iamblichus chose the *Gorgias*, for reasons of pedagogic convenience, for his basic curriculum. This did not in any way rule out the study and use of the *Republic* and *Laws* in his school.[14] But why choose the *Gorgias* for the teaching of 'political' virtue and science in the basic curriculum? In Chapters 8 and 9 it will be seen that the *Gorgias* was thought to express important principles of political philosophy as well as specifying, as we have seen (Ch. 5, 3), its two branches.

3. A Reading List in Political Virtue and Science

We are now in a position to draw up a reading list of the texts that would be studied in the later Neoplatonic schools as teaching 'political' virtue and providing an education in practical philosophy, as a first stage in a process of progressive divinization. The following list of texts is as extensive as our sources allow. Obviously, in some schools and periods, few of the texts would be read, in others much more. The first part of the list (see Table 2) includes texts thought to provide a preliminary non-scientific moral edification ('ethical' virtue) which, however, could also extend to include 'political' virtue;[15] the second part (see Table 3) lists the relevant propaedeutic texts of Aristotle; and the third part (see Table 4) concerns Plato. Facing each canonic text are the names of the Neoplatonists attested as having commented on it. The names given in italics are of those Neoplatonists whose commentaries have survived; the commentaries of the others are lost.

The attribution (see Table 2) to Iamblichus and Proclus of the two commentaries surviving in Arabic on the *Golden Verses* is uncertain. However, the two texts derive from Greek Neoplatonic originals and the one attributed to Proclus may go back to a lost commentary attested for the fourth-century Neoplatonist Proclus of Laodicea.[16] The Isocratean texts are cited by the later Alexandrian Neoplatonists with the *Golden Verses* as illustrating

---

[14] See O'Meara (1999b).

[15] Thus the Pseudo-Pythagorean *Golden Verses* were considered by Hierocles as providing not only basic moral instruction in 'ethical' and 'political' virtue but also as extending even to higher divine life (see Hierocles, *In Carm. Aur.*, pp. 5, 1–7, 1; pp. 84, 7–85, 14). Similarly Epictetus' *Manual* provided elementary moral edification that reached and included 'political' virtue (see I. Hadot in Simplicius, *In Epict.*, Introduction, pp. 51–4).

[16] On this and on the Arabic commentaries, see Westerink (1987), Daiber (1995).

Table 2. *The curriculum of 'political' virtue: preliminary reading*

Texts		Commentaries
(Pseudo-Pythagorean)	*Golden Verses*	(Arabic) *Iamblichus* (?)
		(Arabic) *Proclus* (?)
		Proclus of Laodicea
		Hierocles
Epictetus	*Manual*	Theosebius[a]
		Simplicius
Isocrates	*Ad Demonicum*	
	Ad Nicoclem	
	Nicocles	

[a] Damascius, *Vit. Is.*, fr. 109 (where, however, it is not absolutely clear that Theosebius, over and above making much use of Epictetus, actually lectured on him); see above p. 25.

practical philosophy[17] and there is some evidence of Neoplatonic commentary on them.[18]

If the Aristotelian works in Table 3 (reflecting the tripartition ethics/economics/politics) are all listed as pertaining to practical philosophy by later Neoplatonists,[19] the *Nicomachean Ethics* (which Aristotle himself describes

Table 3. *The curriculum of 'political' virtue: Aristotle*

Texts		Commentaries
Aristotle	*Nicomachean Ethics*	Porphyry[a]
	Eudemian Ethics	
	Magna Moralia	
	Economics	
	Politics	
	Constitutions	

[a] Frs. 165–6, with Ghorab (1972: 78–80).

[17] Ammonius, *In Is.*, p. 15, 21–3; Elias, *In Cat.*, p. 118, 30–1. I. Hadot (1984: 201 n.) first pointed out this use of Isocrates in Alexandrian Neoplatonism.

[18] See Hoffmann (2000: 611–12), who also notes that the three Isocratean texts provide moral edification going, in order, from the private to the political sphere.

[19] Simplicius, *In Cat.*, p. 4, 26–28; cf. p. 7, 17; Olympiodorus, *Prol.*, pp. 7, 34–8, 3; Elias, *In Cat.* pp. 116, 15–28; 113, 31–7; Pseudo-Elias, *In Is.* 22, 1–8; David, *Prol.* pp. 74, 11–75, 2; cf. I. Hadot et al. (1990: i. 65, 69–70 and 84–5). On Aristotle's *Constitutions* cf. also below App. II.

Table 4. *The curriculum of 'political' virtue: Plato*

Texts		Commentaries
Plato	*Apology*[a]	
	Alcibiades	Iamblichus[b]
		Syrianus
		Proclus
		Damascius
		Olympiodorus
	Gorgias	Hierocles[c]
		Plutarch
		Proclus
		Olympiodorus
	Republic	Porphyry[d]
		Theosebius
		Syrianus
		Proclus
		Damascius
	Laws	Syrianus[e]
		Damascius

[a] See above n. 12.
[b] For the Neoplatonic commentaries on the *Alcibiades*, see Dörrie and Baltes (1993–6: iii. 194).
[c] For the Neoplatonic commentaries on the *Gorgias*, see Dörrie and Baltes (1993–6: iii. 195–6).
[d] For this list, cf. Dörrie and Baltes (1993–6: 206–8), who mention other partial commentaries. Proclus' work is a collection of essays on themes of the *Republic*, rather than a commentary. The *Republic* went under the title αἱ πολιτεῖαι in the Alexandrian school (Westerink 1981).
[e] See Dörrie and Baltes (1993–6: iii. 208).

as dealing with 'political science', I, 1, 1094a 27) seems mostly to have been used[20] and the *Politics* sometimes read, for example by Proclus,[21] who responded to the criticism in the *Politics* of Plato's *Republic*.[22]

The list of commentaries in Table 4 is certainly incomplete and does not include the oral lectures given, we may assume, on the *Gorgias* by Iamblichus or by Ammonius, on whose lectures Olympiodorus reports in

[20] To judge from the *Index locorum* of Proclus, *In Alcib.*, Olympiodorus, *In Alcib.*, *In Gorg.*
[21] Marinus, *Vita Procl.* 14.
[22] In the 17th essay of his *In Remp.*; cf. Stalley (1995), (1999). A Platonist and contemporary of Plotinus, Eubulus, had already responded to Aristotle's criticisms of the *Republic*; see Porphyry, *Vita Plot.* 20, 41–3.

his written commentary. Our list is also too extensive in various ways: the use of the *Alcibiades* as relating to 'political' virtue was a matter of debate (above p. 64); the *Gorgias* remained the primary text used in this regard, the study of which might sometimes (but not always) be deepened by a reading of the *Republic* and the *Laws*.[23]

To this reading list based on the canonic dialogues of Plato we might add two bodies of work representing respectively a correct reading of Plato and the ancient sources of Plato: the treatises included in *Ennead* I of Porphyry's edition of Plotinus if, indeed, as suggested above (p. 52, n. 9), Porphyry saw these treatises as relating to 'political' virtue; and Pythagorean political philosophy as represented by Iamblichus, not only in his work *On Pythagoreanism*, but also in the numerous pseudo-Pythagorean texts of ethical and political bearing whose popularity in Late Antiquity, I will argue, is largely due to Iamblichus.[24]

Finally, to this Neoplatonic library of practical philosophy we should add texts which do not concern directly the curricular programme of divinization through 'political' virtue, texts which nevertheless discuss political aspects of practical philosophy, in particular parts of what survives of Iamblichus' correspondence, the 'Mirrors of Princes' of Sopatros and Synesius, and the anonymous sixth-century dialogue *On Political Science*.

To these and to other such texts I will refer in the following chapters, in which the content of political philosophy, as we can derive it from the Neoplatonic curriculum, will be examined in the context of the return of the philosopher, once divinized through education, to the 'cave' of practical life, to the task of the divinization of society through the knowledge acquired of divine life. The most important sources for our reconstruction of the content of political philosophy will be, as the Neoplatonic curriculum suggests, the *Gorgias*, *Republic*, and *Laws* of Plato, as these dialogues were read and interpreted by Neoplatonists.

---

[23] Of course in lecturing on the *Gorgias*, the Neoplatonist teacher could make use of the other dialogues on the same curricular level. Thus Olympiodorus cites the *Laws* and (especially) the *Republic* more often than other Platonic dialogues in his *In Gorg.*

[24] See below p. 97; these texts include not only the *Golden Verses*, but also writings attributed to Archytas, Bryson, Callicratidas, Diotogenes, Ecphantus, Periktione, Phintys, Sthenidas.

Part II
Neoplatonic Political
Theory Reconstructed:
The Divinization of the State

Part II Synopsis

Having ascended the scale of virtues and sciences, having acquired 'political' virtue and political science as a first stage in divinization and thereby attaining yet higher levels of assimilation to the divine, the Neoplatonist philosopher might also then 'descend', like Plato's philosopher-kings, into the cave of political affairs, bringing divinization to political life. This descent of the philosopher, this divinization of political life through philosophy, is the subject of the following five chapters.

We might articulate the theme of descent as a divinization of political life by beginning with questions which are likely to occur to readers of Plato's *Republic* when they meet in Plato's text the idea of the philosopher-king. Why should, or must, philosophers descend to the cave of political action, perhaps at the risk of their lives? Can such philosophers be considered to be happy, given the life of knowledge which they must leave? How is Plato's revolutionary inclusion of women among the philosopher-kings to be understood (Ch. 7)? The basis on which these philosophers will rule should correspond, for the Neoplatonists, to what they considered to be political philosophy or science. This science, we have seen (Ch. 5, 2–3), includes a legislative and a judicial branch. Thus to describe the political science inspiring philosophers in their divinization of the state, we will take first the legislative branch (Ch. 8) and consider the purposes to be achieved in political life, the kinds of political reform that may be sought, the transcendent models that might inspire legislative reform, the role of law in political life, and the constitutional order best suited for divinization. As regards the judicial branch (Ch. 9), we will examine the question of the appropriate use of judicial power and the purpose of punishment. Another matter also relevant to the theme of the divinization of the state will be discussed in Chapter 10: the use to which religion may be put by the philosopher in the context of political reform. Finally, various factors limiting the possibilities of political reform will be discussed in Chapter 11: the problems posed by political action, the nature and limits of practical wisdom, and other factors which contribute to success and failure in politics.

By filling out in this way the accounts of the content of political philosophy provided by Neoplatonist philosophers (above, Ch. 5, 2–3), Chapters 7–11 will complete our outline reconstruction of Neoplatonic political theory.

Philosopher-Kings and Queens

1. Motives

Liberated from the dark cave of ignorance and opinion, brought up to the light of knowledge, the knowledge of the Forms and of the source of the Forms, the Form of the Good, the philosopher in Plato's *Republic* must then return to the cave, descending into it so as to put the knowledge thus acquired in the service of the prisoners in the cave. In short, the philosopher must become king. But why should the philosopher descend? Why must the philosopher become king?[1]

We sense in Plato's text a reluctance in the philosopher to return to the cave (519c–520a). Must the philosopher return by reason of a social obligation arising from the fact that the purpose of the philosopher's 'liberation' (i.e. education) is the common good?[2] Does this mean that the good of the philosopher is to be subordinated to the good of the city (cf. *Rep.* 519e)? Or is the return imposed by the need to prevent evil persons from appropriating political power (cf. *Rep.* 347c)? In other dialogues, Plato suggests less negative grounds than this for the return of the philosopher to politics. In the *Symposium*, the love of beauty expresses itself in the desire to procreate, and the highest form of procreation is that which gives birth to a wisdom which concerns the ordering of cities and households.[3] And if we compare the maker of the world (or 'demiurge') of Plato's *Timaeus* with the maker of political order that is the statesman (and many pointers encourage this comparison),[4] then, as the demiurge makes the world because of his goodness (*Tim.* 29e1–30a2), so too might the true statesman be inspired to act.

---

[1] For a discussion of this question in Plato, with references to further literature, see Mahoney (1992). This section summarizes the content of O'Meara (1999c), developing some of its points.

[2] Cf. Olympiodorus, *In Gorg.*, p. 166, 14–18.

[3] *Symp.* 209a; cf. Iamblichus, *De myst.* III, 3, pp. 107, 15–108, 7.

[4] Cf. Brisson (1974: 51–4); Laks, in Rowe and Schofield (2000: 273).

Plotinus seems to have the descent of Plato's philosopher-king in mind in the following passage:

and having been in [the One's] company and had, so to put it, sufficient converse with it, [the soul must] come and announce, if it could, to another that transcendent union. Perhaps also it was because Minos attained this kind of union that he was said in the story to be the familiar friend of Zeus, and it was in remembering this that he laid down laws in its image, being filled full of lawgiving by the divine contact. Or, also, [the soul] may think political matters unworthy of it and want to remain always above; this is liable to happen to one who has seen much.[5]

Plotinus is describing the ascent of the soul to union with the highest principle, the One, a union that may be followed by an announcing of this union to others, an activity described also as 'political' and compared to the activity of a legendary legislator among the Greeks, Minos, who, having been in communion with Zeus, legislates 'in the image' of this communion. Plotinus could have read the story of Minos' companionship with Zeus in the Platonic dialogue *Minos* (319b–320b) or in the opening of Plato's *Laws* (624a).[6] But in these texts, Minos the legislator simply receives instruction from Zeus, whereas, in Plotinus' version, he legislates, makes laws, as 'images' (εἴδωλα) of his communion with Zeus. The story of Minos thus appears to be interpreted in the light of the activity of Plato's philosopher-kings, who *imitate* the divine (*Rep.* 500c5, 500e3–501b7). Another indication of the influence of this part of the *Republic* on the Plotinian passage is the suggestion that the soul, united to the One, may wish to remain above, a suggestion which has its counterpart in the reluctance of Plato's philosophers to involve themselves in politics (*Rep.* 519c–520a).

But why then, in Plotinus' view, would the soul wish to leave its union with the One, descending to political matters, communicating its union to others, as Minos legislated in the image of the divine? Plotinus merely says that the divine contact so 'fills' (πληρούμενος) Minos that he legislates (7, 25–6). This suggestion of fecundity, of an abundance associated with union with the One and issuing in political activity, is somewhat unclear and requires investigation.

Further light can be shed on the matter if the general relation between knowledge (θεωρία), action (πρᾶξις), and production (ποίησις) in Plotinus

---

[5] Plotinus, *Enn.* VI 9, 7, 20–8; for discussion of another way of construing the Greek text, see O'Meara (1999c: 281).

[6] See also Dio Chrysostom, *Or.* IV, 39–41. The story is reported, quoting the *Laws*, in Proclus, *In Remp.* I, p. 156, 14–20; Elias, *Prol.*, p. 7, 15–22.

is considered. In *Enn.* III 8, Plotinus extends the Aristotelian distinction between knowledge, action, and production beyond the human sphere, so as to apply as a general pattern to all of reality. Aristotle had already done this to the extent that his first principle, divine Intellect, is pure knowledge and that human knowledge and actions, as well as natural processes in general, can be described as imitating in some way divine life.[7] In III 8, Plotinus argues that all action and production is subordinate to knowledge as a by-product of knowledge, a secondary activity accompanying knowledge. Thus the transcendent principles that are Intellect and soul are forms of knowledge which give rise to products, i.e. the lower levels of reality. As regards humans, this means that human action and production can result as by-products, secondary effects, of knowledge, or, if not, as inferior substitutes for knowledge:

Men, too, when their power of contemplation weakens, make action a shadow of contemplation (θεωρία) and reasoning. Because contemplation is not enough for them, since their souls are weak and they are not able to grasp the vision sufficiently, and therefore are not filled (πληρούμενοι) with it, but still long to see it, they are carried into action, so as to see what they cannot see with their intellect. When they make something, then, it is because they want to see their object themselves and also because they want others to be aware of it and contemplate it, when their project is realized in practice as well as possible. Everywhere we shall find that making and action are either a weakening or a consequence of contemplation; a weakening, if the doer or maker had nothing in view beyond the thing done, a consequence if he had another prior object of contemplation better than what he made.[8]

In the case of weakness of the intellectual power of the soul, humans resort to action as a lower substitute for knowledge, not being 'filled' by it (4, 35). But action can also result as a by-product in the case of the soul that does not suffer from this lack, a soul which possesses knowledge. The latter case corresponds to the example of Minos in *Enn.* VI 9, who is 'filled' by his union with the One and consequently acts. Thus political action, as indeed all action, may arise as a result that accompanies the fulfilment of philosophical knowledge.

A further step must be made, however, in the explanation of how knowledge can be fecund so as to issue in political action. Soul, in reaching union

---

[7] See above, Ch. 3, 1.

[8] 4, 31–43. See also V 3, 7, 30–4: 'for its action is simultaneously contemplation, and in its production it produces forms, which are like intellections carried out in practice, so that all things are traces of intellection and Intellect proceeding according to their archetype, the ones near it representing it closely, and the last and lowest keeping a faint image of it'.

with the One, is united with the absolute Good whose nature is such as to 'overflow', to communicate its goodness and thus give rise to the rest of reality.[9] Union with the One must involve sharing in its metaphysical fecundity, its nature as the self-giving and self-communicating Good. For Plotinus' Minos this means that communion with the One is communion with its fecundity as the Good, a fecundity that produces communication of the Good in the form of laws as images of the Good—just as, in general, the lower levels of reality are images of the higher and produced by the higher in a cascading series of images of the One. We can infer from these ideas that the motivation of the Plotinian philosopher-king relates to sharing in the metaphysical fecundity of the absolute Good: the philosopher descends to political matters as a consequence and expression of the union reached with the One.

This explanation of what Plotinus might mean when he speaks of Minos as being 'filled . . . by the divine contact' such that he legislates (VI 9, 7, 25–6) is explicitly expressed by later Neoplatonists, for example by Proclus:

because that which is perfectly good has its completion, not just in conserving itself, but desires, by a giving to others and not being envious, to confer good on all and make them like itself.[10]

Proclus is speaking here of a soul that does not descend from intelligible contemplation and that exercises a kind of cosmic providence as the expression of its knowledge. However the relation between the fecundity of what is good, knowledge, and action is clearly established here in the case of soul, and the relation between knowledge and action can be applied lower down in the scale of reality, in relation in particular to political action:

This is analogous to the political [man]: it is not unclear that he starts from knowledge and examination, and then, in this way, orders the whole state, showing in deeds the conclusions derived from this knowledge. So also does the lover first know the object of love, of what kind it is, and then, in this way, gives it a share of his providential care.[11]

The motivation of the Neoplatonic philosopher-king receives a name in a lost work of Hierocles. In this work (*On Providence*, summarized by the patriarch Photius), Hierocles discussed the distinction, in Plato's *Phaedrus* (248a ff.), between the 'philosopher' and the 'lover'.[12] According to

---

[9] On this metaphysical principle, summarized in the medieval principle *bonum est diffusivum sui* and first systematically used by Plotinus, see Kremer (1987).

[10] Proclus, *De mal.* 23, 21–5.

[11] Proclus, *In Alc.* 95, 19–25. See also 182, 24–5 (quoted below p. 138).

[12] Photius, *Bibl.* 251, 464b.

Hierocles, the philosopher loves contemplation 'without political action', valuing nothing else, seeking, through the purificatory virtues, the perfection of which Plato's *Theaetetus* speaks (i.e. assimilation to the divine). The 'lover', on the other hand, loves the young 'with philosophy', is practised in the 'practical virtues on account of the divine'. He is a true πολιτικός, in fact the philosopher-king of the *Republic*, who, through contemplation, imitates the divine in his private and public action.[13] This 'lover' is not inferior to the 'philosopher', surpassing in respect to 'philanthropy' the life of the philosopher, who in turn surpasses the 'lover' in regard to an individual way of life.

The two figures sketched by Hierocles should not, I think, be opposed to each other. The one corresponds rather to the ascent of the soul to the One or the Good (hence the leaving behind of political action and the cultivation of the purificatory virtues), whereas the other corresponds to the descent of the philosopher to political action.[14] What characterizes the political involvement of the philosopher-king is 'philanthropy'. A banal enough theme in Stoic philosophy and more generally in ancient portraits of the ideal monarch,[15] philanthropy is used here by Hierocles to express the specifically Neoplatonic concept of providential (i.e. political) action as the communication of the absolute Good in which the philosopher, through contemplation, comes to share. If it is god, in the first place, who 'loves humanity', who is 'philanthropic',[16] then, by assimilation to god, by becoming united to the Good and by sharing in it, the philosopher also shares in this divine philanthropy, an assimilation which manifests itself in political action.[17]

In the second century, Platonists explained the goal of philosophy, assimilation to god, as being sought on two levels: on the level of the theoretical

---

[13] There is a problem, I think, in the text of Photius here (p. 201, 40), for which I suggest the correction οὐκ] οὗ.

[14] See also Hermias, *In Phaedr.* p. 221, 10–15: 'For in general the philosopher, whenever he is turned towards intelligible being and the knowledge of intelligibles and of god, having the eye of reason turned upwards, he is the first [i.e. theoretical] philosopher; but when he turns from this knowledge to the care of the city and orders it according to that knowledge, then he becomes a political philosopher'.

[15] See Spicq (1958); Dvornik (1966: 540, 552, 554, 619, 624, 719); Kloft (1970: 136–47 and *passim*); de Romilly (1979).

[16] See Spicq (1958: 173–4), citing in particular Plato, *Symp.* 189d, *Laws* 713d.

[17] Iamblichus also speaks of the philanthropy of the ruler in *Ep. ad Dex.*, excerpted in Stob., *Anth.* IV, p. 223, 9; for the theme in Pythagoreanism, see O'Meara (1993b: 72 n. 11). The link between divine and royal philanthropy (the king being image of god) is common in Hellenistic imperial ideology; see Spicq (1958: 181–4).

life and on that of the practical life.[18] This theme was developed in the introductions to philosophy produced in the later Neoplatonic schools, where the beginning student was told that the goal of philosophy, divinization, involved the following: since divine life has two aspects, knowledge of all things and providential care of the world, assimilation to the divine will consist in imitating these two aspects, which, for the philosopher, means, on the one hand, seeking knowledge, and, on the other hand, undertaking political activity, legislative and judicial.[19] Proclus himself lived this ideal, according to Marinus (*Vit. Procl.* 28):

Consequently he did not live according to only one of the two modes that characterize divinity, that of pure thought and aspiration to the better, but he also displayed a providence in regard to things in the second rank, in a mode more divine than the merely political recorded earlier.

So also did Isidore live, according to Damascius (*Vit. Is.*, fr. 24):

To sum it all up in a word, his actions were a clear illustration of the manner in which Pythagoras conceived of man as most resembling god: eagerness to do good and generosity extended to all, indeed the raising of souls above the multiplicity of evil which encumbers the world below; secondly, the deliverance of mortal men from unjust and impious suffering; thirdly, engagement in public affairs to the extent of one's abilities.

Political action, for the Neoplatonist, as an imitation of the providential aspect of divine life, is linked, as we have seen, to the higher level of divinization represented by the theoretical life, in the sense that it expresses and derives from the theoretical life: political action issues from knowledge, from the fecundity of knowledge in so far as knowledge shares in the fecundity of the absolute Good.[20]

To conclude our enquiry into the motivation of the Neoplatonic philosopher-king, we might take the examples of two active politicians who saw their action in the light of the paradigm provided by Plato's philosopher-

[18] Albinus, *Prol.* p., 151, 2–4; cf. Alcinous, *Did.* 28; Annas (1999: 59 n. 19).

[19] Ammonius, *In Is.*, p. 3, 8–19; Olympiodorus, *In Gorg.*, pp. 166, 14–16; 116, 29–117, 2; cf. 12, 4–6; Psellos, *Omn. doct.* 72, 5–12. Themistius, *Or.* XV, p. 277, 24–7, attributing to Pythagoras the idea of man as image in relation to god, restricts this imitation to the function of beneficial action (εὐποιΐα).

[20] In discussing the Greek text on the virtues of the soul cited in Arabic by Miskawayh, Pines (1986: 13–16) opposes a first part of the text concerning an ascension of the soul through a (Neoplatonic) scale of virtues to a second part, which he considers to be Aristotelian, in which having reached divine life, man acts like god in a primary self-act and in a secondary providential act. However, the Greek Neoplatonic texts we have considered in this section show that this opposition (explained by Pines in terms of a difference in the Greek sources of the Arabic text) is a misconception, at least in terms of Neoplatonic philosophy.

king, the examples of Julian the Emperor and Boethius. Shortly after his accession to power in 361, Julian composed a text in which he recounted an autobiographical myth expressing his political mission. He describes how the god Hermes appeared to the young Julian and led him up towards the mountain where the gods reside. There the god Helios (the sun) appeared to him in a vision. Julian asks to be permitted to stay in the vision of the gods, but he is told that he must return to the murky world below, a world replete with ignorance, impiety, and political chaos. Julian is to return to this world as a ruler sent by Zeus and prepared by instruction in good rulership. As reward for this, he is promised a return to the vision of Zeus.[21] I will suggest below (Ch. 8, 2) that Julian does not go so far as to claim that he corresponds to Plato's philosopher-king: he ranks himself lower than this. However, his mythical account of the origin of his political mission echoes the image of the cave of Plato's *Republic*: he also ascends (through education) from the darkness of ignorance and political disorder to the vision of light, of first principles and of the highest principle, Zeus (corresponding to the Good). He subsequently descends, in possession of the requisite knowledge, to a mission of political reform. Even the hesitation of Plato's philosopher-kings is felt again in Julian's myth. But why does Julian accept his mission? The myth speaks of Julian's piety and obedience to the will of Zeus.[22] The absolute Good and other transcendent principles are personalized as gods in Julian's myth. It is due to the impulsion of the absolute Good that Julian descends.[23]

More than a century and a half later, in 524, Boethius awaited execution in his prison in Pavia. He too had been educated in Plato's ideal of the philosopher-king, but his eminent career in the administration of the Goth emperor Theoderic had been destroyed. Seeking consolation, he describes what motivated his political career as follows:

Was this how I looked, was this my expression, when I used to seek out with you [i.e. philosophy] the secrets of nature? When with your rod you drew for me the paths of the stars? When you shaped my character and the whole manner of my life according to celestial models? Are these our rewards for obedient service to you? It was you who

---

[21] Julian, *Or.* VII, 22, 227c–234c (which I summarize rapidly here). Compare Julian's portrait of Numa, a legendary king of Rome, a Pythagorean, sent by Zeus, who combined vision of the gods and legislative action (*Contr. Christ.* 193c–d).

[22] On piety, see below, Ch. 11.

[23] Compare Julian's myth with the myth of Synesius' *De prov.*, the myth of a good ruler (Osiris) sent by gods, who is compared to an evil ruler (Typhon), a myth structured, as noted by Cameron and Long (1993: 352 n. 96), according to the myth of Plato's *Statesman*. See also Synesius, *De regno* 32 on the 'descent' of philosophy from the company of Zeus to political benefaction.

established through the words of Plato the principle that those states would be happy where philosophers were kings or their governors were philosophers [*Rep.* 473c–d]. You, through that same Plato, told us that this was why philosophers must involve themselves in political affairs, lest the rule of nations be left to the base and wicked, bringing ruin and destruction on the good. It was in accordance with that teaching that I chose to apply in the practice of public administration what I learned from you in the seclusion of my private leisure. You, and God, who has set you in the minds of philosophers, know me well, and that I undertook office with no other motives than the common purpose of all good men.[24]

Boethius refers to two motives for his political involvement: the rather negative reason mentioned by Plato (to prevent power coming into the hands of the evil), and the 'common purpose (*commune. . . studium*) of all good men'. What Boethius means by this second explanation might be explicated as follows, in the light of the ideas which we have met above and to which Boethius himself holds: the good are such to the extent that they share in the absolute Good; their purpose is common to them through this sharing; sharing in the Good means sharing in its fecundity, its communication of goodness.[25] The good will then seek to communicate their share of the Good in political action, just as the absolute Good does this in producing reality as a whole.

In conclusion we can say that the metaphysical necessity of the absolute Good's communication of itself describes the need in those who share in the Good to descend to providential, i.e. political, action: 'divine necessity is when we say "it is necessary for god to benefit the world" . . . It is this necessity that compelled Socrates.'[26]

The impulsion to political action comes in the context of the philosophical soul's relation to the body and hence to other incorporated souls. If the philosopher is part of a political community, as being a ruler (as in the ideal city of Plato's *Republic*), then it will be part of the philosopher's 'political' virtue (as the guiding mind in the community) to rule 'providentially' in the light of transcendent knowledge.[27] The philosopher may have a more restricted role, as part of a more limited group (perhaps a philosophical school) where it will also be part of 'political' virtue to govern others.

---

[24] Boethius, *Cons.* I, 4, 4–8 (trans. Tester).

[25] For these principles in Boethius, cf. *Cons.* III, 9–11 and his *De hebdomadibus*.

[26] Olympiodorus, *In Gorg.* p. 12, 4–6, who also discusses Socrates as statesman at p. 210, 14–19. A 'necessity' for the philosopher to communicate virtue to others is mentioned in Plato, *Rep.* 500d4.

[27] Cf. Proclus, *In Remp.* I, pp. 207, 16–211, 3; p. 130, 5–10; Abbate (1998: 108–9).

However, what will motivate this action will be, in both cases, the desire to communicate the Good to others.[28]

2. The Happiness of Philosopher-Kings

To the extent that Plato's philosopher-king must leave the world of light, of knowledge, to return to the difficulties and dangers of political action, it would seem that this return must involve a loss, a sacrifice of the personal good of the philosopher for the sake of the common good. If this is the case, then this loss must surely demotivate the philosopher. And what could the common good be, if it entails the sacrifice of the private good of the individual? As regards this question,[29] responses can be found in the works of the Neoplatonists. We might begin with the most explicit, if somewhat facile answer given by Macrobius when, in commenting on Cicero's *Somnium Scipionis*, he addresses directly the question of the happiness (*beatitudo*) of rulers.

According to Macrobius, the question arises if it is held (1) that the virtues produce happiness and (2) if the virtues are defined as 'purificatory', involving contempt for this world and a turning towards a transcendent divine reality.[30] In such a case, the rulers of states cannot possess happiness. However, by introducing the Plotinian–Porphyrian scale of virtues (above Ch. 4, 1–2), in which the purificatory virtues represent merely one of a number of levels of virtue, which also include 'political' virtues, Macrobius can say that if rulers exert the latter kind of virtue, since virtue entails happiness, then these rulers are happy.[31]

This answer, however neat, cannot be regarded as a very satisfactory treatment of the matter.[32] For if rulers are happy by practising the 'political' virtues, these virtues, in the Plotinian–Porphyrian scale, are merely a

---

[28] See Simplicius, *In Epict.* 32, 163–234 (I am indebted to I. Hadot for drawing my attention to this passage). On the 'providential' function of the teacher in the Neoplatonic school, see Hoffmann (1998: 229–40).

[29] For Plato, see Mahoney (1992). The proverbial happiness of rulers becomes a question in Plato's *Gorgias* (470e) and *Theaetetus* (175c) and a *topos* in rhetoric (cf. Dio Chrysostom, *Or.* III, 1–3).

[30] Macrobius, *In Somn.* I, 8, 2–3; cf. I, 8, 8, p. 38, 24–6 where these virtues are identified with the purificatory stage in the Plotinian–Porphyrian scale of virtues.

[31] I, 8, 5–12: *si ergo hoc est officium et effectus virtutum, beare, constat autem et politicas esse virtutes: igitur et politicis efficiuntur beati*; cf. also II, 17, 4; Olympiodorus, *In Phaed.* 8, 11, 2–3.

[32] See Flamant (1977: 598–9).

precondition and preparation for access to higher levels of virtue, the purificatory and theoretical virtues, which bring divinization and the ultimate goal, happiness. Thus 'political' virtues provide *means* for attaining happiness, but do not in themselves constitute happiness. Despite the apparent simplicity of his argument, this may indeed be the way Macrobius sees things. In speaking of 'political' virtues as 'making' rulers happy, he may mean that these virtues provide rulers with a means for attaining happiness and he also describes these rulers as preparing, through terrestrial actions, the way to heaven.[33]

A clear position on the question of the happiness of rulers can be inferred from the last chapters of Plotinus' treatise on happiness, or the good life, *Enn.* I 4. Here, having argued in chapter 4 that happiness is achieved on the level of the life of knowledge (the βίος θεωρητικός), Plotinus suggests that happiness is not affected by involvement, at lower levels of our existence, in the affairs of the body and in practical matters. The happiness thus achieved, the happiness of the sage, is a stable condition, independent of the blows of fortune, of external events and conditions (chs. 11–12). From this we can infer that the philosopher-king, if he is in possession of theoretical wisdom, will enjoy happiness, irrespective of political activities and political fortune (cf. 7, 17–22). The philosopher, in descending to the 'cave', will not sacrifice or lose this good or happiness, which will remain intact and immune from whatever political life imposes. The sage 'would like all men to prosper (εὖ πράττειν) and no one to be subject to any sort of evil; but if this does not happen, he is all the same happy' (11, 12–14).

Julian the Emperor refers to the independence and serenity of such a sage in the following passage:

The stability of happiness will want to depend as little as possible on Fortune, and those living in government cannot breathe, as it is said, without Fortune, unless someone were to say that the king and general is grounded somewhere above the realm of Fortune, according to those who truly contemplate the Forms . . . But he whom custom and first of all Homer call 'him responsible for the people and worried so much', how could one preserve his position independent of Fortune?[34]

Julian does not, it seems, consider himself as possessing already the perfect and independent happiness of the Plotinian sage. His hope was more modest:

[33] See I, 8, 12: this text (quoted above, n. 31), continues some lines later with the statement: *rectoribus civitatum, quibus per terrenos actus iter paratur ad caelum.*

[34] Julian, *Or.* VI, 4, 256c–d.

a release (which was to come with his death a year later) from his political mission and a return to the contemplation of the gods. In Chapter 8, 1 (below) I will return to the question of the happiness of rulers who, like Julian, have not (yet) attained the perfection of life of the Plotinian sage.

3. Philosopher-Queens

To the ordinary male reader of the *Republic* in Antiquity, it must have seemed that one of the most outlandish of Plato's revolutionary ideas was that of including women among the rulers of an ideal state.[35] It should not surprise us, however, that Neoplatonists took notice of and defended this idea. It is clear, for example, that women were important members of Plotinus' school.[36] They also assured through marriage the dynastic succession on which the schools of Athens and of Alexandria depended, and two women, Sosipatra and Hypatia, were much admired as philosophers and teachers (above Ch. 2, 2–4). If therefore there were specific examples of women, such as Hypatia, who had ascended to the highest levels of philosophy, a 'descent' to political action was to be expected in principle. The Neoplatonists also had contacts with aristocratic and influential women who could act on their behalf, for example Eusebia, wife of the emperor Constantius II, who protected Julian as a young man and to whom he addressed a panygyric. However, it is not the historical question of the concrete activity of women of rank and power with Neoplatonic affiliations that I wish to consider here, but rather the question of how Neoplatonists interpreted and defended Plato's idea of the philosopher-queen.

The Neoplatonists could find the idea of the philosopher-queen, not only in the *Republic*, but also, indicated briefly, in Plato's *Timaeus* (18c–e) and, in the (pseudo-)Pythagorean literature that Iamblichus did much to promote, in a letter of Periktione.[37] In his eighth and ninth dissertations on the *Republic*, Proclus discusses Plato's proposal that men and women share in common the education that will lead to the knowledge on the basis of

---

[35] See e.g. Philoponus, *De aet. mund.*, p. 325, 3–12. On Plato's attitude to women in the *Rep.* and elsewhere, with a review of earlier studies, cf. Föllinger (1996: 56–117).

[36] Above, Ch. 2, 1; cf. Goulet-Cazé (1982: 238–40). On women in Plato's school, see Anon., *Prol.* 4, 30–2.

[37] *PT*, p. 142, 22–3 (Periktione was the name of Plato's mother); cf. Proclus, *In Remp.* I, p. 248, 24–7 (on Pythagorean women, with Abbate 1998: 67 n. 29). However, see also, in the pseudo-Pythagorean corpus, Phyntis (*PT*, p. 152, 9–11), who confines women to the home.

which they will rule. An education in common means, for Proclus, sharing in 'political' virtue and having, as presupposed by this, a common nature.[38] As opposed to this Platonic thesis Proclus sets, on the one hand, a position, identified as Aristotelian, which concedes a common nature shared by men and women (the human species), but distinguishes their respective virtues, and, on the other hand, a position, ascribed to the Stoics, which denies a common nature, but concedes a community in virtue.[39] Proclus, however, insists on a community both of nature (in which the difference is that of sexual parts) and of virtue: the same virtues (and vices) are found both in men and in women. The importance of the virtues being present in common is that it is virtue, reached to a high degree through education, which constitutes the basis of correct political action. Proclus points this consequence out: it is for this reason that Plato's Socrates speaks of men and women as 'guardians'.[40]

The Platonic claim for a community of virtue shared by men and women had already been defended, according to Proclus, by Iamblichus' pupil Theodore of Asine with arguments which Proclus presents as follows.[41] First, if virtues are not shared in common, then the ideal city will be imperfect, since some of its members will have none or only some of the virtues. Secondly, Theodore argues, the differences between the sexes are 'a product of different modes of life': compare the courage of the Amazons[42] and the Lusitanian women (in western Spain) who govern and command in war, while the men weave. Thus it is local customs, modes of life, and not nature, that divide the social tasks between men and women. Thirdly, the gods include goddesses, in particular Athena, goddess of weaving, but also a warrior goddess: it would be absurd to deny any virtue to any god or goddess, and so also, by analogy, to any human. Fourthly, men and women have the same kinds of souls and parts of soul; why not then the same virtues, which are perfections of the soul? Finally, Theodore refers to women inspired by the gods or in whom divine souls have descended, prophetesses such as Socrates' teacher Diotima: how could they be denied the virtues?

In presenting Theodore's arguments, Proclus adds, however, that the

---

[38] Proclus, *In Remp.* I, pp. 236, 5–237, 3; Plato, *Rep.* 454d–e.

[39] pp. 237, 5–13; 252, 22–6; on the Aristotelian and Stoic positions, see Föllinger (1996).

[40] pp. 237, 28–238, 17. Cf. Olympiodorus, *In Gorg.*, p. 105, 25–9: 'woman differs from man in no respect, excepting the genital parts, so that often a woman might live a superior political life than a man, such as to act like a man and die'.

[41] pp. 253, 1–255, 24.

[42] Cf. Plato, *Laws* 806b.

Platonist case for the access of women to education and virtue (and there-fore political rule) must meet two objections arising from the texts of Plato himself. One objection consists in pointing out that the souls in the *Timaeus* (42a–b) that descend from the intelligible realm enter at first, not the body of a woman, but that of a man.[43] The second objection argues that if Plato makes women rulers in the *Republic*, in the *Laws* he does not admit them to the highest political rank, that of the guardians of the laws.[44] Proclus' answers to these objections[45] are worth noting.

To the first objection Proclus replies that if men and women share a com-mon nature and therefore the same capacity for virtue, there are degrees in this common nature, a 'more' and 'less', such that men are superior.[46] This he regards as corresponding to Plato's own position.[47] The 'more' and 'less' distinguishing the sexes sharing the same nature, Proclus argues, is prefig-ured already among the gods, that is, among the transcendent principles and causes, and indeed throughout the metaphysical structure of things as constituted by pairs of causes, monadic and dyadic, the monad as a princi-ple of unity and limit being prior to the dyad as principle of plurality, both being complementary factors productive of things.[48]

As for the second objection, Proclus sees the political projects of the *Republic* and the *Laws* as situated on different levels (a point to which we will return below, Ch. 8, 2): the *Republic* takes individuals that are pure and edu-cates them, whereas the *Laws* takes people who have already lived in other cities and are less perfect. Thus the city of the *Laws* is inferior in its political ambition to that of the *Republic*: not only does it not foresee the highest posi-tions for women, it also allows private property (banned from the life of the rulers in the *Republic*), which, given woman's weaker nature (in Proclus' view) and thus her presumed preference for the private to the public good, means that it is prudent to exclude her from the highest office at the level of the less perfect city of the *Laws*.[49]

To judge from Proclus' report of Theodore of Asine's views—a report which may not be complete or entirely representative—Theodore's reading of Plato was more radical than that of Proclus, who gave more weight to the

---

[43] Cf. Föllinger (1996: 87).

[44] pp. 255, 28–256, 3; on the position of women in the *Laws*, cf. Piérart (1974: 76); Föllinger (1996: 105); Saunders (1995).

[45] pp. 256, 4–257, 6.   [46] Cf. p. 241, 15–30.

[47] p. 256, 4–15 (cf. Plato, *Rep.* 455d–e); Föllinger (1996: 83 ff.), also emphasizes this aspect of Plato's approach.

[48] pp. 245, 13–246, 21; cf. Proclus, *In Tim* I, pp. 46, 1–48, 5; Abbate (1998: 115–20).

[49] pp. 256, 16–257, 6.

conservative and conventional aspects of Plato's attitude to women. If Theodore argued that it is local custom, specific ways of life, that determine the distribution of social tasks between men and women, Proclus saw a natural difference, or rather a difference in degree in a common nature, corresponding to a universal difference between types of causes, monadic and dyadic. At the same time, however, Proclus insisted on the shared nature, and thus on the shared capacity for virtue and for rule, among men and women. Thus women could accede to virtue and rule, but it would be by reaching the 'male' degree of their nature[50] and this prospect, if included in the ambitious political project of the *Republic*, was not part of the lower-level political programme set out in the *Laws*. The revolutionary and conventional aspects of Plato's ideas about women seem in this way to have found in Proclus some form of theoretical integration.

[50] See *In Remp.* I, p. 248, 13–16; Föllinger (1996: 85–7).

Political Science: 8
Legislative

1. The Finality of the State

Proclus describes 'political science' (πολιτικὴ ἐπιστήμη) as having two aims, the 'possible' (δυνατόν) and the 'advantageous' (ὠφέλιμον). Thus legislation—the first part of political science (above Ch. 5, 3)—considers, in Plato's *Republic*, what is both possible and advantageous as regards philosopher-queens.[1] With respect to what is possible, on the one hand, we might distinguish between limits placed on what can be done in given concrete circumstances and limits which apply in general to political action (below, Ch. 11). As regards the advantageous, on the other hand, it seems to be the goal, properly speaking, of legislation, which seeks to realize, in the realm of the possible, what is beneficial for citizens.[2] Political science, a ruling (or directive) science having a legislative and a judicial part, will aim at promoting the good of those ruled. Thus, in a letter addressed to Dyscolius,[3] Iamblichus defined the purpose of the good ruler as the happiness and welfare of his subjects.[4] This had been specified in Plato's *Republic* (342e, 345d–e) and had been a commonplace of descriptions of ideal rulership since the classical period.[5]

However, Iamblichus goes further in his letter, it seems, in the way he ties the good of the ruler to that of his subjects. He argues indeed that the individual good is linked to the common good such that 'the individual good is

---

[1] *In Remp.* I, pp. 238, 11–21; 239, 24–7. Cf. Plato, *Rep.* 450c, 456b12, 458b, *Laws* 742e; Burnyeat (2000).

[2] Proclus, *In Remp.* I, p. 238, 11–21.

[3] See above Ch. 2, n. 29.

[4] Stob., *Anth.* IV, p. 222, 10–14; see also Synesius, *De regno* 6; Proclus, *In Tim.* II, p. 118, 10–17 and Damascius, *In Phaed.* I, 32, 2, where the ruler is distinguished from the despot (i.e. the tyrant) who seeks his own good.

[5] See Isocrates, *Ad Nicocl.* 9; Aristotle, *Nic. Eth.* VIII, 10, 1160b2–3; *Pol.* III, 7; Dio Chrysostom, *Or.* I, 12, 23.

included in the whole and the part is saved in the whole, in animals, cities, and other natures'.[6] This passage of Iamblichus' letter suggests that he has an organic view of the city or state such that the welfare of each part depends on the welfare of the whole and thus that the ruler's good is linked to that of his subjects, since both are a function of the common good.[7]

What is striking about these claims in Iamblichus is that they appear to be in conflict with the position described above (Ch. 7, 2), according to which the good or happiness of the philosopher who becomes a ruler is *not* dependent on the political sphere, being transcendent.[8] Iamblichus suggests in his letter to Dyscolius that the ruler is heartened, strengthened (εὐσθενεῖ), when his subjects prosper.[9] From this we might infer that the activity of ruling is made more effective by success in attaining the good of citizens, but that this activity would be secondary and non-essential to the transcendent good enjoyed, independently of political life, by the ruler who is a philosopher.

However, it appears that the good of the ruler is more closely tied than this to the common good. Such at any rate is what is suggested by a debate in the school of Athens on which Damascius reports:

> The ruler must do everything for the sake of those he rules. But Hegias maintained that the ruler should not merely take care of those whom he rules but of his own self in priority to them, since everyone desires the good for himself before others.[10] Isidore on the other hand says that the ruler *qua* ruler looks after the ruled and for this reason they obey him; but if he looks after himself as well, he does so as one of the ruled who is in need of being cared for. The ruler in the strict sense of the word needs nothing, though in his capacity as man he may have needs . . . if the act of ruling benefits the ruled it will also benefit those to whom it is assigned.[11]

The ruler, as a human being, is also a beneficiary of good rule: the good of the ruler is, in this respect, the same as that of all subjects of rule. The reference to the ruler's status as 'man', as human, probably points to the definition of man as a rational soul related to body, using body as an instrument (above, Ch. 4, 3). As soul living in relation to body, the good of the ruler is

---

[6] Stob., *Anth.* IV, p. 222, 14–18; see also the extract from Iamblichus' letter on marriage (Stob., *Anth.* IV, pp. 587, 15–588, 2), where political rule is said to concern neither the exclusive interest of the ruler, nor that of the ruled, but the common interest equally. Cf. Plato, *Laws* 715b.

[7] For an organic view of the state, see also Proclus, *X dub.* 59.

[8] Elsewhere, in a letter to Sopatros (in Stob., *Anth.* IV, p. 907, 7–9), Iamblichus says 'he is happy who is assimilated to god as far as possible, perfect, simple, pure, transcending human life'.

[9] See Stob., *Anth.* IV, p. 222, 12–14.

[10] On Hegias, see *DPA* iii. 530–1.

[11] Damascius, *Vit. Is.*, fr. 364. This debate echoes the discussion in Plato, *Rep.* 342e–343c.

the same as that of any other soul in the same condition, whose good is the aim of political science. As purified soul, the ruler may reach a transcendent good possessed in independence of material concerns. However, as soul related to the body and its needs, the ruler's good will be what is affected by political life.[12]

However Iamblichus' view of the link between the individual and the common good on the political level seems even stronger than this: there is, we have seen, an organic relation between them, such that the individual good (the part) is 'saved' in the common good (the whole). To develop this idea further, we might turn to Proclus' interpretation of the nature of a political 'whole', an interpretation given in his seventeenth essay on Plato's *Republic*. Here he responds to Aristotle's critique in the *Politics* (II, 1–5) of the strong unity that Plato advocates for the ideal state.[13] Proclus distinguishes between material (i.e. numerical) unity, in which individuals are not distinct, and the formal unity produced when individuals share in a common goal, the transcendent Good. This shared, common good, creates a political whole, which is organic in this sense, and gives rise to 'fellow-feeling and like-mindedness'.[14] Thus a transcendent good, in which citizens together share, gives unity, wholeness, to their interrelations in such a way that through this each shares in the transcendent good.[15] As a human being, as soul related to the body, the ruler shares through political life in a transcendent good; as purified soul, the ruler may have reached this good

---

[12] Compare Aristotle, *Politics* III, 6, 1279^{a}1–9.

[13] Proclus' essay is translated with notes in Stalley (1995) and given a favourable appreciation in Stalley (1999). See also Narbonne (2003).

[14] Proclus, *In Remp.* II, pp. 361, 30–362, 24; cf. I, p. 187, 5–7; on 'like-mindedness' (ὁμόνοια, described as the goal of political science by Olympiodorus; cf. above Ch. 5, p. 55), a vital concept concerning the preservation of states, not only in Isocrates, Plato, and Aristotle, but also in official inscriptions of cities up to the time of Iamblichus, cf. de Romilly (1972), Thériault (1996), and the extract from Iamblichus on ὁμόνοια in Stob., *Anth.* II, p. 257, 5–17.

[15] Cf. Iamblichus, *In Phileb.* fr. 6 (trans. Dillon): 'it is impossible to partake as an individual of the universal orders, but only in communion with the divine choirs of those who, with minds united (ὁμονοητικῶς), experience a common uplift'. In his letter to Dyscolius, quoted above, Iamblichus states the organic relation between parts and whole as obtaining not only in political wholes, but also in biological and 'other' natures. This suggests that the question of the relation between parts and wholes in political structures involves more general, metaphysical principles concerning parts and wholes. In his *Elements of Theology* (props. 67–9), Proclus distinguishes three levels of relations between parts and wholes, in descending order of being and value: (i) a whole before (i.e. superior to) the parts; (ii) the whole of parts; and (iii) the whole in the part. The part (iii) shares in the whole (i) by becoming part of a whole (ii). Thus it is through being part of a whole that a part can participate in a principle transcending the whole. Applied to political relationships, this means that the citizen shares in the (transcendent) good by being part of a political whole which shares as such in this good.

and possess it in such a way as to be unaffected by whatever occurs on lower levels of existence. If political life can add nothing to the transcendent good, the happiness enjoyed by the purified soul of the sage, it can be beneficial to souls who find themselves at the beginning stage of the scale of virtues, that of the 'political' virtues. And these souls may include, not only citizens, but also rulers.

At any rate, the goal of political science, the common good that includes the individual good on the political level, is 'good' to the degree that it relates to, or participates in, a transcendent Good. In short, the finality of politics is sharing in the divine, i.e. divinization, just as 'political' virtue represents a form and early stage of divinization. Thus the political good, or 'political happiness', is not an ultimate goal, but a stage giving access to the ultimate Good:

> The goal of political happiness . . . is the Good, which supervenes thanks to moderation, justice, and the other virtues.[16]

The purpose of the political philosopher is to promote a political order which favours the development of the 'political' virtues among the citizens and thus the achievement of 'political happiness', as a first stage in the process of divinization. Political life, a life in which soul, as living in relation to the body, is confronted with problems of order both within itself and in relation to others, is thus a school of virtue, an extended version, so to speak, of the philosophical school, the ruler being consequently a kind of mentor or guide who brings order to political life, inspired by a privileged access to the divine.

The conception of the purpose of political science as divinization is clearly stated by Iamblichus in an important extract from a letter he addressed to a certain Asphalius:

> wisdom (φρόνησις) leads the virtues and makes use of them all, like an intellectual eye, arranging well their ranks and measures and opportune disposition . . . Being prior, wisdom originates from the pure and perfect intellect. Generated thus, she looks towards this intellect and is perfected by it, having it as the measure and finest model of all her activities. Now if there is any communion between us and the gods, it comes about most through this virtue, and it is most especially through her that we are assimilated to the gods. The discernment of what is good, useful, fine, and their opposites, is present to us through her, as is the judgement of appropriate actions and correction assured. In short,

---

[16] Olympiodorus, *In Gorg.*, p. 178, 10–11: having to do with 'political' virtue (above, Ch. 6, 3), the *Gorgias* deals with this virtue as yielding a 'political happiness' subordinate to a transcendent Good (p. 5, 8–12). On 'political happiness' see also Proclus, *In Remp.* I, pp. 26, 30–27, 6.

wisdom governs humanity and leads the whole order among humans, painting cities, households, and the way of life of each person by comparison with the divine model, according to the best resemblance, erasing this, adding on that, and in both imitating the model in due proportion. So indeed does wisdom make divine-like those who have her.[17]

The following sections will be devoted to elaborating some of the themes announced in this passage. We may note already that Iamblichus links humanity to the divine through the virtue of wisdom. Wisdom derives from a transcendent divine intellect, and, inspired by this model, divinizes human institutions through the order she brings. The passage follows closely in its imagery and wording the text in Plato's *Republic* (500e), where philosopher-kings are compared to painters who imitate a divine model and thus, in their action, divinize the *polis*.[18] We can assume then that the wisdom in question, in the extract from Iamblichus' letter, is the wisdom of the philosopher who has descended to political life.[19] In consequence we can ask: what precisely is the model that inspires the philosopher's political science? How does the model translate into the details of political organization, as regards legislation in particular?

2. Levels of Political Reform

The translation of a transcendent paradigm into a political order presupposes the choice of an appropriate model, a choice which in turn depends on the degree of political ambition, the level of political reform that is sought. It will thus be useful to take account first of the range of different levels of political reform that might in theory be envisaged, since this range conditions the identification and choice of a divine model which is to be given political expression.

Later Neoplatonists distinguished between three levels of political reform. The first level has to do with 'political' reform in the individual soul; the second concerns a constitutional order which takes account of, and integrates, already existing laws and customs; the third is a political

---

[17] Stob., *Anth.* III, pp. 201, 17–202, 17.

[18] An even closer version of *Rep.* 500e (quoted above, p. 35) is given by Hierocles in his work *On Providence* (Photius, *Bibl.* 251, 464b).

[19] Olympiodorus (above, p. 55) describes wisdom (φρόνησις) as the efficient cause of political science.

order which involves no such restrictions. The first level corresponds to a moral reform through the practice of the 'political' virtues, to be achieved, we may suppose, in the Neoplatonists' schools and which is represented, they believed, in Plato's *Letters*; the second level they took to be the political project sketched in Plato's *Laws*; the third level was seen as describing the ideal city of Plato's *Republic*, a city characterized for them by the doctrine that all goods are shared in common.[20]

The relation between the ideal city of the *Republic* and that proposed in the *Laws* was, for the Neoplatonist, far from what it is often supposed to be today, that is, that the ambitious political reformer of the *Republic*, disappointed by his experience in Sicily, produced in his old age a more modest project, that of the *Laws*.[21] Rather, the later Neoplatonist read the relation between the two cities in the light of a passage in the *Laws* (739b–e), which distinguishes between the best constitution (where all is held in common); a second-best constitution which seeks to approach the best, but admits of private property and family units; and a yet lower, third-best city.[22] Thus, in the *Laws*, a political project is sketched which approximates to the ideal, while at the same time making concessions to human nature as regards the need for private property and family. The ideal, best constitution, on the other hand, makes no such concessions and seems indeed hardly possible for humans, since it is described as a 'city of gods or of children of the gods' (*Laws* 739d). The Neoplatonists understood this city of the gods mentioned in the *Laws* as corresponding to the project of an ideal city of the *Republic*.[23]

These ideas suggest that, for the Neoplatonist, the ideal city of the *Republic* could hardly have represented a project for realization among

---

[20] Anon., *Prol. Plat.* 26, 45–58 (and the excellent n. 226, pp. 77–8), English trans. in Dillon (2001: 244); cf. already Alcinous, *Did.* 34; Proclus, *In Remp.* I, pp. 9, 17–11, 4; II, p. 8, 15–23. The Anon., *Prol. Plat.* 5, 44–5 says that Plato discovered the second order (of the *Laws*); but who then discovered the third order (of the *Rep.*)? The principle of communal sharing, by which the Neoplatonists characterized the ideal city of the *Rep.* (see *Laws* 739c2–3) corresponds to a Pythagorean dictum, 'friends share all in common' (κοινὰ τὰ φίλων; see Plato, *Lysis* 207c10, *Rep.* 424a1, *Laws* 739c2–3; Iamblichus, *Vit. Pyth.* 6, 29; Olympiodorus, *In Phaed.* 1, 13, 14–16). I argue that Iamblichus saw the city of the *Rep.* as Pythagorean in O'Meara (1999b).

[21] For a decisive critique of this view, see Laks (1990); Schofield (1999: ch. 2).

[22] On this passage of the *Laws* cf. Schöpsdau (1991). We have seen above (Ch. 7, 3) that Proclus uses the distinction of levels of reform represented by the cities of the *Rep.* and the *Laws* in order to explain the place given women in the one city as compared to their place in the other. For another example of this use, see Proclus, *In Remp.* I, pp. 161, 14–163, 9.

[23] However, in the *Rep.* the sharing of all goods in common seems to concern the ruler-group in particular. The ideal city of the *Rep.* does not then correspond fully to the highest city sketched in the *Laws*; cf. Föllinger (1996: 92) and especially Vegetti (1999) for discussion of the differences between the ideal city of the *Rep.* and the accounts given of it in the *Timaeus* and *Laws*.

humans.[24] It had rather the function of an ideal, a 'divine' state which lower projects for political reform could seek to approximate, while allowing compromises imposed by the human condition, compromises such as those represented in the 'second-best' constitution of the city of Plato's *Laws*. The Neoplatonist had good reason, then, not to be tempted by impossible political dreams, by the vain hopes of which Damascius speaks, hopes that tempt the educated who 'sketch out the best societies and delight in these fictions'.[25] If the philosopher were to seek political reform, it would then be at best at a level corresponding to the second-best constitution of Plato's *Laws*, or perhaps at a yet lower level dictated by the circumstances.

After Julian the Emperor's death, as the pagan philosopher became more and more marginalized by a power that, by the time of Justinian, was seeking to become exclusively Christian, it may have seemed that the possibility of political reform had dwindled to nothing. The philosopher could then, following Socrates' suggestion (*Rep.* 496c–d, quoted above p. 6), lay low, taking shelter, as if behind a wall, from the raging storms of injustice. Olympiodorus emphasized this option a number of times and interpreted the 'storm' as signifying democratic politics,[26] an interpretation which is in line with Plato's anti-democratic conservatism, but which could also be applied, for example, to the rule of Christian mobs in Olympiodorus' city, Alexandria.

However, even in this late period, a high official in the Justinianic court elaborated along Neoplatonic lines, in a dialogue *On Political Science*, a novel constitutional programme. This programme will be seen (below Ch. 13, 2) to correspond to the level of reform represented by the second- or third-best cities of Plato's *Laws*, as did, I believe, the political reform attempted, two centuries earlier, by Julian during his short reign. An indication of the level of Julian's political ambition is the systematic importance given to religion as a part of political organization, a feature prominent in the city of the *Laws* (and far less so in the *Republic*) and which will be examined in detail below (Ch. 10). Another indication of Julian's moderation in his political ambition is his refusal to consider himself a

---

[24] On this question in Plato cf. Burnyeat (2000).

[25] Damascius, *In Phileb.* 171, 5–7; cf. *Rep.* 458a1–b1, discussed by Burnyeat (2000: 783–4); Marcus Aurelius IX, 29.

[26] Olympiodorus, *In Gorg.* pp. 143, 5–10 (saying that both Socrates and Plato took shelter in this way); 165, 17–23; 207, 27–208, 6; Simplicius, *In Epict.* 32, 193–4. Cf. Van den Berg (2003), on the motto 'Live unnoticed' in later Neoplatonism. Simplicius also suggests (186–93), if it is possible, that the philosopher leave an evil political context for a better one, as did Epictetus under Domitian's tyranny (and indeed as Simplicius himself did, above, Ch. 2, 3).

philosopher-king: he felt his own philosophical limitations to be too great to justify such pretension.[27] Rather than that of a philosopher-king, his role was that of a political executive, guided by 'political philosophers' acting as advisers and legislators, who could remain free for philosophical contemplation while he was taken up with the daily exercise of power.[28] Among these advisers we can include Aedesius and other members of the Iamblichean school whom Julian had invited to his court. Finally, we might add that Julian's reform was that, not of a radical revolutionary, but of a traditionalist advocating a return to old inherited institutions revised and made to function in the interest of greater justice in general,[29] a spirit of reform much closer to that of the *Laws* than to that of the *Republic*.

3. Models

What is the divine model, the transcendent paradigm, which the ruler or political philosopher should imitate in bringing about political reform?[30] How does this model translate into specific legislation? The first question can be made especially acute if we return to the passage in *Enn.* VI 9, 7 where Plotinus describes soul as descending from her union with the One so as to communicate her vision, just as Minos legislated 'in the image' of his commerce with Zeus (above, p. 74). How can the One be thus communicated? How can it be the model of which legislation is an image, if the One, as first principle, transcends all knowledge and is ineffable?[31]

This question is explicitly raised and answered by the anonymous Justinianic dialogue *On Political Science*, as will be seen below (Ch. 13, 2). However, limiting ourselves for the moment to earlier Neoplatonists, we can already find indications of how the question might be handled. We can

---

[27] Julian, *Or.* VI, 2, 254b–255c, 266c–d; cf. Bouffartigue (1992: 454–5).

[28] See 263d. Cf. Plato, *Statesman* 259a–b. Julian's distinction between the advisory and legislative action of political philosophers and his own executory role recalls Plato's distinction between the ruling, directive, architectonic function of political (or royal) science and the instrumental, productive function of subordinate arts and skills (*Statesman* 260c, 305c10–d5). The broader theme of the philosopher as counsellor of monarchs in the Hellenistic and early Roman imperial period is developed by Flinterman (1995: ch. 4).

[29] Cf. Athanassiadi-Fowden (1981: 103–18) for a survey. For Julian's conservatism, see Browning (1976: 134); Smith (1995).

[30] For general statements of this idea, see e.g. Plotinus, *Enn.* V 9, 11, 21–5; Iamblichus, *Prot.* 10; Julian, *Or* VI, 8, 262b; Damascius, *In Phaed.* 19, 2–4.

[31] See Balaudé (1990: 90).

infer immediately that, as regards Plotinus at any rate, if the One is indeed unknowable and ineffable, it nevertheless expresses itself in intelligible form in the transcendent Intellect which derives from it. The One, as unknowable and ineffable in itself, is expressed and known in its products and, in the first place, in the immediate 'image' of it which is divine Intellect. Thus the political wisdom that inspires reform of soul's life in the body can imitate and express the One as knowable and expressed in divine Intellect. Our inference is consistent with the extract from Iamblichus' letter to Asphalius quoted above (p. 90), where wisdom is described as the product of 'pure perfect intellect', which is the model for wisdom's political activity.

Since, for Plotinus, divine Intellect is identical with the transcendent Platonic Forms, the philosopher who imitates this Intellect imitates the Forms. This corresponds to Plato's own indications in the *Republic*, in particular where he compares (500e–501b) the philosopher-kings to painters who imitate the Forms as a divine model. Does this mean then that the philosophers, in their work of political reform, imitate a divine city? Plato refers later in the *Republic* (592a10–b4) to his ideal city as a paradigm that may be 'in heaven', since it may be found nowhere on earth.[32] Neoplatonists identified the 'heavenly city' of the *Republic* with the 'city of gods' of the *Laws*, as we have seen. It is not surprising thus that they speak of heavenly, transcendent, intelligible cities.[33] But what is the relation between such cities and the divine models that inspire political science? What are these models?

This kind of question might appropriately be handled, in later Neoplatonism, by recourse to distinctions between levels and intermediate stages, an approach encouraged by the increasing hierarchical differentiation of the later Neoplatonic metaphysical universe. We should thus take into account the multiplicity of levels of transcendent reality (intelligible, intelligible/intellectual, intellectual, etc.) in asking what will become of Plotinus' divine Intellect/Forms, as political model, in Iamblichus, Proclus, and their successors. We should expect there to be many possible divine models for political reform, corresponding, on the one hand, to the many levels of the divine, and, on the other hand, to the different levels of reform that might be envisaged. Thus Proclus distinguishes between levels of divinity imitated in the different levels of political reform, the highest

---

[32] See Burnyeat (2000), who distinguishes between the heavenly city and the Forms.

[33] See Hierocles, *In carm. aur.*, p. 19, 13; Proclus, *In Tim.* I, p. 32, 11–19; Plotinus, *Enn.* IV 4, 17, 34–5.

level producing the 'city of gods' (in which all is shared) of the *Republic*, subordinate divine levels providing models for the second-best city of Plato's *Laws* and for the third-best city.[34] Thus, to each level or project of political reform corresponds a transcendent model.

In referring to three levels of divinity providing models for three levels of political reform, Proclus describes these divine models as 'demiurges', identified as Zeus, Dionysus, and Adonis. This allows us to determine precisely the place of these models for politics in Proclus' metaphysical world: they are found at a comparatively subordinate rank of divinity, below the levels of the One, of the henads, and of intelligible and intelligible/intellectual reality.[35] While not going further into the baroque details of Proclus' system of demiurges, we might nonetheless note that Minos' model in Plotinus (the One as Zeus) is now placed at a considerably lower level of divine reality.[36] Proclus also tells us that the three paradigmatic demiurges are to be found in the myth of Plato's *Gorgias*.[37] Thus the *Gorgias* not only contains political philosophy and instructs in political virtue: it also refers, in its myth, to the divine models which the philosopher in politics will attempt to imitate.[38] Should we think that each divine order contains within it, as a special feature, a model city? Proclus suggests rather that it is the order itself that constitutes the model: human cities assimilate themselves to the order of the gods.[39]

For later Neoplatonism, therefore, the question of the model to be imitated in political reform may be answered by referring to the level of political reform attempted and to the corresponding level of divine reality, the corresponding order of gods. This order was relatively low in the hierarchy of divinity, as compared to what Plotinus had suggested, being found, not in the ultimate principle, the One, as he had indicated, but in the ranks of demiurgic principles as described, for example, by Proclus in his *Platonic Theology*. This greater modesty in the identification of possible divine models of political reform has to do no doubt with the far greater complication of the transcendent world in later Neoplatonism and with less ambitious views about the possibilities of human reason.

---

[34] See *In Remp.* II, p. 8, 15–23. Cf. I, p. 16, 20–4.

[35] See Dillon (2000), Opsomer (2000).

[36] This may be true already of Iamblichus (see Dillon 2000: 342–3); the reference in Iamblichus' letter to Asphalius to political imitation of a transcendent intellect seems thus to avoid the technicalities of a fuller exposition of Iamblichus' views.

[37] Proclus, *Theol. Plat.* VI, 6–8 (*Gorg.* 523a–524a); cf. Tarrant (1999); the Zeus of the myth of the *Protagoras* is identified as a demiurge, source and paradigm of political science in *Theol. Plat.* V, 24.

[38] See Proclus, *Theol. Plat.* V, 24. [39] *In Remp.* I, p. 247, 15–27.

In the *Timaeus* (90b–d), Plato mentions a closer, more accessible, visible source of inspiration for the assimilation of the soul to the divine, the observable motions of the heavens which, in their harmonious order, provide us with patterns for the motions of our soul.[40] Indeed the universe as a whole, as a cosmos, an order brought out of disorder, after the model of the Forms, can itself be considered as a natural paradigm for ethical and political order for humans. This idea became very influential in Antiquity, in particular in its Stoic version, in which *imitatio dei* was conformity to nature, the cosmos itself being a *polis* writ large. The Stoic idea of imitation of the cosmic order influenced the Hellenistic 'mirrors of princes' attributed to various Pythagoreans,[41] and was popular also in texts on ideal rulership of the Roman imperial period such as those of Dio Chrysostom.[42] The Pseudo-Pythagorean 'mirrors of princes' are preserved in the form of excerpts in a fifth-century anthology composed by John Stobaeus. Among the sources of this anthology are materials ultimately deriving from a Iamblichean library.[43] It is possible that Stobaeus' Pseudo-Pythagorean excerpts relate thus to Iamblichus' programme to promote Pythagorean (or supposedly Pythagorean) texts as the ancient sources of Platonic philosophy.[44] A sign perhaps of the use of these Pseudo-Pythagorean texts in Neoplatonic circles is Olympiodorus' reference to a political imitation of the cosmos, a theme he combines, as do the Pseudo-Pythagorean texts, with an analogy between king and state, god and the universe,[45] an analogy which will be considered below in section 4. The idea of the cosmos, the 'cosmic city', as model of political order is also to be found in Proclus.[46] Indeed it is an idea that can be related to the conception of transcendent demiurges as political models to the extent that the world, the cosmic order, is an expression of these divine demiurgic natures. The political consequences of the use of the cosmos as model will be dealt with in the next section.

---

[40] Boethius uses this passage in *Cons.* I, 4, 4.

[41] Cf. Diotogenes, *On Kingship* (*PT*, p. 72, 21–2): 'for the city, a harmony of many different [elements], imitates the coordination and harmony of the world'.

[42] *Or.* I, 42–43.

[43] Stobaeus is the source of our extracts from Iamblichus' correspondence, his *De anima*, and other lost works of Porphyry. Piccione (2003) suggests that Stobaeus' anthology has a propaedeutic function and relates to a milieu influenced by Iamblichean teaching.

[44] See *PR* 96–7, 102–3. On the political theory of the Pseudo-Pythagorean texts, see Goodenough (1928), Chestnut (1979), and, among other more recent studies, Squilloni (1991) and Centrone in Rowe and Schofield (2000: 570–5).

[45] Olympiodorus, *In Gorg.* p. 221, 1–11; cf. p. 5, 6–8; Diotogenes, loc. cit. (above, n. 41).

[46] See Proclus, *In Remp.* II, pp. 3, 5–10; 99, 10–100, 28; 325, 22–326, 2; Philoponus, *De aet. mund.*, p. 35, 16–24.

Between the divine order immanent in the universe and the divine transcendent orders of the demiurges, an intermediary level of political models might finally be mentioned, the level of mathematical principles which, for Iamblichus and Proclus, are innate truths that soul discovers within herself and which constitute conceptual images of divine realities.[47] Both philosophers claim that mathematics provides paradigms for political philosophy, in particular for constitutional structure, political equality and harmony, and the calculation of the appropriate times (καιροί) for actions and for procreation.[48] The mathematics of constitutional order (which includes equality and justice) will be discussed below in section 5, where the sources in Plato will be indicated. The important role played by mathematics in Plato's *Republic* and *Laws* (the 'nuptial number' of the *Republic*,[49] for example, or the mathematics of land distribution in the *Laws*) should make it less strange that the Neoplatonists could think that mathematics might have so much to contribute to political philosophy.

4. The Primacy of Law

Later Neoplatonists, in distinguishing (following Plato's *Gorgias* 464b) two branches of political philosophy, the legislative and the judicial, subordinated the latter to the former, since justice is administered according to canons formulated by the legislator (above, Ch. 5, 3). A subordination is also suggested by Olympiodorus in his commentary on the passage of the *Gorgias*, in which he describes the legislative as preserving the soul, the judicial as having a corrective function.[50] The legislative branch may be taken to include fundamental principles of political organization (what we could describe as constitutional order) to be followed by other laws and dispositions, to judge at least by Plato's procedure in the *Laws* Book VI. We may therefore begin, following some general considerations about the nature and importance of law, with questions relating to constitutional order, taking up judicial matters in the next chapter.

Plato's play on the word 'law' (νόμος) as a 'disposition of intellect' (τοῦ νοῦ διανομή, *Laws* 714a1–2) is cited by Proclus as if it were a definition of

---

[47] On this see *PR* 80, 167–8.

[48] Above, Ch. 5, 2. On the notion of καιρός, see below, Ch. 11, 1.

[49] 546b–c; cf. Mattéi (1982).

[50] Olympiodorus, *In Gorg.*, p. 77, 15–18; see also Iamblichus, *Vit. Pyth.* 30, 172.

law and he infers that legislative science is a kind of particular intellect, in other words that law is a determination of reason deriving from, and subordinate to, transcendent divine Intellect.[51] It corresponds thus to the wisdom of Iamblichus' philosopher-kings which derives from, and has as its model, transcendent intellect, or, more precisely, Zeus as demiurge.

In a letter to a certain Agrippa, Iamblichus provides a veritable encomium of law:

Law is said to be 'king of all'.[52] Now law seems to prescribe what is good and forbid the opposite.[53] By what beauty, therefore, by what greatness, does a good order assimilated to law exceed all things? The prescriptions of the laws spread throughout, in respect to as much and as many kinds of what is fine as there are genera and species of the virtues, and so the benefit they bring extends[54] over all orderings of cities and all lives led by humans. Law is therefore a common good, and without it no good can occur.[55]

As the primary expression of political science, the expression of a divine model, a transcendent good, law communicates the good, as a common good, to lives lived on the human level. It expresses moral values and makes possible the benefits which they bring.

Elsewhere Iamblichus emphasizes the benefits brought by the excellent legislation of Charondas, Timares, Zaleukos, and others to the cities of southern Italy and Sicily, lawgivers who were granted divine honours by their cities.[56] Disciples of Pythagoras, these legislators had been educated in the divinely inspired 'political science' that Pythagoras transmitted to humanity.[57] The ideal legislator is described by Julian thus:

having purified his mind and soul, in legislating [he] keeps in view, not the crimes of the moment or immediate contingencies, but learns the nature of government (τὴν τῆς πολιτείας φύσιν) and has observed the essential nature of justice, what might be the nature of injustice, and then transfers as far as possible the knowledge thence acquired

---

[51] Proclus, *In Remp.* I, p. 238, 22–5; II, pp. 307, 20–308, 2; cf. Olympiodorus, *In Gorg.* p. 139, 17–21 (also quoting *Laws* 714a1–2); Iamblichus, *Protr.*, p. 98, 14–15; Proclus, *In Alcib.* 220, 18–19 (p. 273 with further references on p. 410 n. 3). Cf. Aristotle, *Nic. Eth.* X, 9, 1180ª21–2. For Plato, see Neschke (1995: 156–8).

[52] Pindar fr. 169 quoted by Plato, *Gorgias* 484b. On the success of Pindar's fragment and the variety of interpretations of it, see J. de Romilly (1971: 62–9) (with bibliography).

[53] The same account of legislation is given by Iamblichus in *Vit. Pyth.* 172, p. 96, 16–17.

[54] Cf. Pseudo-Archytas, *On Law*, in *PT*, p. 35, 2–3.

[55] Stob., *Anth.* IV, p. 223, 14–24.

[56] *Vit. Pyth.* 7, 23; 27, 130; 20, 172; Ehrhardt (1953: 474). Legislative preambles attributed to Charondas and Zaleukos are preserved in Stobaeus' anthology (edited in *PT*).

[57] Iamblichus, *Vit. Pyth.* 30, 173; cf. p. 3, 24–7. On Zeus as the divine source of political science, see Proclus, *In Remp.* I, p. 68, 24–6.

to the present task and frames laws which have a general application to all the citizens without regard to friend or foe, neighbour or kinsman.[58]

Plato himself was a descendant of Solon, the legislator of Athens, and hence, Olympiodorus suggests, wrote the *Republic* and *Laws*.[59] If law is not absent from Plato's *Republic*,[60] one nevertheless has the impression that, in the ideal state, such is the perfect and total knowledge possessed by the philosopher-kings that they themselves are, to use a phrase that would be used in the Hellenistic and Roman periods, 'living law':[61] they hardly need a body of laws to which to refer in their action; in the state, they are unconditionally sovereign. In the *Laws*, the situation is different. Accompanying the concessions made in the second-best state (private property, family units) is a less sanguine view of the capacities of the highest officers of the state. These officers are named after their primary function as 'guardians of the law' (752dff.). Law is thus sovereign in Plato's second-best state (cf. 715d) and a distinctive aspect of the *Laws* is, of course, the elaboration of a legislative code that it undertakes.

In what immediately follows the praise of law in Iamblichus' letter to Agrippa, we find the guardian of the law:

However, the ruler responsible for the laws must be fully pure in relation to the highest standard of the laws, neither deceived through ignorance by deceptions and impostures, nor yielding to force, nor trapped by any unjust pretext. For the saviour and guardian of the laws must be as incorruptible as humanly possible.[62]

The emphasis Iamblichus gives to law can be better understood, I suggest, if some account is taken of the relevance of a second-best state such as that proposed in Plato's *Laws* for the level of political reform that can, at best, be sought for humans. If the 'city of gods' of Plato's philosopher-kings is humanly beyond reach, then law becomes the key to the divinization of the state. Through law, Iamblichus claims, are expressed the virtues; through law all goods are achieved. We can infer that the virtues in question are the 'political' virtues, the promotion of which in human, political life allows sharing in a transcendent good and thus divinization.

---

[58] *Or.* VI, 262a–b.

[59] Olympiodorus, *In Alcib.* 2, 18–20. Solon is associated with Pythagoras and Lycurgus in Proclus, *In Remp.* I, p. 200, 21–4. On Solon, see also below Ch. 9, n. 32.

[60] Cf. Morrow (1960: 578–83).

[61] See Aalders (1969), Squilloni (1991: 107–36, with bibliography at 25 n. 9).

[62] Stob., *Anth.* IV, pp. 223, 24–224, 7; cf. the Pythagorean saying in Iamblichus, *Vit. Pyth.* 32, 223: 'Always help the law and fight lawlessness'.

5. Constitutions

The Neoplatonists were familiar with Plato's theory of constitutional types as developed in the *Republic*, types which comprised (in descending order of value) aristocracy, timocracy, oligarchy, democracy, and tyranny.[63] This list of five types can be extended to six, so as to include monarchy, although Plato himself sees little major difference if the leadership of his ideal state, the philosopher-king(s), is one (monarchy) or many (aristocracy) in number.[64] All other constitutional forms are regarded as degradations or perversions of the primary (monarchic–aristocratic) type. However, in the *Laws*, the constitutional form proposed is of a mixed type, combining monarchic and democratic elements: here also one might detect an aspect of the account taken of human nature characteristic of the second-best state.[65] Which of these constitutional orders should the Neoplatonist prefer? How would this order (which we could describe as positive law[66]) reflect the model provided by natural, mathematical, or divine law?

If we start at the lowest paradigmatic level, that of natural law, then it would seem that monarchy (or aristocracy) is the constitutional type recommended by the order of the universe. So, at least, ran a traditional argument which goes back to Isocrates[67] and which is very prominent in the Hellenistic Pseudo-Pythagorean 'Mirrors of Princes': as the universe is ruled by god, so the king ought to rule the state.[68] The cosmic analogy is taken up by Olympiodorus, who quotes in support of it the Homeric verse (*Od.* II, 204) 'many leaders is not good, one leader let there be'. Olympiodorus concludes: 'so a multitude of commoners should not rule, but one who is wise and political', immediately adding that this supports

---

[63] *Rep.* 445c–d and Book VIII; Olympiodorus, *In Gorg.*, p. 14, 8–21; Pseudo-Elias, *In Is.* 22, 10–11.

[64] *Rep.* 445c–d; *Statesman* 292c. Sallustius (*De dis*, ch. 11) distinguishes more strongly between monarchy and aristocracy, the former corresponding to the rule of reason in the soul, the latter to the rule of reason and spirit. Olympiodorus, *In Gorg.*, p. 221, 11–17 (citing Ammonius) is more orthodox.

[65] See *Laws* 693d–702b; Aalders (1968: 38–49); Stalley (1983: 77–9, 116–20).

[66] Porphyry distinguishes between divine, natural, and positive law (θετός; *Ad Marc.* 25, p. 120, 8–10); cf. Olympiodorus, *In Gorg.*, p. 240, 21–3; Calcidius, *In Tim.* VI, p. 59, 19–20 (*iustitia positiva* and *naturalis*) seems to have inspired the distinction between positive and natural law in the medieval West (cf. Kuttner 1936).

[67] Isocrates, *Nicocles*, where the superiority of monarchy to other régimes is argued by reference to the monarchy of Zeus.

[68] Diotogenes, in *PT*, p. 72, 18–19.

aristocracy as well as monarchy, in Plato's view.[69] A similar preference for an aristocratic and especially monarchic constitution can be found in Plotinus.[70] Proclus, too, finds in the cosmos a hierarchy of the type expressed in the (monarchic or aristocratic) ideal city of the *Republic*, a hierarchy of many ranks, however, as we would expect in a later Neoplatonist approach.[71]

The preference for a monarchic or aristocratic constitutional order should not be seen, I think, as endorsing the actual political régime, on the imperial or local level, of the late Roman Empire. Autocratic rule not based on philosophical knowledge and perfect virtue is tyranny, not true monarchy or aristocracy in the Platonic sense.[72] The possibility of a ruler perfect in knowledge and virtue, at that time, or any other, must have been considered very small, if not non-existent. A more human and attainable form of constitution, of the level of the second-best city of the *Laws*, would have been a mixed constitution such as that of the *Laws*, to which I shall return a little later.

Going up the scale of political models, from the model provided by natural law to that provided by mathematical principles, we can read suggestions on this subject in Plato which were developed by the Neoplatonists. It is in particular the mathematical concept of 'geometrical proportion', a proportion between terms such that the *ratios* between terms are equal (e.g.: $1 : 2 = 2 : 4$), applied by Plato in a political context, that interested the Neoplatonist.[73] Plato introduces this concept in the *Gorgias* (508a):

Now the wise men[74] say . . . that heaven and earth, gods and men are bound by community and friendship and order and moderation and justice; and that is why they call this whole universe the 'world order' (κόσμος) . . . You haven't noticed that geometrical equality has great power among gods and men . . . (trans. Irwin)

---

[69] Olympiodorus, *In Gorg.*, p. 221, 1–17; cf. pp. 166, 6–18; 167, 17–18; 208, 5–7 (Olympiodorus, p. 236, 3–13, speaks of the Pythagorean preference for an aristocratic constitution). The Homeric verse is quoted by Boethius, *Cons.* I, 5, 10–12 in a similar anti-democratic context; it had, of course, been given prominence long before by Aristotle as supporting a view of the universe organized in relation to one primary principle (*Met.* XII, 10).

[70] Plotinus, *Enn.* IV 4, 17, 24–36.

[71] Proclus, *In Remp.* II, pp. 99, 10–100, 28.

[72] Cf. Iamblichus, *Vit. Pyth.* 32, 214–22; Proclus, *In Alcib.* 165, 9–11 (cf. Plato, *Statesman* 292e9–293a1); Sallustius. *De dis* XI, 2. Tyranny, rather than reflecting the natural order, in fact reverses it: Proclus, *In Remp.* II, p. 176, 11–15. It puts the good of the ruler before the common good (above n. 4).

[73] The proportion is stated as a general metaphysical principle by Proclus, *In Alcib.* 3, 5–13.

[74] Plato is referring, it seems, to the Pythagoreans.

The political significance of 'geometrical equality' (or geometrical proportion) is that it concerns an equality of ratios and not an equality of quantities as in arithmetic proportion (e.g. $4 - 3 = 2 - 1$): the latter relation means, in political terms, that each receives the same amount, the former that each is assigned what is appropriate or due.[75] We recognize here the founding principle of Plato's ideal state in the *Republic*, the principle that to each should be assigned the social function (as ruler, auxiliary, or producer) which is appropriate to one's capacity, in other words, Plato's principle of justice, 'to do one's own'.[76] It is not strange, in view of this, that Plato objects, in democracy, to the indiscriminate equality it confers on unequals (558c). Iamblichus excerpts the passage from the *Gorgias* quoted above,[77] which is commented on in detail by Olympiodorus, who adds a full mathematical account of geometrical proportion[78] and specifies that what is intended is a distribution (διανομή) in terms of what is appropriate and merited.[79]

The same idea of proportional equality is defined by another mathematical concept that Iamblichus attributes to Pythagoras. Among Pythagoras' scientific contributions to humanity was political science[80] and, in particular, the 'the best constitution', which is explained, rather obscurely, as constructed like a scalene right-angled triangle, of which the important characteristic seems to be the harmonic unity of unequal sides. This triangle is cited later, again as a model of the equality and justice reached through equal proportions of unequals.[81]

Does the principle of proportional equality mean that the constitution of Plato's ideal state in the *Republic*, which exemplifies this principle, is to be chosen? Not necessarily, it seems: the scheme of the *Republic* presupposes rulers capable and worthy of the monarchic function with which they are invested. If such persons are not to be found, then the principle of proportional

---

[75] Cf. Dodds's very useful note, (1959: 339), to the *Gorg.* passage, quoting Isocrates, *Areop.* 21; Harvey (1965: 107–10), who thinks that Plato derived the political application of geometrical equality from Archytas (105–7, 145).

[76] *Rep.* 433b4 (cf. Neschke 1995: 129–30, 134); cf. Iamblichus, *Vit. Pyth.* 30, 179; Proclus, *In Remp.* I, pp. 216, 21–217, 5. On the principle of justice ('geometrical equality') on the cosmic level, see Proclus, *In Remp.* II, p. 236, 1–4; Calcidius, *In Tim.* VI, pp. 59, 22–60, 3.

[77] Iamblichus, *Protr.*, p. 90, 7–14.

[78] Drawn from Nicomachus, *Intr. arith.* II, 22–7, a textbook which was made a central part of the Neoplatonic curriculum by Iamblichus (cf. *PR* 51–2).

[79] Olympiodorus, *In Gorg.*, pp. 181, 24–183, 13; cf. Proclus, *In Tim.* II, p. 227, 5–6.

[80] Above n. 57.

[81] Iamblichus, *Vit. Pyth.* 27, 130–1; 30, 179; cf. Iamblichus, *De comm. math. sc.*, p. 69, 4–22 (especially p. 69, 15–16).

equality requires another constitutional scheme. How this can be achieved may be seen in Plato's *Laws*, where it is vigorously argued that the mixed constitution (monarchic and democratic) of the second-best city aims at achieving the equality of geometric proportion.[82]

It is in this context, I believe, that a mysterious and surprising passage in Boethius[83] finds its place. In his *Introduction to Arithmetic* (II, 45), Boethius says:

> And thus the arithmetic [mean] is compared to a state ruled by a few, because a greater proportion is in its smaller terms. They say that the harmonic mean is the state ruled by the best (*optimates*), because a greater proportion is found in the greater terms. In the same fashion the geometrical mean is of a state that is democratic (*popularis*) and equalized. For it is composed of an equal proportion of all, both in its greater and in its smaller terms, and among all there is a parity of mediation that preserves in proportions an equal right (*aequum ius*).

Three constitutional structures are related here to three kinds of mathematical proportion: oligarchy to arithmetical proportion, aristocracy to harmonic proportion, and democracy to geometric proportion. What is surprising in Boethius' text is the link made between democracy and geometric proportion, since traditionally, as we have seen, democracy is associated (to its disadvantage) with arithmetical proportion.[84] What is mysterious is the source, presumably Greek, that Boethius is following here and which is not, it seems, the standard mathematical manual of Neoplatonism which Boethius usually uses in his book, Nicomachus' *Introduction to Arithmetic*.[85]

Boethius' source is very probably a text *On Law and Justice* going under the name of the Pythagorean Archytas,[86] where we find that the aristocratic constitution represents harmonic proportion, the oligarchic arithmetical proportion, and the democratic geometrical proportion.[87] The Pseudo-Archytas makes clear that what is compared is not simply equal and unequal quantities (of merit), but also equal and unequal ratios, in which geometric proportion represents equal ratios of unequal quantities. This

---

[82] Plato, *Laws* 756e–757c, quoted by Proclus, *In Tim.* II, p. 227, 1–9; cf. Dillon (2001: 249). For Plato see Neschke (1995: 157–8).

[83] Discussed in somewhat general terms by Silvestre (1996).

[84] See Plato, *Rep.* 558c, *Laws* 756e–757c.

[85] See Silvestre (1996).

[86] Excerpts preserved in Stobaeus (*PT* p. 33 f.). Boethius refers to Archytas by name earlier in his *Instit. arith.* (II, 41, 3). Harvey (1965: 125), suggests, but without adequate argument, that rather than using Pseudo-Archytas, Boethius shares a common source with Pseudo-Archytas.

[87] *PT*, p. 34, 4–10.

difference in the terms of the comparison between mathematical proportions means that a new pairing of types of proportions and constitutions results, in which democracy is shifted so as to correspond to geometrical proportion and arithmetic proportion (representing unequal ratios and unequal quantities of merit in inverse proportion) is assigned to oligarchy.[88]

In this second variant on the theme of political proportionalities, it does not follow that the geometrical proportion that democracy now represents entitles it (as it would have in the first and more well-known variant of the theme) to be considered as superior to other constitutional forms. In fact, if we read further in Boethius' source, the Pseudo-Archytas advocates as best a *mixed* constitution made up from democratic, oligarchic, monarchic, and aristocratic elements.[89]

We can detect, then, the presence in Neoplatonic circles of theories of a mixed constitution which were consonant with Plato's approach in the *Laws*, theories proposed, it was thought, by ancient Pythagoreans and in particular by Archytas, a leading politician of Tarentum and a friend of Plato.[90] An example of a Neoplatonic mixed constitution, situated on the level of political reform represented by Plato's *Laws*, will be examined below in Chapter 13.

---

[88] The passage is explained by Moraux (1984: 670–1) and compared with the political interpretations of geometrical proportion in Plato and Aristotle.

[89] *PT*, p. 34, 16–20. Another Pseudo-Pythagorean work preserved in part in Stobaeus and attributed to Hippodamos (*PT*, p. 102, 10–20) prefers kingship as most divine-like, but since it is easily perverted, recommends a mixed constitution. Boethius' own preference seems to be for the régime of *optimates* that he mentions in the passage quoted above, if account is taken of another, anti-democratic text, in the *Cons.* (above n. 69). The mixed constitutions of Pseudo-Archytas and Pseudo-Hippodamos are discussed by Aalders (1968: 15–21), as are other theories of mixed constitutions in the Hellenistic and Roman imperial periods.

[90] For Iamblichus' use of Archytas, cf. O'Meara (1999b).

Political Science: Judicial 9

The primary, legislative part of political science aims at the good of citizens. This good is understood in moral terms: as members of a political whole, citizens are educated in the virtues expressed by laws. These virtues, 'political' virtues, constitute in turn a stage leading to a transcendent good, the divinization of the soul. As imitations of divine models (cosmic, mathematical, or demiurgic), laws also divinize political life. A divinized political whole represents, in its structure, in its distribution of social functions, an image of the structural principle of geometrical equality which governs the cosmos and the orders of the divine transcending the cosmos.

The secondary, judicial part of political science has a corrective function: it restores conformity to the laws in cases of transgression. Olympiodorus also suggests that the legislative is distinguished from the judicial in the sense that the former has to do with what is general, whereas the latter deals with particulars.[1] This presumably has to do with the generality of legislation,[2] as compared to the particulars of individual cases of transgression. The judicial part of political science thus requires a form of practical wisdom closely tied to knowledge of particular cases, a theme to be taken up below (Ch. 11, 2).

As regards judicial theory as such, in order to recover aspects of the Neoplatonists' approach to themes in this area, we can turn to a variety of sources. Concrete examples are provided by the activities of Plotinus as judge and arbiter of disputes in the life of his school and by Proclus' practice, as described by Marinus, of the 'political' virtues.[3] Iamblichus also supplies examples of 'Pythagorean' justice in his *Pythagorean Life*, examples which would have been regarded as relevant by the later Neoplatonist.[4] We might also turn to Julian the Emperor's policies in the judicial area, to the extent that it could be argued that these policies reflect Julian's philosophical views.

---

[1] Olympiodorus, *In Gorg.*, p. 78, 10–15.
[2] See Plato, *Statesman* 294a–c; Julian, as quoted above p. 99.
[3] Above, Ch. 2, 1 and 3.
[4] *Vit. Pyth.* 17, 124–6.

However, rather than attempting in this way to work back from practice to the theory that this practice might be taken to exemplify, it may be better first to establish, independently of practice, some elements of Neoplatonic judicial theory.

As seen above,[5] the eschatological myths of the *Phaedo* (107d–115a), *Gorgias* (522e–527e), and *Republic* (614a–621d) could be considered as illustrating the judicial part of Platonic political science. This suggests that for a Neoplatonic account of judicial themes we may turn to the Neoplatonic commentaries on these texts, of which those by Proclus, Damascius, and Olympiodorus are extant. However, the eschatological myths illustrate *divine*, not human justice. Yet as such they may be treated as paradigms for human justice. Neoplatonic interpretation of the myths will allow us to describe some general aspects of judicial theory, in particular the nature of the 'corrective' function of justice. We will then move to considering a little-read text which provides information on the subject, not only on the administration of human justice, but also on the particulars of the exercise of power in real conditions, Sopatros' letter to Himerius.

1. The Penology of Plato's Eschatological Myths

The three eschatological myths of Plato's *Phaedo*, *Gorgias*, and *Republic* could be considered as concerning judicial theory.[6] There is a difficulty here, however. If Plato emphasizes in general the therapeutic, reformative purpose of justice and punishment,[7] it can be argued that, precisely in the three eschatological myths, he takes a different approach: in these myths *retribution*, not reform, is the primary purpose of punishment, and, as primary objectives, retribution and reform are incompatible.[8] Such incompatibility was not, however, felt by Plato's Neoplatonist readers, who

---

[5] Ch. 5, 3.

[6] The three myths were seen by later Neoplatonists as constituting a whole, the *Phaedo* dealing with the places assigned to souls that have been judged, the *Gorg.* concerning the eschatological judges, the *Rep.* relating to the souls judged: Damascius, *In Phaed.* I, 471; II, 85 (cf. Westerink's note on I, 471, pp. 241–2, collecting many other references). This scheme goes back to Proclus (cf. *In Remp.* I, p. 168, 11–23; II, p. 128, 3–23) and perhaps even to Porphyry (Macrobius, *In Somn.* I, 1, 6–7). The myths of the *Phaedo* and *Rep.* were associated by Iamblichus in a letter cited by Olympiodorus, *In Gorg.*, pp. 241, 25–242, 9.

[7] See Mackenzie (1981: chs. 11–12). A brief statement of Plato's position is found in *Gorg.* 525b.

[8] See Mackenzie (1981: 223, 237, 239).

interpreted eschatological punishment as essentially therapeutic and reformative, consistent therefore with Plato's general attitude to punishment.
Their approach emerges especially clearly in the explanations that they
attempt to give of Plato's mention, in the myths, of incurable souls and of
an eternal punishment. Having considered these explanations, I will then
suggest briefly what, in Proclus' view, eschatological justice and punishment actually are.

In his *De anima*, Iamblichus provides a review of differing opinions, in
particular those of Platonists and Pythagoreans, concerning eschatological
judgement and punishment.[9] He distinguishes between the judgement
(κρίσις), the effect of judgement (δίκη), i.e. punishment, and purification.
In Iamblichus' account, the purpose of judgement, according to some, is to
separate what is good from what is bad, affirming the good's absolute superiority.[10] This seems to come near to another view, next mentioned by
Iamblichus, which speaks of the judgement as putting in correct order the
better and the worse,[11] in other words putting each in its proper place. As for
the effect of judgement, it is precisely to bring about the triumph of what is
better and the repression of evil, producing an equality proportional to
worth.[12] To this view Iamblichus adds the opinion of those who refer to the
effect of justice as retributive (a fault being paid for by its equal or its multiple in punishment), as a removal from vice or some other such benefit.[13]
These last views are close to what Iamblichus then reports concerning the
utility of eschatological purification: it purifies the soul from earthly accre-
tions, liberating it so it may rise to a higher existence.[14] Iamblichus' own
ideas on these matters do not emerge clearly from his review of these various opinions. However, two theses are prominent in his survey: eschatological judgement and punishment are corrective in the sense of restoring
and enforcing correct moral order in the universe; souls, in receiving their
due, may also morally benefit from their punishment and reach a higher
life.[15] But is *all* eschatological punishment therapeutic and productive of
moral reform in souls that are punished?

An interesting passage in Hierocles' *Commentary on the Golden Verses* certainly goes a long way towards suggesting a positive answer to this question.
Hierocles describes the criminal soul which is aware of its evil and, in dread

---

[9] In Stob. *Anth.* I, pp. 454, 10–457, 6.   [10] p. 455, 7–11.
[11] p. 455, 12–15.
[12] p. 455, 15–19 (on justice as geometric equality, cf. above, Ch. 8, 5).
[13] p. 455, 15–25.   [14] pp. 455, 26–456, 11.
[15] For these two theses, as concerning cosmic justice, cf. already Plotinus, *Enn.* IV 4, 45, 47–52.

of punishment in Hades, condemns itself to nothingness,[16] to self-destruction, as its only 'cure', as an escape from eschatological judgement. This self-annihilating sentence that the criminal soul passes on itself is excessive in its severity, Hierocles adds, since the judges in Hades condemn to nothingness, not the soul itself, but its vice, punishing the soul for its own salvation, using punishment as a doctor uses excision and cautery, to cure the soul of its vice, to purify it of its evil passions and lead it up to a fuller existence.[17] Plato's conception of punishment as a therapy, comparable to medical therapy in that it restores moral health,[18] certainly seems to apply here in Hierocles, at least to some criminal souls. However, in his eschatological myths, Plato does not seem to extend this reformative function of punishment to certain incurable souls, which are said to suffer eternal punishment.[19]

Proclus rejects the idea that certain souls could be absolutely incurable, for this would mean that all souls, or all of a certain type of soul, would no longer be present in this world, having become confined forever to Hades. This consequence being, in his view, absurd, he interprets the incurability of certain souls as relating to their incapacity to cure themselves, to become aware (as are Hierocles' criminal souls) of their crime and repent as a first step to moral reform within. Such souls are cured by cosmic providence over a certain period; they depend on this external help for their salvation.[20]

If even these, the most evil of souls, are not incurable, neither can their punishment be without end. Proclus thus interprets the eternal punishment of such souls as spanning the totality of a certain period of time.[21] His opinion is referred to by Damascius, who disagrees with the identification of the particular period concerned. Damascius also mentions other interpretations of eternal punishment. One of these claims that Plato's mention of eternal punishment is political: the suggestion is that Plato's myth of eternal punishment is intended to have a political function, as a deterrent to crime in present moral life. Other views stress the notion of the helplessness

---

[16] οὐδένεια; Iamblichus refers to our consciousness of our nothingness, οὐδένεια, in *De myst.* I, 15, 47, 17.

[17] *In carm. aur.* p. 65, 5–25.

[18] *Gorg.* 477e7–479c6; the medical analogy is found, for example, in Plotinus, *Enn.* IV 4, 45, 47–52 and in Iamblichus, *De myst.* IV, 5, 189, 1–3.

[19] *Gorg.* 525c, e; *Phaedo* 113e; *Rep.* 615e.

[20] Proclus, *In Remp.* II, p. 178, 5–24; cf. Damascius, *In Phaed.* I, 546, 9–10. On the salvation of 'incurable' souls, cf. also Proclus, *In Remp.* II, p. 184, 14–28.

[21] *In Remp.* II, pp. 178, 2–8; 179, 9–19.

of certain souls, or the continuity of their punishment.[22] All of these views, in short, reject a literal interpretation of eternal punishment.

We might give the last word on this subject to Olympiodorus. He argues that if souls were punished forever, they would never enjoy the good, being always in vice. Yet 'punishment has some good as its purpose'. Consequently, if punishment were not to benefit us, improving our lives, it would be in vain. However, neither god nor nature works in vain. A scholiast, no doubt Christian, added to Olympiodorus' argument this remark in his manuscript: 'Eternal punishment being absolutely true, note how this fellow misinterprets it!'[23]

2. Eschatological Judgement and Punishment

But what do eschatological judgement and punishment actually amount to? In explaining the myth of Er at the end of the *Republic*, Proclus interprets eschatological justice essentially along the lines suggested already by Plotinus and Iamblichus:[24] it is a principle of order in the cosmos, whereby to each soul is assigned its due, its proper place, above or below, in the order of being. This order governs the whole. In this reign of justice, the good find an elevated place corresponding to their merit, whereas the evil reach the lowest of conditions, conditions of suffering in proportion to their fault. The implementation of the universal principle of justice, in the case of particular souls, is the result of the combination of the autonomous motions of the souls themselves seeking their proper places and of the actions of corresponding demons representing the providential world-order.[25] Thus,

[22] Damascius, *In Phaed.* I, 547 (with Westerink's important note, pp. 279–80) and especially II, 147 (a fuller account).

[23] Olympiodorus, *In Gorg.*, p. 263, 13–25, with the scholion on 263, 26. Augustine, *City of God* XXI, 13 also criticizes the Platonists' view that all punishment is therapeutic, purifying the soul of evil. However, when he was younger he had written (*De ord.* II, 8, 25): *nihil puniant quod non valeat ad melius*. For some Christian thinkers such as Origen, the question of eternal punishment remained open. A corollary of the therapeutic view of punishment was the claim that a lack of punishment was to be considered a greater evil for the culpable soul, since it amounted to the lack of a cure; cf. Plato, *Gorg.* 476a–479e; Proclus as quoted in Olympiodorus, *In Gorg.*, p. 130, 9–10; Proclus, *X dub.* 52.

[24] Proclus, *In Remp.* II, pp. 145, 15–148, 15; 150, 9–151, 3; 151, 25–152, 26; 182, 9–183, 25; cf. above p. 108 and Clarke (1998: 226–339) on Julian and Sallustius.

[25] See already Plotinus, *Enn.* IV 8, 5, 22–4 (punishing demons); Iamblichus, *De myst.* IV, 1, 181, 13–19; *De anima* in Stob., *Anth.*, pp. 454, 25–455, 5. On the relation between cosmic justice and fate, see I. Hadot (1978: 121–5).

with the exception of Plato's 'incurable' souls, souls make their own 'hell' for themselves through their passions (as do Hierocles' self-annihilating souls), or their own heaven, in conjunction with the divine agents of cosmic justice. This is essentially what Plotinus had already suggested:

But since there are many places for each as well [as many bodies], the difference between them must come from the disposition of the soul, and must come also from the justice in the nature of things. For no one can ever evade what he ought to suffer for his unrighteous doings: for the divine law is inescapable and has in itself together with the judgement already pronounced its execution. He too who is to suffer punishment is carried unknowing to what he has to suffer; on his unsteady course he is tossed about everywhere in his wanderings, and in the end, as if utterly weary, by his very efforts at resistance he falls into the place which suits him, having that which he did not will for his punishment as a result of the course which he willed. But it is stated in the law how much and how long he must suffer, and again there come together the release from punishment and the ability to escape up from these regions by the power of the harmony which holds the universe together. (*Enn.* IV 3, 24, 5–20)

Neoplatonic eschatology includes many other questions. For example, which part of the soul is guilty of vice and is punished? Are all souls judged, or only evil souls? Can there be a release from the cycle of reincarnations of the soul, of punishments and rewards? These questions might also be pursued,[26] to the extent that they might have a bearing on the use to which Plato's eschatological myths may be put as expressions of the judicial part of political philosophy. That these myths may be put to use in this way is made possible by the coherence which the Neoplatonists sought to establish between Plato's therapeutic conception of justice and punishment and the same conception which they believed they could find in his eschatology.

Of course allowance must be made for the difference between divine cosmic justice, in its perfection, omniscience and power, and human political justice, in its many limitations. The workings of divine justice can escape our understanding and it has in any case a much broader, higher purpose than has human justice. 'Men define justice as the proper activity of each soul and the distribution of worth according to the laws in vigour and the prevailing constitution. However the gods, looking to the order of the whole cosmos and the contribution of the souls to the gods, determine the appropriate punishment.'[27]

---

[26] See e.g. Smith (1974: chs. 4–5).
[27] Iamblichus, *De myst.* IV, 5, 187, 13–188, 1.

3. Sopatros' Letter to Himerius

Later Neoplatonists read Plato's eschatological myths so as to find in them a theory of divine justice and punishment which was consistent with what Plato said elsewhere about the deterrent and therapeutic functions of justice and punishment. Divine justice is corrective in the sense that it restores and ensures correct moral order in the cosmos, while curing transgressing souls, in part through the autonomous actions of these souls, in part throught the action of the divine (demonic) agents of cosmic justice. We can infer that human justice should seek to imitate divine justice as far as possible and that it will have the same corrective function.

An interesting text concerning the administration of human justice, its therapeutic function, its exercise of a practical wisdom concerned with particulars, is a letter addressed by a certain Sopatros to his brother Himerius on the occasion of the latter's accession to a position of power. This letter survives in the form of roughly six pages of excerpts preserved in Stobaeus' anthology.[28] Its author can be identified as the son of Iamblichus' pupil Sopatros (i.e. 'Sopatros 2'), who was a philosopher, decurion of Iamblichus' city Apamea and brother of a Himerius whose own son was named Iamblichus (= 'Iamblichus 2') and who occupied, according to Libanius, various unspecified positions of power prior to 357.[29] The names indicate the Iamblichean intellectual milieu to which Sopatros 2 and Himerius belonged, a Neoplatonist milieu in which family relationships often went with philosophical affiliations.[30] A Neoplatonic milieu is also suggested by the context in which Sopatros' letter survives in Stobaeus' anthology, where it is followed by excerpts from the Pseudo-Archytas' *On Law and Justice* and from Iamblichus.[31]

In the excerpts from Sopatros' letter we might note the following ideas. In the first excerpt, Sopatros distinguishes between the praise of virtue based on the highest precepts, and praise related to actions (πράξεις), in

---

[28] IV, pp. 212,13–218,9. In this section I summarize points argued in more detail in O'Meara (2003b). The only earlier study of this text is that by Wilhelm (1917–18), who supplies a running commentary, in part paraphrase, in part quotation, including many useful but somewhat indiscriminate references to sources and parallel texts in Isocrates, pseudo-Pythagorean texts, Dio Chrysostom, Iamblichus, and others.

[29] Cf. *PLRE* i. 437 and 846–7. Wilhelm (1917–18: 401–2) identifies the author of the letter excerpted in Stobaeus as Sopatros 1 (i.e. the pupil of Iamblichus), but the relation to a brother Himerius argues against this (*PLRE* i. 846).

[30] On the dynastic aspect of the later Neoplatonic schools, see Proclus, *Theol. Plat.* I, Introduction (xxvi–xxxiv).

[31] On the Iamblichean connections of some of Stobaeus' sources, see above, p. 97.

which the best of what is given is to be preferred to what is best 'by nature', i.e. absolutely.[32] Sopatros thus suggests that, when it comes to political action, the highest principles must be relativized in connection with given circumstances and indeed, in the following excerpts, he provides much advice concerning this practical relativization of the absolute. The 'Mirror of Princes' that Sopatros presents to his brother in his letter[33] thus speaks to a middle position, between a morally absolutist ideal and an unprincipled conformity to the given. Sopatros recommends a moderate level of political ambition (above Ch. 8, 2).

Sopatros' letter also refers to a middle position in the sense that the position of power now occupied by his brother is not absolute, but subordinated on the one hand to a higher authority, yet set over others on the other hand. (One might imagine a position of primary political responsibility on the provincial level.) Sopatros thus provides his brother with advice relating (i) to his handling of his superiors, and (ii) to his relations to his subordinates and subjects.[34]

(i) As regards superiors, Sopatros distinguishes between three sorts of tasks (ἔργα) assigned to a higher official by his superiors: those that cannot be refused, but that may be mitigated in their unbearableness by the mode and moment of their execution and by persuasion; those that cannot be accepted under any circumstances,[35] but everything is to be endured by the official who will prefer to suffer evil rather than do it;[36] and those which might be avoided, or put off, by the use of astute suggestions.[37] This last point may be related to another theme in Sopatros' excerpts, that of the use of opportune free speech (παρρησία) and appropriate respect shown to superiors: free speech may be used sometimes, if not harmful to those who are ruled; respect is appropriate when shown for the benefit of those ruled. Sopatros has in mind then a political objective—the good of citizens, the advantage of the ruled—in discussing how the middle-rank ruler is to deal with the sometimes unacceptable duties imposed from above. This objective

---

[32] p. 213, 1–6 (this excerpt seems to derive from the beginning of Sopatros' letter). See Proclus, *In Tim.* I, p. 81, 5–7 who reports Solon as having said that his laws were not the best, but what was possible, although he knew what was better.

[33] Wilhelm (1917–18) entitles the letter a 'Regentenspiegel'.

[34] (i) pp. 213, 8–215, 10; (ii) pp. 215, 12– 218, 9.

[35] Sopatros here quotes Aristotle, *Nic. Eth.* III, 1, 1110ª26–7.

[36] See Plato, *Gorg.* 474b3–4, 475d–e, 479c 4–5, 508e4–6; Boethius, *Cons.* IV, 4, 32: *infeliciores eos esse qui faciant quam qui patiantur iniuriam.*

[37] pp. 213, 16–214, 3.

is the 'best life',[38] the morally 'beautiful', to which the high official can bring his subjects, by means of his moral courage and political wisdom (πολιτικὴ φρόνησις) weaving a harmonious whole.[39]

(ii) As regards Himerius' relations to his subordinates and subjects, the excerpts from Sopatros' letter stress two virtues that should be demonstrated, generosity and justice. The virtue of generosity corresponds to the virtue of philanthropy so often extolled in Hellenistic and late antique 'Mirrors of Princes' and that had already been discussed by Iamblichus in his letter to Dyscolius (another high official, it seems), where the largesse of the powerful is related to the common good and to the greater efficacy of the ruler with regard to the common good.[40] As for the practice of justice, Sopatros recommends a therapeutic, edificatory approach adapted to the differences in moral character of Himerius' subjects.[41] What this means is that while an uncompromising enmity to evil is to be demonstrated so as to avoid the promotion of permissiveness, the law, as regards the full rigour of the penalties it prescribes, is to be applied with moderation and humanity, neither with anger, nor with relentless attention to every small fault, as if human nature were infallible, for 'to sin is in human nature'.[42] Rather, attention should be paid to the moral correction and reform of those judged, grace may be appropriately shown, and in general subjects are to be ruled with an adapted approach, 'the decent with measure, the supine with vigour, the bold with austerity and the timid with gentleness'.[43]

Sopatros, as regards the administration of justice, follows in general, we might conclude, Plato's approach to penology in that he advocates a combination of deterrence and moral reform or therapy, the emphasis being placed particularly on the latter aspect. However the excerpts that remain from Sopatros' letter hardly allow us to go very much further than noticing this tendency. At any rate, the high official is asked to keep in mind the principles we have found emphasized already by Iamblichus in

---

[38] ἀρίστη ζωή, an Aristotelian description of divine life (*Met.* XII, 7, 1072^{b}28) used by Plotinus to refer to the human goal of divinization, the life of intellect (*Enn.* I 4, 3, 30–5; IV 8, 1, 4).

[39] pp. 214, 8–9 and 15–20; 215, 1–4; 212, 16–213, 1; cf. Plato, *Statesman* 279a–b, for the image of political weaving.

[40] See above p. 77; Iamblichus in Stob., *Anth.* IV, pp. 222, 7–223, 12; Sopatros, pp. 215, 12–216, 3.

[41] pp. 216, 15–218, 9, of which I summarize some points in what follows.

[42] p. 217, 20–2. For praise of moderation in the administration of justice cf. Julian, *Or.* III, 30. On avoiding punishment in anger Proclus cites examples provided by Plato and by the Pythagoreans Archytas and Theano (*X dub.* 54). For an impression of the judicial practice of provincial governors in the fourth century, cf. MacMullen (1990: ch. 20).

[43] p. 217, 7–10.

his correspondence:[44] the primacy of the good of those ruled and of the common good; the objective of promoting the 'best life' through virtue; the use of law as the expression of virtue and the means to achieve virtue in the state. Sopatros clearly expects from his brother the highest moral standards, as did Iamblichus from the guardian of the law, an integrity combined with a political wisdom showing a flexibility adapted to the particulars of the situation and to the differences in individuals. With Sopatros' recommendations we can compare the moral inflexibility demonstrated later, and with poor results, in a position similar to that of Himerius, by Severianus.[45]

---

[44] See above, ch. 8, 1 and 4; Iamblichus' letters to Dyscolius and Agrippa, excerpted in the same chapter of Stobaeus as that of Sopatros, may also have been epistolary 'Mirrors of Princes'.

[45] Damascius, *Vit. Is.*, fr. 278, 280.

The Political Function 10
of Religion

In the Greek city-state of the classical period, it would have been difficult to make sense of the modern separation of church and state, so closely linked were the religious and political aspects of the lives of its citizens. The very identity of the city-state, its origin, its collective coherence, its well-being found expression in religion, and the days of its citizens were filled with religious festivities, including what we consider today to be cultural and athletic events, all testifying to the bonds uniting the community with its gods. Whatever their real motivations, the charges of impiety brought against philosophers such as Socrates appealed to the political danger represented by criticism of the gods. The specific character of each city-state was expressed in its particular religious myths and rituals, even if the classical Greek city-states shared to some extent a common pantheon.

With this public or civic religion, in its local diversity, we might compare various initiatory rites and movements, in particular the mysteries of Eleusis and the Orphic movement, which responded not so much to the needs of the community as to those of the individual, for example that of the salvation of the individual in an afterlife.[1] If we were to develop this comparison into a distinction between (i) civic religion which divinizes the city through the uninterrupted presence of the gods in the life of the collectivity, and (ii) a more individual religious practice which divinizes the individual in the afterlife, then we could relate this distinction in turn to (i) the divinization of the state sought in Neoplatonic political philosophy, and (ii) the divinization of the soul that, in Neoplatonism, represents access to a higher level of divine life. In Neoplatonism, the two forms of divinization are not opposed: they represent different degrees of divinization, the lower (civic divinization) being presupposed for access to the higher (divinization

---

[1] These two religious tendencies should not be distinguished to the extent of opposing them as mutually exclusive; cf. Burkert (1987: 10–11).

of the soul), the higher making possible in turn the lower. Transposed in terms of religion, this would mean that civic religion has an important function in the divinization of the state, as preparatory to a transition to higher levels in the divinization of the soul.

In this chapter, the question of the political function of religion will be explored as regards the Neoplatonic conception of the divinization of the state and its relation to higher forms of divinization. Since the question, for the Neoplatonist, will express itself, not in the very general way in which I have sketched it above in connection with the classical Greek city-state, but more specifically, in connection with the interpretation of texts in Plato dealing with the political function of religion, it may be useful to recall briefly some relevant aspects of Plato's treatment of religion in the *Republic* and the *Laws*.

1. The Political Function of Religion in Plato

Civic religion is not absent from the ideal city of the *Republic*. At its origin, its members, living an idyllic pastoral life, feast together, singing hymns to the gods (372b). When the city is founded, the most important legislation, that concerning temples, sacrifices, service of the gods, demons and heroes, services for the dead, is briefly mentioned, but left aside as being properly assigned to the god Apollo at Delphi (427b–c). What receives much more attention in the *Republic* is the question of the educational function of religious myths such as those sung by Homer and Hesiod, as these might shape the malleable souls of the young. Strong objection is taken to the immoral and unworthy behaviour attributed to the gods in these myths, and a number of guidelines, or norms (τύποι),[2] are formulated, as constituting the basis on which appropriate religious myths might be told. These norms stipulate that the divinity is good and the cause of good, not of evil (379b, 380c); that the gods deceive us neither in word nor in deed (382e); that they exemplify the virtues and thus are not open, for example, to bribery (390e). The gods should exemplify in this way the moral values of the ideal city, the primacy of the good and of the life of virtue, values which should also be expressed in mythical tales concerning demons and heroes (392a). Plato's overriding interest is thus the political education, through religious myths,

---

[2] 'Norms' is Burnyeat's translation (1999). These norms are discussed by Proclus, *In Remp.*, diss. IV.

of the moral character of children, by means of their imaginative imitation of paradigms (395c–d), at a stage prior to that of the education of reason through the sciences which the future rulers of the city will receive.

Besides the prominence of law, the acceptance of private property, the relative lowering of women's status and the project of a mixed constitution, another point on which the city of Plato's *Laws* differs from that of the *Republic* is the extensive attention given to civic religion.[3] The fundamental importance of religion is already made clear in the formal opening address that is directed to the future members of the projected city: the well-being of individual and state are said there to depend on taking god, not man, as the 'measure of all things', on 'following god',[4] or becoming 'like' god. This basic principle translates as the practice of the virtue of piety, i.e. the constant service of the gods (θεραπεία θεῶν), a service which respects the hierarchical order of the gods and extends to the service of demons and heroes. Parents should also be honoured, obeyed in their lifetime, and paid appropriate service after death (716a–718a). If the fundamental political importance of piety is kept in view, the severity of Plato's legislation against impiety (907d–910d) can better be explained. It is claimed in the *Laws* that impiety arises from one of three erroneous opinions: (i) that the gods do not exist; (ii) that they do not care for humans; (iii) that they can be swayed (i.e. bribed) by sacrifices and prayers (885b, 907b). Plato's argument against the first of these opinions (888e–899d) tends to be read today as if it were an early form of proof for the existence of God, an argument read in abstraction from its political context. However, it should be noted that the argument seeks to establish a scale of values (the priority in the cosmic order of reason, soul, and virtue[5]) which corresponds to the scale of values on which the projected state is based: the priority of reason and virtue and the freedom and harmony that these bring.[6] Such is the link between the cosmic and political order, spelled out very clearly in *Laws* 889b–e in relation to a position Plato rejects, that the 'atheist' in effect rejects the fundamental principles on which the projected city is based: his impiety represents a serious internal menace to good political order. In contrast, the extensive religious programme proposed in the *Laws* represents the translation into

---

[3] See Reverdin (1945) for a general account. On the relation to actual religious institutions in Greece and in particular in Athens, cf. Morrow (1960), Piérart (1974).

[4] See *Laws* 716b; on this Pythagorean precept, see above Ch. 3 (the whole context of the passage in the *Laws* has a strong Pythagorean tonality).

[5] *Laws* 892b, 896c–d, 898c.

[6] *Laws* 688a–b, 693b–c, 701d, 963a.

religious practice of the grounding principles of the state. The gods who, in the *Republic*, provide educational models of political and moral values for children, serve the citizens in general in the *Laws* as expressions of the purpose of the community. A philosophical elite may well conceive of the gods in the highly abstract terms used in Plato's argument against atheists, but general access to the same values is provided at a lower level by religion,[7] the constant practice of which is vital for the cohesion and good functioning of the state.

The particulars of the religious institutions proposed in the *Laws* cannot be taken up here. However, we should recall some aspects that will be of importance to Plato's Neoplatonic readers. The legislator of Plato's *Laws* is essentially conservative in dealing with gods and temples: he will not presume to go against what is inspired by the oracles of Apollo at Delphi, of Zeus at Dodona and of Ammon, or by ancient traditions concerning cults indigenous or imported (738b–c). The organization in space of the cult and temples of the gods will correspond to the spatial disposition of the state: a group of principal gods (Hestia, Zeus, Athena) will be worshipped in sanctuaries at the centre of the state, on the acropolis, from which radiate the divisions of the land on which will be found a multitude of local cult centres and temples dedicated to local gods.[8] Filled as it is in space by the places sacred to gods and demons, the life of the citizens is also filled in time by a multitude of religious festivities, rituals, games, cultural events.[9] The priesthood in charge of the sacred places and ceremonies is headed by priests of Apollo and Helios presided over by a 'high priest'.[10] These and the other members of a multitudinous clergy, including priests and priestesses, exegetes, treasurers of the temples, diviners, are appointed by election or by the drawing of lots.[11] Candidates for religious office are screened for their moral qualities. The public, collective purpose of this unified yet locally differentiated religious institution emerges clearly in the prohibition of private shrines that escape and might even defy state control (910b–d): Plato's 'Church' is a state institution, at the service of the political goals of the community.

---

[7] See Reverdin (1945: 244–5).

[8] See Reverdin (1945: 57–60) for a summary.

[9] See Reverdin (1945: 62–8).

[10] See Piérart (1974: 315–54 (and pp. 321–3 on the question whether the 'high priest' was an innovation in Plato).

[11] The drawing of lots is seen as leaving the choice of the person to the god (759b–c).

2. Julian the Emperor's Religious Programme

In the second-best model of political reform projected in the *Laws*, piety is emphasized as the fundamental virtue, since it brings about the assimilation of the citizens to the divine whereby the citizens become virtuous and godlike. We have seen that in a passage suggestive of Pythagoreanism, Plato associates piety with 'following god' and with service rendered, in proper order, to the gods, demons, heroes, and parents. The same conception of piety is expressed in the speech Pythagoras gave, according to Iamblichus, to the youth of Croton,[12] and is developed at considerable length by Hierocles in his commentary on the first four verses of the Pseudo-Pythagorean *Golden Verses*. For Hierocles, it is no accident that the *Golden Verses* exhort us first to piety, to honour, in proper order, the gods, demons, heroes, and parents, for piety is the leading virtue, elevating us to the divine cause of the cosmos.[13]

The connection between political reform and piety is made very clear by Julian in the autobiographical myth in which he explains his political mission. This mission, described as a 'descent' to imperial rule subsequent to a transcendent vision of the gods,[14] originated in a reign of impiety, that of Constantine, in which the Empire was afflicted by many evils.[15] It is in obedience to the highest god, Zeus, that the young Julian descends from his contemplation of the gods in order to reform the Empire, following instructions in matters among which proper service of the gods is fundamental.[16] This means that political reform will entail the reversal of the 'atheism' that had become rampant under Constantine (Julian is thinking primarily of Christianity),[17] and the strengthening of state-controlled religious institutions appropriate to the practice of proper piety in relation to the gods. If then we keep in mind Plato's *Laws* and recall that Julian's ambition is not that of the philosopher-king of the *Republic*, but is more modest,

---

[12] *Vit. Pyth.* 8, 37–38, pp. 21, 20–22, 20; cf. p. 50, 20 ('follow god'). On Pythagoras' piety see 28, 134–7, pp. 75, 27–77, 15 (ὁσιότης (p. 75, 28) is equivalent to εὐσέβεια (p. 77, 12)). Cf. the preambles to legislation attributed to the Pythagorean Zaleukos in Stobaeus, *PT*, pp. 228, 24–32; 227, 23–5.

[13] Hierocles, *In Carm aur.*, pp. 7, 23–8, 16; cf. the Arabic commentary on the *Golden Verses* attributed to Proclus, pp. 9–23, Iamblichus, *De myst.* V, 21, 230, 9–10 (service of the gods in proper order). Hierocles refers to εὐσέβεια, but seems to consider this term, θεοσέβεια, and ὁσιότης to be synonyms (p. 14, 9–10).

[14] See above, Ch. 7, 1.

[15] Julian, *Or.* VII, 22, 228d–229b; a connection between (Christian) impiety and political disaster is also suggested in Proclus, *In Tim.* I, p. 122, 8–12.

[16] *Or.* VII, 22, 233c–d; on Julian's piety cf. also 212b and *Ep.* 89, 299b–300c.

[17] See also Julian's prayer at the end of *Or.* VIII (180b).

corresponding more to the second-best political project of the *Laws* or to a project of yet lesser scope,[18] the importance that he gives to piety and religion in the context of political reform makes good sense.

Can we go so far as to claim, over and above this general relationship, that Julian's religious policies, in their detail, were inspired by the politics of religion of the *Laws*? Without going quite so far, we can at least notice that Julian's religious programme may be compared in a number of respects to that of the *Laws*.[19]

(i) Julian's religious policy is as conservative in principle as that of the *Laws*: ancient traditions should not be disturbed.[20] This means, for example, that Jewish religion, in its fidelity to ancient tradition, can be accepted, whereas Christianity, as innovating on Judaism, cannot.

(ii) Local gods have their rightful place for Julian, as they have in the *Laws*. There are many gods for Julian, gods corresponding to geographical, cultural, national differences. But these gods have no exclusive or universal claim:[21] local gods such as that of the Jews are part of a large number of regional gods, themselves subordinate to the major gods of the Greek pantheon. If, in the *Laws*, the local gods are integrated in the city-state in a centralized system presided over by the gods of the acropolis, in Julian's empire, as gods of different regions and nations, they are presided over by the supreme gods of the Greek tradition that also correspond to the primary principles in the later Neoplatonic metaphysical hierarchy.[22]

(iii) Julian embarked on an extensive programme of restoring temples (including the temple of Jerusalem), altars, and cults, including sacrifices.[23] The importance to him of this programme, the density of cult that he sought to promote (including on occasion animal sacrifices of Homeric proportions),[24] becomes clearer, if the vital political function of piety, as indicated in the *Laws*, is recalled.

---

[18] See above, Ch. 8, 2.

[19] Cf. the diverging positions of Athanassiadi-Fowden (1981) and Smith (1995: chs. 2, 7, critique of Athanassiadi). Neither takes account, however, of the relevance of political philosophy to the subject and of the importance of the *Laws* in this context. Smith's discussion also suffers from a caricatural view of later Neoplatonic philosophy ('abstruse', 'recondite', reduced to Iamblichean theurgy) and does not see how it relates to traditional polytheistic religion.

[20] Julian, *Ep.* 89, 453d; the Romans have preserved Greek religious traditions (*Or.* XI, 39, 152d–153a).   [21] Julian, *Ep.* 89, 454a.

[22] See above n. 8. For subordinate regional gods in Plato, see *Statesman* 271d, 272e–273a (with further references to Plato in Riedweg 1999: 78); cf. Iamblichus, *De myst.* V, 25, 236, 6–7 (divine ethnarchs), Athanassiadi (1981: 166).

[23] For a survey of the evidence, see Athanassiadi (1981: 110–11).

[24] Ammianus Marcellinus 22, 12.

(iv) The restoration of cult entailed the appointment of clergy on the regional and local level. In this connection, in his capacity as Pontifex Maximus, Julian sent an important letter, a kind of encyclical, to Theodore, High Priest of the province of Asia.[25] The letter contains much of interest concerning Julian's conception of a pagan clergy, its appointment, qualifications, and duties. The political importance and status of this clergy are repeatedly stressed, as standing in relation to man's nature as a 'political animal'.[26] With this Julian contrasts the anti-political, misanthropic behaviour of 'atheistic' Christian ascetics, which he explains as a result of submission to evil demons, not to transcendent benevolent gods.[27] The appointment of clergy is 'top down': Julian, as Pontifex Maximus, on the advice apparently of the Iamblichean philosopher Maximus, a member of his court,[28] appoints provincial high priests who themselves appoint lower clergy. This method of appointment is not that proposed in the *Laws* (appointment by election and by lot), but evokes rather, in its approach, a Neoplatonic metaphysics of emanation in which all good, power, and knowledge are transmitted vertically, through intermediaries, from higher to lower levels.[29] The appointments are made purely on the basis of the moral and intellectual qualities of the candidates. Here also, a difference should be noted in relation to the programme of the *Laws*, where candidates must meet certain physical and social, as well as moral requirements (759c). Julian insists on this last requirement, explaining at length, as if writing a 'Mirror of Princes' for clergy, the virtues which should distinguish priests, virtues related to their role as intermediaries between gods and humans. Priests should be particularly pious, dedicated to the service of the gods, as well as 'philanthropic', dedicated to the benefaction and care of humanity.[30] This priestly philanthropy, as Julian understands it, need not be a pagan version of the Christian practice of charity, as is often supposed in modern studies:[31] it can be explained more simply as an extension of the philanthropy, the beneficence characteristic of the gods: emulation of the gods, becoming divine-like, means practising the gods' philanthropy.[32] The

---

[25] *Ep.* 89. The high priests of Lydia were Chrysanthius and his wife. On the Iamblichean connections of Julian's high priests, see Athanassiadi (1981: 185–6), who also discusses Julian's reform of the clergy (pp. 181 ff).

[26] Aristotle's famous expression (*Pol.* I, 2): Julian, *Ep.* 89, 288b; cf. 292d (man as 'social animal') and above p. 44.

[27] *Ep.* 89, 288b–c.   [28] See Athanassiadi (1981: 185–6).

[29] See below, Ch. 13, 1, ii. Julian's practice of course corresponds to autocratic rule.

[30] *Ep.* 89, 453a, 293a, 305b.   [31] For a recent example see Smith (1995: 43).

[32] *Ep.* 89, 289a–290a.

philanthropy of Julian's ideal priest is thus the same as that of the later Neoplatonic philosopher-king.[33]

From these comparisons we may conclude that, in its general lines, Julian's conception of the political importance of religion corresponds to what can be found in Plato's *Laws*: the primacy of piety as a political virtue; the political centrality of religious institutions and the menace represented by 'atheism', a position which involves religious ideas incompatible with political order; the necessity of establishing a dense network of active cults in a structure that is both centralized and regionally diversified; the traditionalism that is to be observed in religious organization. However, it does not appear that Julian's approach is *simply* that of applying the religious programme of the *Laws*. Quite apart from historical contingencies, in particular the presence of Roman religious institutions and the imperial extension of the state, some new elements in Julian's programme seem to derive from Neoplatonic philosophy, in particular the conception of a descending hierarchy in the transmission of the good, a conception also influential, we have seen (Ch. 7, 1; Ch. 8, 2), in Julian's vision of the philosopher-king and of the less exalted philosophical emperor that he aspired to be.

3. Religious Cult in Iamblichus

Among the functions of the religious institution of Plato's *Laws* is that of teaching, as it is of Julian's clergy. In the *Republic*, theological myths, appropriately designed, are taught to children as a form of pre-rational, imaginative education in moral and political values. In the *Laws*, this religious instruction is general, as if most citizens are not expected to progress much beyond the stage of infantile imagination.[34] Julian speaks in a similar way of the appeal of theological myths to the lower, childish parts of our soul and of the masses incapable of a purer reception of divine truths.[35] At this level, that of elementary, general, pre-rational moral education, theological myths require, as they did in Plato's *Republic*, purging of the immoral and unworthy traits that they might attribute to the gods, traits which Julian criticizes in the 'myths' of the Jews and Christians.[36] In

---

[33] See above, Ch. 7, 1.

[34] Cf. Morrow (1960: 468–9).

[35] Julian, *Contr. Christ.* 39b; *Or.* VII, 2, 206c–d; cf. Plato, *Statesman* 268d–e.

[36] *Contr. Christ.*, *passim* (e.g. 75b, 106e, 155e, 171e); Julian alludes in 44a–b to Plato's critique of theological myth in the *Rep.*

the structure of philosophy, however, myths pertain not only to the function of elementary moral edification: they can also have a higher intellectual function in both suggesting and concealing superior theological truths.[37] This higher function must also presumably be part of the work of Julian's clergy.

Besides teaching, Julian's clergy is responsible for other traditional religious functions: prayers, hymns, sacrifices, and other rites. On the subject of the material aspects of religious cult, Julian suggests that this relates to our corporeal condition: material signs and images are required by the material condition in which we find ourselves, as intermediaries linking us to the transcendent immaterial divinity.[38] We may consequently infer that just as the human condition as embodied soul involves political life and requires 'political' virtue as a first stage in the divinization of the soul, so too does this condition require religious cult, in its materiality, as part of the first level of divinization. However, the interpretation of the function and importance of religious rites varied among Neoplatonist philosophers, as can be seen, for example, from the following comparison between Plotinus and Iamblichus.

If Plotinus attributes some importance to the 'political' virtues as means for setting in order the life of the soul as embodied, and thus as a preliminary stage presupposed by higher levels of divinization, some discontinuity remains between the reform of the embodied life and the true divinization of the soul.[39] We can explain this by noting the strong independence and exteriority of soul, in Plotinus, in relation to its embodied condition. Whatever its condition, soul *always* remains rooted and present (even if unconsciously) in the transcendent life of divine Intellect, to which it can at any moment return by the practice of the virtues and philosophy.[40] Materiality does not contribute positively to the divinization of soul, but represents rather an obstacle to be transcended by the soul in its return to the Good. It is perhaps for this reason that Plotinus, much to the bewildered surprise of his pupils Amelius and Porphyry, had so little interest in attending various religious ceremonies in Rome.[41]

For Iamblichus, however, the descent of soul into the body usually

---

[37] Julian, *Or.* VII, 11, 216c; cf. Proclus, *In Remp.* I, pp. 79, 18–81, 21; Sheppard (1980: 157–9); Clarke (1998: 344) (Sallustius); Lamberton (1986: 197) (Proclus).

[38] *Ep.* 89, 293b–296b.

[39] Above, Ch. 4, 1.

[40] See *Enn.* IV 8, 8, 1–6.

[41] Porphyry, *Vit. Plot.* 10, 33–8; on this text cf. Van den Berg (1999).

resulted in an embodied condition that was of profound significance for the soul. If certain souls can remain 'pure' in their descent into the body—souls such as that of Pythagoras—retaining thus their relation to transcendent divine being,[42] many others lose this relation: they descend entirely and their embodied state becomes constitutive of their identity.[43] This means for them that materiality is of much greater significance in the question of the divinization or salvation of the soul. Most human souls no longer enjoy the proximity and accessibility of the divine that Plotinian souls possessed. Rather, they are estranged from the divine, cut off from it, weakened in this distance from it and bound up in their identity with different types and at different levels of material existence. The material condition of souls, in its variety, is thus of primary importance to the divinization of souls, which must at first be realized through and by means of material conditions.[44] This entails in turn that political and religious life, in their materiality, must be of much greater instrumental value in Iamblichus than in Plotinus. The importance of soul's relation to the body, in the divinization of soul through political life, has already been noted[45] and it can be observed also in respect to religious practices, if we turn to Iamblichus' De mysteriis.

The correct title of the De mysteriis is 'The Response of the Teacher Abammon to Porphyry's Letter to Anebo, solving the difficulties it contains'.[46] In this work Iamblichus assumes the personage of an Egyptian priest whose pupil, Anebo, was the recipient of Porphyry's letter.[47] To judge from the passages that Iamblichus quotes from Porphyry's letter, it seems that Porphyry sought information and explanation concerning a large number of practices, in particular those which we would describe as magic, involving the manipulation, seduction, and even bullying of gods and demons through various procedures. Other questions concerned divine epiphanies and the intervention of evil and deceiving spirits. Augustine, who summarizes Porphyry's letter to Anebo,[48] wonders what Porphyry's own attitude in this inquiry is: is he genuinely seeking instruction from

---

[42] See PR 37–8. [43] See above, Ch. 3, 3.

[44] These material conditions include the material 'vehicle' of the soul, whose function in the elevation of the soul assumes greater importance in later Neoplatonism. See Dodds's survey in Proclus, El. Theol., pp. 313–21.

[45] Above, Ch. 8, 1.

[46] De myst. 1, 1–3: the modern title goes back to the title given the work by Marsilio Ficino (De mysteriis Aegyptiorum Chaldaeorum Assyriorum).

[47] On Iamblichus' authorship and the reasons why he chose to speak as 'Abammon', see Saffrey (1971). Saffrey (2000a) provides a helpful analysis of the structure of De myst.

[48] Augustine, City of God. X, 11.

Anebo? Or is he, in bringing out the scandalous assumptions behind various sorts of magical practices, providing thereby an implicit criticism of them?

We can identify more precisely what, for a Platonist, would be scandalous in such practices, if we refer to the norms that Plato had applied in his critique of religious myths in the *Republic* and the principles of piety formulated in the *Laws*: that the divine is good and the source of good, not of evil; that the divine cannot be influenced, bribed, corrupted by human practices; that the divine is not deceiving and fraudulent.[49] Iamblichus shares these principles entirely, as Porphyry must have done: authentic religious practice, as opposed to malpractice, must be explained, in its necessity, form, and efficacy, consistently with the goodness of the divine, its power as the source of all that is good and of no evil, its transcendence and incorruptible sovereignty over all that is inferior, including human acts, and its truthfulness.[50] It might be added that the religious practices which Iamblichus wishes to defend, as consistent with these Platonic principles, are not exclusively of the type in which Porphyry, in his *Letter to Anebo*, seems most interested, practices which are marginal, strange, extreme. Iamblichus also wishes to cover more conventional, collective public cults.[51] In fact his approach concerns all religious practice, properly conducted, whether Egyptian, Chaldaean, or Hellenic, whether public or private. He is concerned with all true service of the gods and of their subordinate demons.

Iamblichus' explanation of correct religious practice as consistent with Plato's norms and principles includes further premises concerning the gods and human souls which derive more particularly from his Neoplatonic metaphysics. Not only are the gods incorporeal, perfect, good, the source of all good and of no evil: as the origin of all power, form, and structure in material reality, they and their power are omnipresent throughout material reality, being received in proportion to the varying receptivity of material beings.[52] They constitute a hierarchy which extends down

[49] Above, s. 1; cf. Julian's criticism of Jewish and Christian theology as violating these principles (above s. 2).

[50] *De myst.* IV, 1, 181, 1–10; V, 4, 205, 9–206, 14; I, 11, 37, 14–38, 13; I, 12, 42, 1–5; IV, 6, 189, 4–11; IV, 10, 194, 15–16; I, 21, 64, 13–65, 14; I, 18, 53, 2–5; II, 3, 70, 12–17; II, 10, 90, 7–91, 7; II, 10, 94, 1–5; III, 31, 178, 2–179, 12; IV, 6, 189, 4–11; IV, 10, 194, 15–16. Julian also uses (*Ep.* 89, 301a) the principles of piety of the *Laws* (cf. Riedweg 1999: 63–4).

[51] Cf. *De myst.* V, 10, 211, 6–18; V, 15, 219, 18–220, 6; Van Liefferinge (1999: ch. 1), a useful recent study.

[52] *De myst.* III, 12, 129, 1–13; V, 23, 232, 10–233, 10. The theory of intelligible omnipresence differentiated by varying material receptivity was developed by Plotinus in *Enn.* VI 4–5.

through intermediary (in particular demonic) levels to link with human souls in a graduated series, constituting thus a 'community (κοινωνία) of gods and men'.[53] As for human souls, they are also differentiated by the degree of their descent and involvement in corporeality. Their divinization or salvation will accordingly require various appropriate means: for 'pure' souls, a pure 'immaterial' cult; for souls plunged in materiality, a material cult corresponding to their particular condition; for those in between, an appropriate intermediate cult.[54] Thus divine service operates on the principle of 'like to like', the similarity that links the practitioner of a rite with a corresponding divinity,[55] in correspondence with the order of souls as well as with the proper order of the gods.[56]

Given these Platonic and Neoplatonic principles, how then are religious practices, correctly conducted, to be understood? The general purpose of such practices, as indicated already, is the elevation and divinization of the fallen soul, a purificatory, therapeutic function which Iamblichus compares with the cathartic function of comedy and tragedy.[57] Thus prayers invoking the gods elevate the soul by bringing it to a greater similitude to the god to whom the soul prays.[58] The greater union with the divine thus achieved through prayer means a greater sharing in divine life, thus in the perfections of divine life or in those of demons and heroes, if these intermediate levels are addressed.[59] Prayer is in this way both a method of ascent for the soul and a source of benefits for it; no manipulation or coercion of the divine is involved and the divine remains the source of all good and power, including that which elevates the soul.

Iamblichus stresses the importance of prayer in sacrifices, which have the same purpose of purifying and elevating the soul.[60] He strenuously rejects the suggestion that the burnt offerings of sacrificial rites can sway or

---

[53] De myst. V, 10, 211, 16–18.

[54] De myst. V, 15, 219, 1–220, 18; V, 18, 223, 10–225, 11; V, 20, 227, 1–228, 12. On pure souls' transcendent cult, cf. also V, 22, 231, 1–2; for a daring hypothesis as to what the immaterial cult practised by pure souls might be, see Shaw (1993).

[55] De myst. V, 20, 227, 17–18.

[56] De myst. V, 21, 230, 10. On the importance in piety of respecting proper order, as stipulated in the Laws, cf. above p. 120. Shaw (1995) provides a very good analysis of the differentiated use of ritual in the divinization of soul in Iamblichus.

[57] De myst. I, 11, 40, 1–15.

[58] De myst. I, 15, 47, 16–48, 4; I, 12, 42, 6–15.

[59] De myst. V, 26; II, 9, 87, 14–88, 16. On the Neoplatonic theory of prayer, cf. also Proclus, In Tim. I, pp. 210, 30–212, 11; Esser (1967). On Neoplatonic hymns as a form of prayer (and therefore of philosophy, as a divinizing of soul), see Van den Berg (2001: ch. 2).

[60] De myst. V, 26, 237, 8–15; V, 11, 215, 1–7.

even 'feed' the demons or gods to which they are directed. Rather, it is the superior (gods, demons) that 'nourishes' the inferior (souls), in that the sacrifices operate a purification (by burning materiality), elevation, and assimilation of the inferior to the superior.[61] Thus, by performing ritual sacrificial burning, the soul purifies itself of materiality and assimilates itself to a greater participation in the transcendent, which means having a greater share in the goods of which the transcendent is the source. The good that comes down in this way from the gods, through the elevation of soul effectuated by sacrifice, not only benefits the individual soul, but is also of general advantage, to cities, peoples and nations.[62] These benefits differ, depending on the level of the souls concerned, on the types of offerings made, and on the level of divinity to which they are directed. It seems that it is rare, in the case of some few souls, that an immaterial relation with the highest levels of divinity is established. Yet the lower levels of sacrifice, more adapted to the condition and needs of most souls, are also a stage to higher levels of sacrifice.[63] In all cases, Iamblichus insists, the efficacy of sacrifices, their operative power, derives, not from the human agents involved, the priests, but from the gods, source of all power. Human agency is merely auxiliary, in the sense that it can produce appropriate dispositions for the participation in divine power.[64] Linked thus by correspondence, by assimilation, through appropriate instruments, at different levels of materiality and immateriality, the different levels of souls and of the gods constitute a 'community', a cosmic and trans-cosmic system of sympathy and 'friendship' whereby, in unison with appropriate human religious rites, the good derived from the transcendent is shared at different levels and in different ways.[65]

4. Theurgy and the Retreat to Private Cult

Throughout the *De mysteriis*, Iamblichus uses, in connection with the service of the gods, the terms 'theurgy', 'theurge', 'theurgic'. The term

---

[61] *De myst.* V, 10, 212, 1–214, 3.

[62] *De myst.* V, 10, 211, 8–16.

[63] *De myst.* V, 9, 209, 11–210, 14; V, 14–18.

[64] *De myst.* II, 11, 97, 2–98, 15. Cf. III, 1, 100, 10–101, 7; III, 7, 115, 2–10 (on divination). For the term 'auxiliary', συναίτιος (97, 15), see Plato, *Tim.* 46c7–e2, where primary intelligible rational causes are contrasted with secondary material causes (cf. also *De myst.* III, 1, 101, 8–9).

[65] *De myst.* I, 12, 42, 6–15; I, 13, 43, 8–12; V, 9.

'theurge' was coined, it seems, by the authors of the *Chaldaean Oracles*, a collection of oracles, dating to the second century AD, which was fully accepted and integrated into Neoplatonic philosophy by Iamblichus as a source of divine revelation of the highest value, equal to other (supposedly ancient) sources of such revelation, Greek and barbarian, philosophical and religious.[66] Today, scholars tend to associate theurgy with the magical practices indicated in the *Chaldaean Oracles* and have been inclined to see the emphasis on theurgy in Neoplatonism, from Iamblichus on, as a departure from the rationalist philosophy of Plotinus, indeed a capitulation to irrational magical practices. However, if the term 'theurge' is indeed a neologism first found in the *Chaldaean Oracles*, it does not, in Iamblichus and in later Neoplatonism, have a meaning restricted to certain magical rites. This can be seen in later Neoplatonic explanations of theurgy as a process for making man god (θεουργεῖν = θεοποιεῖν).[67] In a broader sense, then, 'theurgy' can be compared to divinization and thus regarded as a term for the assimilation to god by which Neoplatonists defined their goal.[68] In this wider sense, Iamblichus uses the term in the *De mysteriis*, not just as regards the practices of the *Chaldaean Oracles*, but also for other sorts of religious cult.[69]

The same point can be made with respect to two other terms closely associated with the vocabulary of theurgy, 'telestic' and 'hieratic'. They also need not designate exclusively Chaldaean practices.[70] An interesting example of this wider application can be found in Hierocles:

so that the theoretical part of philosophy is prior, as intellect, whereas the practical part follows, as power. But we distinguish two forms of the practical [part of philosophy], the political and the telestic, of which the first purifies us of the irrational by means of the virtues, whereas the second eliminates material illusions by means of sacred rites. A prime example of political philosophy is the established laws of the community, and of telestic philosophy the holy rites of the cities. And the highest part of all philosophy is theoretical intellect; in between comes the political [intellect]; and third the telestic [intellect]; the first having the function of an eye in relation to the others, the others

---

[66] On the term θεουργός, cf. Lewy (1978: 461), and, on the *Chaldaean Oracles*, Majercik (1989). In this section no attempt is made to do justice to the complicated issue of Neoplatonic theurgy (for a useful survey see Van den Berg 2001: ch. 4), my purpose being merely to indicate the way in which theurgy fits into religious practice, as this practice relates to political philosophy.

[67] Psellus, *Omn. doct.* 71 and 74, quoted by Lewy (1978: 461), who identifies Psellus' source as Proclus; however, these chapters may be derived from Iamblichus' *On Virtues* (above, Ch. 4, n. 21).

[68] Psellus, *Omn. doct.* 71. Cf. Van den Berg (2001: 74).

[69] See *De myst.* I, 8, 28, 6–9; III, 20, 149, 13–17; V, 14, 217, 17–218, 10; V, 18, 224, 11–225, 10; VIII, 4, 267, 6–10; X, 6, 292, 15–18; Van Liefferinge (1999: 124).

[70] See Lewy (1978: 495–6).

coming after it having in relation to it the value of a hand and foot, all related to each other, so that any one of these would be imperfect and almost useless without the collaboration of the others.[71]

Hierocles therefore refers to traditional civic cult as 'telestic'.[72] He also links this cult very closely, and subordinates it, to political philosophy, itself subordinated to the theoretical part of philosophy, as required by the Neoplatonic scale of sciences and virtues: whereas political philosophy and virtue correct irrationality in soul's life in the body,[73] religious cult seems to correct materiality at a lower level. We might refer here to the materialistic, concrete religious acts that Iamblichus interprets in the *De mysteriis*.

Iamblichus did not confine 'theurgy', as a process of divinization, to the lower registers of the enmattered existence of the soul. He also refers to a theurgy which goes beyond the human condition of cosmic existence and represents an act of union with transcendent immaterial divinity, a union beyond that reached by intellect and philosophy.[74] Indeed it seems that in the scale of assimilation to the divine, the levels of 'political', purificatory, and theoretical virtues are surpassed by a supreme degree of divinization, 'theurgic' virtue, whereby man truly becomes god.[75]

While Iamblichus could still envisage, towards the beginning of the fourth century, the elevation of enmattered soul in the context of traditional civic cults, as well as in relation to Chaldaean practices, and Julian undertake, later in the century, as part of his political reform, an ambitious programme to revive these public cults, civic religion was to become more and more the domain of Julian's 'atheists', the Christians. The progressive desertion and destruction of pagan temples and sacred places limited the public, civic sphere in which religious life could be cultivated according to Platonic principles. The Neoplatonist philosopher, suffering political and religious exclusion, was obliged more and more to live forms of religious as well as of political divinization in the narrow bounds of the philosophical school and of private life.

A vivid illustration of this is provided by a story Marinus tells of Proclus. Athens had been affected less than other cities by the destruction of temples. Pagans could still live there and practise their cults relatively undisturbed.

---

[71] Hierocles, *In Carm. aur.*, p. 118, 4–17.

[72] Cf. K. Harl (1990: 12–13).

[73] Above, Ch. 4.3.

[74] *De myst.* IV, 2, 184, 1–13; II, 11, 96, 14–97, 19.

[75] Psellus, *Omn. doct.* 71 and 74 (on Psellus' source, see above n. 67); see above, Ch. 4, n. 33.

However when, between 482 and 484, the statue of Athena was removed from the Parthenon,[76] the goddess appeared in a dream to Proclus, asking him to prepare his house for her: it was now in his private home that she would reside.[77] The goddess of the city of philosophers, of Plato's city, had withdrawn from the acropolis, to live a clandestine life in the private sphere of the philosopher.[78]

[76] See Trombley (1993–4: i. 81–2).

[77] Marinus, *Vit. Procl.* 30.

[78] On Proclus' religion see Festugière (1966), Saffrey (1984), and, on his relations with Christianity, Saffrey (1975).

The Limits of Political Action   11

In this chapter, the outline reconstruction of Neoplatonic political theory proposed above (Chapters 4–10) will be completed by consideration of factors relating to the possibility and limits of political reform. As before, the question at issue is not that of concrete historical events, of the extent to which Neoplatonists actually achieved (or failed to achieve) something in real politics. Rather, we will consider features which were identified in Neoplatonic philosophical theory as limiting the possibilities and affecting the success or failure of political science in general. The question of what is possible, as regards the political ambition of the philosopher, was not ignored in Neoplatonism (above, Ch. 8, 1). A range of levels of political reform was set out (above, Ch. 8, 2), going from the 'city of gods' believed to be represented in Plato's *Republic* (but this was hardly a possible option in relation to the human condition), through levels of political reform such as that expressed in the second-best city of Plato's *Laws*, to more modest projects of political improvement. It has been suggested that Julian's political programme might appropriately be situated on the level of the second-best or on a more modest level. The project that Sopatros proposes to Himerius (above, Ch. 9, 3), concerning as it does the exercise of power under higher authority, is even more limited in scope and provides an example of a flexible, discriminatory approach to the adaptation of the philosophical ideal to particular given circumstances. The level of political reform, of the project considered possible, is thus determined, on the one hand, by the limits imposed by the human condition, as soul living in body, and, on the other hand, by the specific circumstances in which the philosopher lives. Of course these circumstances may sometimes be such that no action is possible and abstention is to be recommended (above, Ch. 8, 2).

Political reform is limited further in its possibilities, in what it can achieve, (1) by the dependence of our actions, in the material world in which they occur, on factors outside of our control and (2) by difficulties in translating knowledge (θεωρία) into action (πρᾶξις). In the following pages these additional limiting factors and difficulties will be presented in more detail and will lead to some brief remarks on what the Neoplatonist judges to be success or failure in political action.

1. The Heteronomy of Action

In *Enn.* III 8, Plotinus describes action (πρᾶξις) as a by-product or substitute for knowledge (θεωρία). It is a substitute for those of us who, incapable of pure knowledge, resort to action as a kind of shadowy expression of what we have difficulty in grasping. For those, however, who have reached pure knowledge, becoming transcendent intellect, action derives from knowledge as a by-product and expression of knowledge (above, Ch. 7, 1). In both cases, however, our actions escape our control: they are outside the soul (*Enn.* I 5, 10, 21–2), are related to another (πρὸς ἄλλο) and affected by others, taking place in the context of the material world (*Enn.* IV 4, 43, 16–24). This other-relatedness of our actions means that, even if they are autonomous, as originating from an autonomous decision within us, within the soul, they are not autonomous as related to external factors of which we are not masters, the exterior circumstances that necessitate action and that affect them.[1] This heteronomous dimension of action means that in many cases, for Plotinus, we are open to being influenced by external factors, by objects which provoke passions and desires in us: we may fall under the 'spell' of the world. However, even if we retain our liberty, our autonomy, our actions are still in part necessitated and conditioned by what is not in our control.[2] Thus, 'everything in the sphere of action, even if reason is dominant, is mixed and cannot have "being in our power" in a pure state' (*Enn.* VI 8, 2, 35–7). Actions arising from philosophical knowledge are therefore in part autonomous, as derived from autonomous reason, in part heteronomous, as taking place in, necessitated, and conditioned by the material world. This heteronomy is expressed by the popular notion of 'fate', which Plotinus interprets as the rational organization and rule of the material world by the world-soul, itself expressing the transcendent law of divine Intellect to which Plotinus refers as 'providence'.[3]

---

[1] *Enn.* VI 8, 1, 22–30; 5, 1–27; for this theme in Stoic philosophy, cf. Annas (1992: 99–100).
[2] See *Enn.* IV 4, 44, 16–25.
[3] See *Enn.* III 3, 5 for the distinction between fate and providence.

This other-directedness of the political life, as contrasted with the self-directedness of the life of purification and knowledge, was elaborated by Proclus and by other later Neoplatonists,[4] as was the theme of the mixture of autonomy and heteronomy in political action. As regards the last point, Proclus introduces some noteworthy ideas into the discussion.[5] In his *De providentia* (34), he finds the three factors that condition human actions in Plotinus (providence, fate, and human reason) in Plato's *Laws*, in the following passage (709b5–c1):

> God is all, while chance (τύχη) and opportunity (καιρός), under God, set the whole course of life for us, and yet we must allow for the presence of a third . . . skill (τέχνη). (trans. Taylor)

Whereas the first factor in Plotinus, providence, corresponds to god, the second factor, fate, is described variously by Proclus as 'chance' and 'opportunity' (as in the quotation from Plato above), as the revolution of the cosmos and 'opportunity', or as fate and 'opportunity'.[6] The third factor, 'skill' in the passage from the *Laws*, corresponds to human autonomous agency, in particular 'political' skill.[7] Two points require further discussion here: the significance of the theme of 'opportunity', which receives considerable emphasis in Proclus, and the idea suggested by Proclus that political skill can collaborate with opportunity, ' "for the skill of the pilot can contribute to the opportunity of a storm" [*Laws* 709c1–2], medical skill to healing, and in general political skill to practical affairs'.[8]

The linkage Proclus makes between opportunity, chance, fate, and the revolution of the cosmos shows that the first terms refer, not to some fortuitous or arbitrary aspect of the world, but to the natural law governing the universe, in particular in relation to its temporal dimension. As the world exists in time measured by the celestial movements, so also do actions, which have their appropriate moments, opportunities.[9] This conception of opportunity is well brought out by Proclus in another text,[10] where he cites the Pythagoreans as having called 'opportunity' the first cause, as that from

---

[4] See Damascius, *In Phaed.* I, 74 (with Westerink's note ad loc.); Olympiodorus, *In Phaed.* 4, 2–3; 5, 1.

[5] See Brunner (1992).

[6] See the table in Brunner (1992: 176).

[7] Proclus, *De prov.* 34, 25–30; the three factors are also found in Iamblichus' letter to Macedonius, in Stob., *Anth.* II, p. 174, 5–11.

[8] Proclus, *De prov.* 34, 28–30.

[9] Aristotle classifies 'opportunity' (καιρός) as a good in the category of time (*Nic. Eth.* I, 4, 1096ᵃ23–7).

[10] *In Alc.* 120, 12–121, 26.

which things derive their perfection:[11] opportunity is the source of good in medicine, for example, since the right moment is critical in the treatment of a disease. As each body has its appropriate place, so each action has its appropriate moment. As different periods in the time of the world are appropriate to successful procreation among living things,[12] so certain actions can be successfully completed at certain moments.[13] Thus, we may infer, opportunity is part of fate, that is, a moment which, in the temporal succession of things, is appropriate for a particular action. Success in political action therefore involves acting in complicity with fate by choosing the right moment for an action, a moment fixed by fate, just as the successful doctor chooses the right moment for intervention in the evolution of a disease.[14]

The political skill involved in choosing the right moment for action may entail mathematical knowledge, as can be seen from Proclus' revision of Iamblichus' *On Pythagoreanism* III, 15: where Iamblichus speaks of mathematics as 'leading the ordered movements of actions', Proclus writes of the measures of 'the opportunities (καιρούς) for actions and of the varied cosmic cycles, the numbers appropriate for procreation'.[15] Proclus consecrated a lengthy discussion, his thirteenth essay on Plato's *Republic*, to this last point: the mathematical, in particular astronomical, knowledge required of the philosopher-rulers of the *Republic* in their regulation of marriages and births. The *Republic* suggests that it is due to errors in their policy here that a decline of the ideal state begins (546a–d). The Platonic text therefore gives great political importance to a mathematically inspired policy of procreation, a policy which, as Proclus stresses, must choose the right moments for its actions, as these moments are determined by the revolution of the cosmos.[16]

Proclus also notes that events may go contrary to the choices we make. In these cases it turns out that we fail to act in accordance with the natural law and we must accept our failure and the wisdom of nature that governs everything.[17] Before Proclus, Julian had quoted at length the passage from

---

[11] For the Pythagorean sources see Segonds's (1985) note to the passage (194, n. 6).

[12] On this see Iamblichus, *Phys. arith.* 10–11, 33–64 (in *PR* 218–20).

[13] On the classical background to this cf. Trédé (1992: chs. 3–4).

[14] Cf. also Proclus, *X dub.* 51.

[15] Iamblichus, *De comm. math. sc.*, p. 56, 5–6; Proclus, *In Eucl.*, p. 23, 14–16.

[16] Proclus, *In Remp.* II, pp. 79, 6–80, 5; at p. 73, 27–9 Proclus speaks of a 'science of καιροί' that the rulers should acquire. Cf. Plato, *Statesman* 284e6–7, 305d2–4 and Lane (1995: 278–80); (1998: pt. iii).

[17] Proclus, *De prov.* 34, 15–22.

Plato's *Laws* (709b) interpreted by Proclus. Julian emphasizes the other term in Plato's text that, together with 'opportunity', constitutes fate for the Neoplatonists, 'chance' (τύχη), stressing its importance for those active in politics, as well as the necessity to accept whatever it brings.[18]

The mixed character of political actions, both autonomous and heteronomous, seeking on the basis of knowledge to achieve the best possible results in complicity with the natural law, has to do with the mixed realm in which these actions take place, the realm of soul present in the body, related to the body, and using the body. As separated from the body, however, soul, living the life of the higher levels of virtue, transcends the realm of fate; the autonomy of its life is no longer conditioned by and enmeshed in the cosmic law.[19]

2. Practical Wisdom

Political action, to be appropriate, must be inspired by knowledge: by knowledge of the universe, by mathematical and also perhaps by metaphysical knowledge (above, Ch. 8, 3). But attention must also be paid to the particular circumstances, the world of changing material objects concerned by this action. Thus deficiency in an action may derive, not from inadequate theoretical knowledge, but from lack of attention to particular circumstances. These points had been explored long before by Aristotle in his analysis of practical reasoning, which he distinguishes from theoretical knowledge (*Nic. Eth.* VI, 5 and 7). The idea of practical reasoning is taken up by Plotinus (*Enn.* V 3, 6, 35–7), who stresses the relatedness to the 'outside' (ἔξω) that it shares with action. Iamblichus also speaks of wisdom (φρόνησις) concerning contingent (i.e. material) objects, a wisdom which he describes as 'practical deliberation'.[20]

---

[18] Julian, *Or.* VI, 4–5 (where the Platonic theme is combined with the imperial theme of the emperor's Τύχη/*Fortuna*). This theme in Julian is emphasized by Candau Morón (1986). Simplicius, citing *Laws* 709b9, refers to Τύχη as a divinity (*In Phys.*, p. 333, 5–17; cf. also Sallustius, *De dis* IX, 7).

[19] Cf. Brunner (1993). Describing how soul, living in the world, is involved in what the world necessitates, Proclus compares soul to a philosopher who embarks on a boat, thus becoming subject to the orders of the sailors and pilot and to the weather (*In Remp.* II, p. 345, 19–25; for the image see Epictetus, *Discourses* II, 5, 10–11).

[20] *Eth. arith.* 31–2 (in *PR* 224); cf. Aristotle, *Nic. Eth.* VI, 10, 1142^{b}31–3; Hierocles, *In carm. aur.* pp. 63, 12–64, 10; Schibli (2002: 84–8). On φρόνησις in Plotinus and Iamblichus, see also above pp. 40, 90.

It is not simply the case, then, that appropriate political action issues directly from theoretical knowledge (some consideration of the contingencies concerned by the action is also required), although a passage in Proclus might be taken to suggest this:

The political [man] starts from knowledge and examination (ἐξέτασις), and then, in this way, orders the whole state, showing in deeds the conclusions derived from this knowledge.[21]

It is possible that Proclus' reference to 'examination' might concern some intermediary process of deliberation. We should note also the suggestion that political actions constitute in some way the 'conclusions' (συμπεράσματα) of an argument of which the major premiss is provided by knowledge. This in turn reminds us of the Aristotelian conception of the 'practical syllogism', a conception clearly formulated by Olympiodorus:

The statesman . . . draws his conclusions from a universal major premiss based on reflection and from a particular minor premiss, because he uses the body as an instrument and is therefore concerned with actions, and actions are particular, and the particular is individual, so that the statesman depends on one particular premiss for his conclusion.[22]

The practical wisdom of the political man therefore involves theoretical knowledge (the major premiss) and knowledge of material particulars (the minor premiss), from which, taken together, derive, as if conclusions, his actions.[23]

Knowledge of particulars, in Aristotle, involves sense-perception (*Nic. Eth.* 1143[b]5): this is where deficiency in action may also arise, since sense-perception, for the Neoplatonist, is unreliable and misleading. The point is made by Plotinus' pupil Amelius, taking up a suggestion in Plato (*Rep.* 546b1–2), in connection with the philosopher-kings of Plato's *Republic*:

Amelius says that virtue is double, one living within, such as knowledge (θεωρία), the other living outside, such as practical [virtue], and that the guardians are named 'sages' [*Rep.* 546a 8] on account of knowledge, but that they make mistakes in their practical activities based on reflection combined with sense-perception, an unreliable criterion.[24]

---

[21] Proclus, *In Alc.* 95, 19–23.

[22] Olympiodorus, *In Phaed.* 4, 4; cf. 4, 3: the universal major premisses are λόγοι in the soul of the statesman. On the practical syllogism see also Iamblichus, *De myst.* V, 18, 223, 15 and Iamblichus in Ammonius, *In De interpr.*, p. 135, 19–25, and, for the source in Aristotle, *Nic. Eth.* VI, 12, 1143[a]32–1143[b]5.

[23] On the judicial branch of political science as involving knowledge of particulars, see above p. 106.

[24] Proclus, *In Remp.* II, p. 29, 7–9.

The mistakes of the rulers deriving from sense-perception are those concerning procreation which lead to the decline of the ideal city of the *Republic*.[25] More generally, then, to the extent that actions depend on perception of material particulars, political philosophers can fail, however strong their theoretical knowledge.

The possibility of failure may be found, not only in an unreliable grasp of particulars, but also in inadequate knowledge of universal physical, mathematical, or metaphysical principles. In the absence of a full knowledge of such principles, another kind of deliberation will be required, a collective deliberation shared by different minds deciding an action. It is in this way that Proclus explains the need for deliberative assemblies, which, by bringing together a number of deficient thinkers, constitute together a greater intelligence, a theory to be found in Aristotle which seems to have reached Proclus through Plotinus.[26] However, Proclus immediately adds that knowledge is distributed unevenly and that a superior mind will appear, 'sharing more in the Good and filling (πληρώσας) his soul with intellect' (182, 24–5), who may act as counsellor (σύμβουλος) to others, in other words, we may suppose, the Platonist philosopher.[27]

3. Success and Failure

Various reasons have been noted above that might explain failure in political action: defective theoretical knowledge, a defective grasp of contingent particulars, the heteronomy of action, an overriding of action by the rule of 'fate'. But whatever the outcome of the philosopher's action, the measure of failure and success cannot be such criteria as power, prosperity, pleasure, or fame; it can only be the common good, which is itself subordinate (as corresponding to 'political' virtue) to higher goods, those represented by the higher levels of the virtues. The greatest imaginable political success cannot therefore go beyond the realization of a general condition of 'political' virtue, as a first, preparatory stage leading to higher levels of divinization.

---

[25] See also Proclus, *In Remp.* II, p. 56, 10–15; pp. 70, 28–71, 2; p. 79, 16–17. However, Proclus describes such errors, like those involving other kinds of practical expertise, as rare (p. 9, 20–5).

[26] Proclus, *In Alc.* 182, 12–20 (Segonds 1985 ad loc. refers to Aristotle, *Pol.* III, 11, 1281^{b}1–10 and to Plotinus, *Enn.* VI 5, 10, 18–26, perhaps Proclus' source). The need for such assemblies explains the design of corresponding buildings: Proclus, *In Alc.* 182, 18–19. The Anon., *Prol. Plat. phil.* 5, 40–3 tells us that Plato invented circular halls for political assemblies.

[27] See Plotinus, *Enn.* VI 4, 15, 23–32.

In relation to the realities of political action in Late Antiquity, we have seen that there were many reasons for the Neoplatonist to be pessimistic as regards the possibility of achieving the form of success specified by Neoplatonist political philosophy. Julian indeed suggests that, through teaching and example, the philosopher can benefit human life more than the combined action of many kings.[28] The domain where political divinization could best be achieved in practice often remained, then, that of the philosophical school and the influence it could have.

[28] Julian, *Or.* VI, 11, 266a–b; cf. Damascius, *Vita Is.* fr. 366: 'that a philosopher is a greater benefactor of human life than an excellent king' (Athanassiadi 1999 ad loc. suggests that this was a subject of school debate).

Part III
Platonopolis in Christianity and Islam

Part III Synopsis

Neoplatonic political philosophy, as reconstructed in outline in this book, may be seen to have been of importance for the political theories of Christian and Islamic thinkers in Late Antiquity and in the early medieval period. In what follows, I would like to show this and suggest also that the study of the impact, critique, and transformation of the Neoplatonic Platonopolis in the works of these thinkers may also help extend what has been reconstructed so far from the texts of the Neoplatonist philosophers themselves.

A selection of examples, relating to different periods and contexts, will be discussed in what follows. In Chapter 12, I begin with the Christian theocratic ideology formulated for the Emperor Constantine in the early fourth century by Eusebius, bishop of Caesarea in Palestine. Almost a century later, in North Africa, Augustine, bishop of Hippo, rejected Eusebius' political programme. Our question will be: to what extent might Eusebius' and Augustine's ideas be related to the political theories of the Neoplatonic philosophers of their time? Towards the beginning of the sixth century, in the Greek East, the Pseudo-Dionysius elaborated a theory of the Church which will be shown in Chapter 13 to be a Christian ecclesiological transposition of Neoplatonic political ideas. Chapter 13 will also concern texts associated with the court of the Emperor Justinian, the *Ekthesis* of Agapetus and an anonymous dialogue *On Political Science*. The latter work will be found to contain interesting political ideas of Neoplatonic origin. Finally, in Chapter 14, al-Farabi's ninth-century project of a 'perfect state' will be analysed as an Islamic version of a Neoplatonic Platonopolis, a striking example of a largely unexplored theme which cannot be examined more fully here, the continuity between the political thought of the Late Antique Neoplatonic schools and that of philosophers living in the early medieval Islamic world.

The examples discussed in the following chapters represent some significant moments, not a complete history, of the *fortuna* of the Neoplatonic Platonopolis. We will be concerned with the impact of Neoplatonic theory, not on historical events, but on the ideas of some Christian and Islamic thinkers. And of course the study of this theme could be extended into the later medieval period, in Byzantium, for example, up to the Italian Renaissance, as will be suggested very briefly in the Conclusion.

Eusebius and Augustine 12

1. Eusebius' Praise of Constantine

Roughly a generation younger than Iamblichus, bishop of Caesarea, not very far south of Iamblichus' school at Apamea in Syria, Eusebius reminds us in some respects of the pagan philosopher. He also produced large programmatic works of learning, compiled from extracts taken from a wide range of earlier writers. As compared to Iamblichus' work *On Pythagoreanism*, Eusebius' *Preparation for the Gospel*, for instance, selects and adjusts to his purposes, not only Greek philosophical (in particular Platonic) literature, but also, of course, Jewish and early Christian sources.[1] However, it is not so much the vast learning displayed by Eusebius in his monumental biblical, historical, and polemical works which is of particular interest here. Of more relevance is the speech he composed near the end of his life, his *Praise of Constantine*.

Eusebius delivered this speech in the presence of the Emperor at the festivities, marking thirty years of Constantine's reign, which took place in Constantinople on 25 July 336.[2] Eusebius may not simply be giving voice to the official imperial propaganda of Constantine's court.[3] However, his speech must have represented at least an acceptable interpretation and justification of the Christian Emperor's long rule,[4] of which Eusebius saw no end (Constantine would die the following year). In its elaborate language, a seamless texture of pagan and Christian vocabulary, studded with glittering erudition and magnificent imperial and cosmic imagery, Eusebius' speech must have matched perfectly the visual splendour of the imperial court ceremony in which it was delivered.[5] As the contents of the *Praise of*

---

[1] Cf. Barnes (1981: 168) for a comparison between Iamblichus and Eusebius as compilers.

[2] Cf. Barnes (1981: 253) and Cameron and Hall (1999: 184) on the date and occasion of the speech.

[3] Barnes (1981: 267–8) argues against the common assumption that Eusebius was a close and constant adviser of Constantine.

[4] Straub (1939: 118).

[5] Straub (1939: 120).

Constantine have been summarized elsewhere,[6] it might suffice to empha-
size here some themes of more specific interest.

Eusebius proposes to celebrate Constantine's kingship in so far as he sees
it as 'true' (cf. p. 204, 15), that is as correctly modelled on the universal kingship of the Christian god, as opposed to counterfeit regimes, modelled otherwise we may assume.[7] His subject is then essentially the universal
kingship of the Christian god[8] and the way in which Constantine's kingship
images it. The kingship of God is that of an absolute monarchy recognized
by all men and all creation (I, 3–5), but transcendent, beyond all (ἐπέκεινα
τῶν ὅλων, p. 196, 18), reigning over a heavenly kingdom of angelic hosts
separated from the earthly domain by the celestial bodies, the sun, moon,
and stars (I, 2). Such is the august transcendence of this god, his inaccessi-
bility (I, 1), that his earthly image, the true king of men, is not modelled
after him directly, but rather after God's Logos, the second person of the
Christian Trinity, who expresses him, mediates and administers for him not
only the heavenly kingdom, but also all earthly creation (III, 6; cf. VI, 9).
Constantine is thus a true king to the extent that he images the transcendent
intelligible rulership of God's Logos, Christ.

The relation between image and model, between the true king of men
and the divine Logos, requires more attention. Eusebius suggests that the
king, having been shaped in the image of the divine kingdom, looks up, as
if to an archetypal Form (ἀρχέτυπος ἰδέα) according to which he governs
his realm (III, 5), much, we might note, like the philosopher-kings of the
Republic. Eusebius also suggests (V, 4) that it is by being modelled on the
'archetypal Form' of the supreme king, sharing in the virtues that derive
from it, that Constantine becomes a true king. Is this archetypal Form the
Logos of God? Is the Logos the paradigm of Constantine's virtues? Is the
Logos the paradigm of Constantine's action, or, more broadly, is it rather
the heavenly kingdom which is, through Christ's mediation, the model of
Constantine's political action?[9]

It is not entirely clear how such questions might be answered.[10] Perhaps
we should not oppose, as different models, the supreme god's kingship,

---

[6] Cf. Barnes (1981: 253–5); Cranz (1952); Farina (1966). The speech includes only the first ten
chapters of the text translated by Drake (1976); cf. Maraval (1997) on the relation of the speech to
the text that follows it. Cranz (1952), Farina (1966), and Barnes (1981) are also helpful in relating
the ideas of the *Praise of Constantine* to those found in the earlier works of Eusebius.

[7] *Praise* V, 4; prologue, p. 196, 8–11.

[8] This is how he describes his speech in his *Life of Constantine* IV, 46.

[9] Cf. I, 6; III, 6; IV, 2.

[10] The difficulty is noted by Straub (1939: 124).

kingship as mediated by the Logos, and the heavenly kingdom. At any rate Eusebius does list certain actions of the divine Logos that are imitated by Constantine (II, 1–5): as the Logos prepares the entire universe for his Father, so Constantine leads his subjects to Christ and prepares them for the heavenly kingdom; as the Logos protects human souls from evil forces, so does Constantine subdue by conquest the enemies of truth; as the Logos gives souls the rationality allowing them to know the Father's kingdom, so Constantine calls all humans to knowledge of God and piety; as the Logos ushers departed souls to the higher world, so Constantine purifies his realm of impiety and seeks to save humanity. While conquering impiety, instructing and preparing his subjects for salvation, for the heavenly kingdom, Constantine, as Christ's image, is yet a human soul which also seeks this heavenly kingdom, setting no value on power, prestige, and evanescent material goods (V, 5 and 8).

With this portrait of the 'philosopher-king' (V, 4, p. 204, 21), Eusebius contrasts the counterfeit rule of those not modelled on the Christian god. To the monarchy of the Christian god, Eusebius opposes the 'polyarchy' of pagan polytheism.[11] As polyarchy is anarchy and social strife, so is polytheism atheism, to which is opposed the one god, the one king of the universe and his Logos, one royal law (III, 6). The ruler who denies this god and is not formed in his image is not ruler, but a slave to his passions, subject to all vices, tyrannized from within and the author of all crimes (V, 2–3), a figure that reminds us of Plato's portrait of the tyrannical man (*Rep.* 571a–575a).

2. The Philosophical Background to the *Praise of Constantine*

An investigation into the philosophical sources used by Eusebius in elaborating the theocratic programme of the *Praise of Constantine* is not simply of interest as determining the range of erudition manifested by Eusebius in writing his speech. It might also help to situate this theocratic ideal in relation to

---

[11] For the earlier Patristic sources of Eusebius' attempted unification of Christian monotheism and the universal monarchy of the Christianized Roman Empire, see Peterson (1935), who also traces the influence of Eusebius here on later Greek and Latin theologians, as well as the breakdown of the analogy between God's universal monarchy and political monarchy, a breakdown he links to Trinitarian doctrine (see pp. 82–97).

a philosophical background to which it may, in part at least, be responding. The task is not made simpler by the breadth of Eusebius' learning and the rhetorical ability he displays in integrating and exploiting this learning.[12]

An obvious and major source of inspiration for Eusebius is Plato's *Republic*. In summarizing parts of the *Praise of Constantine* above, it has been difficult to avoid reference to Plato's philosopher-kings who rule after a transcendent archetype and are contrasted by Plato with the tyrannical man. Such references to the *Republic* and to passages in other dialogues of Plato could easily be multiplied. Eusebius' familiarity with Plato is in any case very well attested by the extensive extracts from the dialogues that he incorporated in the *Preparation for the Gospel*.[13] However, if Constantine is Eusebius' philosopher-king, he is clearly not the philosopher-king of the *Republic*: he rules over a vast empire, in fact all of humanity, not over a city-state; his model is the heavenly kingship of the Christian god expressed by the Logos; his purpose is the salvation of humanity by bringing souls through teaching to the heavenly kingdom beyond this world.

Besides Plato, other sources have been found for Eusebius' theocratic ideal, in particular the monarchic ideologies formulated in the Pseudo-Pythagorean 'Mirrors of Princes' of Ecphantus, Sthenidas, and Diotogenes.[14] It is true that there are striking resemblances between Eusebius' *Praise* and these texts: the king is the image of god and mediator between god and man; the king is to his realm as god is to the universe; the king is all virtuous by imitating god, is beloved of god, a moral paradigm for his subjects, who brings them to divine assimilation. It is also true, however, that some of these ideas are fairly banal and can be found throughout the literature of mirrors of princes, from Isocrates' *Nicocles* to Dio Chrysostom's orations (I–IV), where we find the comparison between Zeus' monarchy and that of the king, a similar emphasis on the king's paradigmatic virtue and his imitation of god.[15] In any case, these ideas are situated by Eusebius in a metaphysical system which is clearly more elaborate

[12] An inventory of Eusebius' Greek pagan sources can be found in Farina (1966: 270–8).

[13] Book XII, for example, contains extracts from the *Laws*, *Republic* (including, in XII, 19, the passage in *Rep.* 500–1 on philosopher-kings imitating an intelligible model), *Gorgias*, and *Statesman*. On Eusebius' use of Plato, see Des Places (1981: 199–219, 223–8, 249–58).

[14] See Baynes (1934); on these texts see above, Ch. 8, 3.

[15] See Calderone (1973: 235–9), who contests Baynes's thesis that Eusebius is using the Pseudo-Pythagorean texts (it should be noted, however, that Baynes expresses his thesis as a question (1934: 18)) by showing that much that is common to Eusebius and these texts is quite banal. Nonetheless, Calderone's argument that the monarchic theories of the Pseudo-Pythagorean texts are different from Eusebius' position does not prove that Eusebius did not use these texts: Eusebius could very well adapt and change ideas derived from them.

than that either of the Pseudo-Pythagorean texts or of other conventional mirrors of princes, a Platonic metaphysics in which a supreme ineffable first principle is represented by an intelligible Logos ruling over a transcendent world to which is subordinated the world of evanescent materiality. This metaphysics brings us close to the interpretations of Plato to be found in second-century Platonists such as Numenius, a philosopher also well known to Eusebius, who is responsible, through the excerpts he cites, for preserving almost all of the fragments we have of Numenius' work.

Is second-century Platonism the proximate philosophical background of Eusebius' thought?[16] Or should some account be taken of Platonists nearer him in time, Plotinus, Porphyry, and Iamblichus, for example? Perhaps we might note that the Platonic metaphysics sketched above is not exclusively second-century, but could also pass as a simple expression of the world of Plotinus and even of Iamblichus.[17] Eusebius indeed consulted the writings of Plotinus, of which he preserved valuable extracts,[18] and of Porphyry, whom he also used and to whose critique of Christianity he responded at great length. Eusebius does not quote excerpts from his near-contemporary Iamblichus, but it seems likely that he would have been aware of the activities of Iamblichus' important philosophical school not far away in Apamea.[19] We might note furthermore that Iamblichus' leading student, Sopatros, had become a close adviser of Constantine (above, Ch. 2, 2) and, finally, that if Eusebius did indeed use the Pseudo-Pythagorean texts on kingship, this would be less surprising if, as suggested above (p. 97), these texts had more recently been given prominence by Iamblichus as part of his promotion of a Pythagorean background to Platonic philosophy.[20]

The philosopher-king of Plato's *Republic* had been discussed by Iamblichus in his works and interpreted in a way that anticipates Eusebius' approach: the salvation of mankind, divinization, is achieved in a political structure governed by the philosopher-king whose inspiration is a transcendent intelligible model. The assimilation of souls to the divine[21] goes

[16] See Ricken (1967), (1978), Barnes (1981: 183).

[17] See *PR* 34, 42–4, 79, 84 for the pedagogically simplified metaphysics of the earlier books of Iamblichus' *On Pythagoreanism*.

[18] Henry (1935). Kalligas (2001) suggests that Eusebius got access to the library of the Platonist Longinus, Porphyry's former teacher and Plotinus' critic, subsequent to Longinus' execution in 272.

[19] Barnes (1981: 168, 183).

[20] Calderone (1973), in arguing against Baynes (1934), does not notice the contemporary relevance which these texts would have had in the Iamblichean schools.

[21] The famous phrase of Plato's *Theaetetus* (cf. above, Ch. 3) is quoted by Eusebius in *Praep. Ev.* XII, 29.

beyond this political level, which leads through the virtues to a higher existence in an intelligible world, itself subordinate to a supreme ineffable first principle.[22] These ideas were to be encountered in educated pagan circles in the Greek-speaking East in the earlier part of the fourth century, circles touched by Iamblichus' teaching and which included high-level administrators such as those addressed in Iamblichus' correspondence.[23] Eusebius' theocratic programme becomes all the more relevant if it is seen as reacting in part at least to a pagan philosophical theory circulating in his time.[24]

Eusebius' programme matches Neoplatonic theory in its structure, but with one important difference: the occupants of the structure have changed. The Christian god, the Christian Logos, and a heavenly court of angels and saints have replaced the philosophers' ineffable first principle, their divine Intellect presiding over an intelligible world: the same structure with different inhabitants. This change means that the true philosopher-king is not whosoever is inspired by and imitates pagan divine principles, but he who imitates the Christian god. Constantine is the 'true' philosopher-king, not a ruler such as the Neoplatonists, in their most optimistic moments, might imagine. And just as Eusebius in general believes that Christianity has superseded Greek religion and philosophy, including the best of Greek philosophy, Platonism (this is part of the argument of the *Preparation for the Gospel*), so has the reign of the first Christian emperor superseded and annihilated the pretensions of any hypothetical Platonist philosopher-king. I would like to suggest in this way that Eusebius is not simply an erudite compiler working up fairly conventional and irrelevant materials into an empty rhetorical display designed to please Constantine. He is using texts of Plato discussed and interpreted by the pagan philosophers of his time, texts which he interprets as they do, but in a way that is intended to make their position obsolete.

Did Eusebius really believe that Constantine was the ideal philosopher-king? Did he really think that Constantine had achieved or could achieve a higher level of political reform than that which the Platonists thought humanly possible (above, Ch. 8, 2)? Perhaps he believed in his description of Constantine as much as it is possible for the author of a mirror of princes to believe what he says of the ruler he addresses. Most important to him,

---

[22] See above, Ch. 4, 3; Ch. 8, 1.   [23] Above, Ch. 8, 1 and 4; Ch. 9, 3.

[24] The political importance of the presence of this philosophical theory would be illustrated some thirty years later by Constantine's nephew Julian. Sopatros 2's letter to Himerius (above, Ch. 9, 3) is even nearer Eusebius' *Praise* in time.

perhaps, is his theological commitment to the triumph of Christianity over pagans, including the Platonists.[25]

3. 'Pythagorean' Politics in the Early Augustine

The purpose of this and of the next section is not that of attempting to derive a 'political philosophy', if such there be, from Augustine's works. In a far more limited approach, it will be suggested that in the earliest surviving writings of Augustine, written at the time of his conversion in 386, traces can be found of ideas which come close to what has been reconstructed of Neoplatonic political philosophy in the earlier parts of this book. However, Augustine scarcely developed these ideas and certainly abandoned them as he came gradually to adopt a very different point of view, set forth in particular in the *City of God* (written between 413 and 427). This new position is of interest as antithetical not only to the structural function given to political life in Neoplatonism (political life as a stage in the hierarchical assimilation of the soul to god), but also to this function as given a Christian application in an ideology of Christian empire such as that propounded by Eusebius. In this, as in other areas, Augustine was close at first to the Neoplatonists, but in the end radically opposed to them, a complicity turned into conflict of great consequence for the Latin West.

Like Eusebius, Augustine read works of Plotinus and Porphyry. A crucial stage in Augustine's conversion was his reading, in Latin translation, of what is likely to have been a selection of treatises from Plotinus' *Enneads* and from Porphyry.[26] Augustine continues to quote the *Enneads* throughout his life and pays particular attention to Porphyry, for example in the polemics of the *City of God*. He was not necessarily confined completely to the use of the Latin translations which he at first read, but was in a position to consult, if in a limited way, Greek originals.[27] Knowledge of Iamblichus' works has yet to be proved: Augustine certainly knew of Iamblichus and perhaps knew more about him than is apparent.[28]

[25] On the role of the Church in all of this, see Cranz (1952: 61–4); the function of the Church is not specified in the *Praise of Constantine*; elsewhere Eusebius tends to bring Church and State together, as images of the heavenly kingdom. Dagron (1996: 145–7) argues that Eusebius is wary of subordinating the church hierarchy to Constantine.

[26] See Madec (1996: 38) for a reading-list of the debate on this question; O'Daly (1999: 257–9).

[27] See *City of God* XIX, 23; Altaner (1967: 129–53).

[28] *City of God* VIII, 12. Cf. O'Brien (1981), who refers (426, nn. 10–11) to earlier discussions of Augustine's relation to Iamblichus. Jerome refers to Iamblichus' commentary (no longer extant) on the *Golden Verses* in *Ep. adv. Ruf.* 39.

In one of Augustine's earliest surviving works, *On Order*, a dialogue written in connection with the philosophical discussions he led with a circle of friends at Cassiciacum following his conversion, a curriculum of studies is described which represents an itinerary for the soul in its ascent to God. The curriculum is quite clearly of Neoplatonic inspiration[29] and mathematical in its emphasis: the study of the mathematical sciences reveals the cosmic importance of number, a discovery that leads soul up to knowledge of pure intelligible numbers and of the nature of soul itself.[30] One of the participants in the dialogue, Augustine's close friend Alypius, refers in the conclusion of the work (II, xx, 53) to the mathematical ascent presented by Augustine as a venerable, almost divine discipline properly attributed to Pythagoras. Alypius' reference to Pythagoras is accepted and his praise of Pythagoras redoubled by Augustine, who describes himself as extolling the great man almost every day (II, xx, 54) in respect in particular to an important matter which he had omitted in his account of the itinerary of the soul, and for which he refers to Varro as a source, namely Pythagoras' practice of conveying the art of political rule (*regendae reipublicae disciplina*) to his disciples once they had completed the itinerary, once they were already knowledgeable, perfect, wise, and happy. For only as such can they resist the turmoil of political rule. In the words of Virgil (*Aen.* VII, 586) 'Such a man resists, as an immobile rock in the sea'.[31] With this the dialogue ends.

The communication of political science to his disciples is one of the benefits brought to humanity by Pythagoras according to Iamblichus.[32] As Augustine describes it, this instruction follows the completion of a mathematical curriculum which is an ascent to moral and intellectual perfection, to wisdom. The underlying overall pattern would seem thus to be that of the ascent from the cave of the *Republic* followed by a descent, the return to political rule. If the pattern is seen as characteristically 'Pythagorean', this diminishes in no way for Augustine, as for Iamblichus, its contemporary relevance as an ideal, an ideal belonging to a theory of education, knowledge, and reality which is Neoplatonic.[33]

---

[29] See I. Hadot (1984: 101–36).   [30] *De ord.* II, xiv, 39–xvi, 44.

[31] Compare Marcus Aurelius IV, 49. Frend (1989: 252–4) connects this part of the *De ord.* with the mention in the *Confessions* (VI, xiv, 24) of the project of a community, in which all is shared in common (cf. above, Ch. 8, 2), which was planned by Augustine and his friends in Milan, before his conversion. Difficulties in discussions about the integration of women in the community led to their abandoning the project.

[32] See above, Ch. 8, 4.

[33] For another echo of the Neoplatonic curriculum in Augustine's dialogues of Cassiciacum, cf. *Cont. Acad.* III, xvii, 37 (the 'political' virtues are images of true virtues known only to the wise; this

Augustine's reference to a Pythagorean political instruction following a mathematical curriculum does not make clear what specific relation there may be, if any, between the mathematical and metaphysical knowledge attained in this curriculum and the content of the political instruction subsequently given. Do Pythagoras' disciples learn the mathematical and metaphysical principles and models which then will guide them in ruling? Or is the curriculum of ascent to mathematical and metaphysical knowledge, of Neoplatonic inspiration, not related in Augustine's mind to the idea of Pythagoras' political instruction, an idea Augustine took from Varro and simply added to his text?[34]

An earlier section of On Order (II, viii, 25) refers to a knowledge of divine order possessed by the wise, the divine law immutably fixed in God and so to speak 'transcribed' in wise souls,[35] the observance of which determines the perfection of their contemplation and of their mode of life. The young who desire to reach this wisdom are called to practise virtuous behaviour in their personal lives and in activities which belong rather to the political sphere: they should punish with moderation and for the purpose of reform, be generous in pardoning and intolerant of corruption, command those subject to them as if in their service.[36] But, Augustine adds, they should not aspire to govern the state unless they are already perfect (*rempublicam nolint administrare nisi perfecti*). We have here then the 'Pythagorean' practice presented later, at the end of the work, where political rule follows the completion of a moral and intellectual ascent to wisdom. The suggestion is made that this rule is subordinate to a knowledge of the divine law attained in the soul of the sage, and that this knowledge is reached through the cultivation of a virtuous life in the bodily condition and in social relations, a moral education[37] which we may add to the mathematical curriculum referred to at the end of the dialogue.

Taken together, these sections of Augustine's On Order sketch a coherent and fairly complete picture of the moral and intellectual training sought in a Neoplatonic curriculum, a training intended to lead to wisdom, a transcendent knowledge which in turn inspires the political functions that the wise might thereafter assume.

is the Plotinian–Porphyrian hierarchy of virtues that functions as an itinerary of the soul, above Ch. 4). For Neoplatonic divinization in the early Augustine, see Folliet (1962: 233–5), and Bonner (1986) for Augustine's later views.

[34] On the question of Augustine's use of Varro in *De ord.* II, see I. Hadot (1984: 132–5, 156–90).

[35] For the Neoplatonic theory of the transcription of divine knowledge in human souls, see Steel (1978: 148).

[36] See above, Ch. 9, 3.   [37] See above, Ch. 4.

4. The Rejection of Neoplatonism in the *City of God*

These passages in Augustine's early work may show little more than a temporary flirtation with Neoplatonic themes.[38] In the following decades, between 390 and 410, Augustine seems to have shared with his Christian contemporaries optimistic views about the role of the Christianized Empire in the salvation of mankind, views such as those expressed in Eusebius' theocratic ideology.[39] However, Augustine came to reject such views: neither pagan political structures, in particular those proposed by the Neoplatonists, nor a Christianized Empire represented the means for the return of the soul to God, for the salvation of mankind.

This rejection seems to have resulted both from the evolution of Augustine's theological positions and from his own experience as a powerful bishop in North Africa. In the early fourth century, Eusebius' sanguine optimism could appeal to the dramatic spread of Christianity, to the Christian Church's survival of persecution under Diocletian, and to the victory and long reign of the first Christian Emperor. Since that time, the Christianization of the Empire had become massive, notwithstanding Julian's efforts, and in Augustine's time, under Theodosius (379–95), pagans were persecuted, their temples destroyed, and pagan religious practices severely punished. If Augustine approved of these measures and also came to approve the use of state force against Christian heretical movements, in particular against the Donatists in North Africa, he was also aware that, if very many citizens were now Christian, many were so by necessity or through convenience. The depth of their religion could be doubted. It was also becoming clear that the Empire itself, now Christianized, was not the cosmic order that Eusebius had thought it could become under Constantine. A demonstration of this, all the more striking in its symbolic value, was the sack of Rome by the Goths of Alaric in 410. Pagan critics did not fail to see this event as the consequence of abandoning the Roman gods who had made Rome's power and glory, in favour of the Christian god, an impiety which had brought disaster.[40]

The *City of God* responds in the first instance to these critics, while covering a range of subjects far wider than the arguments which had provoked its writing. In the first part of the work (Books I–X), Augustine claims that the pagan gods and demons are to be credited neither with what terrestrial

---

[38] Augustine rejects his praise of Pythagoras in *Retract*. I, 3, 3.

[39] See Markus (1970: chs. 2–4), whom I follow in this and in the next paragraph.

[40] For a similar criticism of Christianity in the East (in Julian and in Proclus), see above, Ch. 10, 2.

goods Rome achieved (for which Roman virtue is responsible), nor with a role in souls' attaining a transcendent good in a life hereafter (here Neoplatonism, in particular Porphyry, is Augustine's target). In the second part of the work (Books XI–XXII), Augustine traces the origin and history of two cities, the city of God and the city of Satan, the heavenly Jerusalem and Babylon, in such a way as to exclude the pretensions of any empire, even a Christian empire such as that advocated by Eusebius, to being an anticipatory image or stage in realizing the heavenly Jerusalem. As the theme of two cities can serve to express both the explicit rejection of the pagan and in particular Neoplatonic political use of religion and the implicit rejection of a Christian theocratic ideology such as that of Eusebius, it will be of use to consider this theme very briefly here.

Augustine developed his theory of two cities over a long period of time prior to the writing of the *City of God*.[41] He suggests a relation between the intelligible world, the transcendent 'fatherland' to which Plotinus calls us, and the kingdom of God.[42] And of course Plato himself refers to a heavenly paradigmatic city in the *Republic* and, in the *Laws*, to the 'city of gods and children of the gods'.[43] The transcendent city and its earthly image reappear in Neoplatonism.[44] However, Augustine's theory of two cities will be seen below to be quite different from a Platonic or Neoplatonic conception of an intelligible paradigmatic city and its earthly image. Augustine's theory seems rather to be an original synthesis, inspired by many sources, including Jewish and early Christian texts; Augustine himself (*City of God* XI, 1) refers to the city of God of the *Psalms* (86, 3; 47, 2.3.9).[45]

What distinguishes the city of God from that of Satan is a difference in orientation, in the object of love for its members: on the one hand God, the one true good, loved in faith and humility, and, on the other hand, the negation (and opposite) of this orientation, a love of false goods, of the self, of false gods and demons (fallen angels), a perverted love characterized by pride.[46] The city of God is thus constituted of angels and of human souls turned to God on their way, in this mortal existence, towards or already enjoying the true good in eternal life. Augustine agrees with the philosophers that felicity is 'social' (*socialis*), the common good completely shared

---

[41] See Lauras and Rondet (1953) for a very useful study of this development.

[42] See Fuhrer (1997: 99, 101–2) (with Augustine's later rejection of this comparison).

[43] Above, Ch. 8, 3.   [44] Above, Ch. 8, 3.

[45] See van Oort's (1991) extensive survey of Augustine's possible sources (199–359); O'Daly (1999: 53–62).

[46] *City of God* XIV, 28; XIX, 17; J. O'Meara (1961: 41–6); Markus (1970: 60, 66–9).

in friendship, a life, however, in which partake only the members of the city of God.[47] Their community is also the only one founded on justice, to the extent that its orientation to God represents what is *due* to each (to God and to souls): the community is hierarchical in structure, each receiving a rank in relation to merit, a rank fully accepted in a completely harmonious whole.[48]

To the city of God Augustine opposes the false orientation represented by the material goods sought by the agency of the false gods of Roman polytheism (Books I–V) and by the reliance on false gods and demons for reaching felicity in the hereafter (Books VI–X). In the latter respect, Augustine singles out Platonists such as Plotinus and Porphyry who had reached through philosophy a knowledge of the true good, but had referred the non-philosophical majority to the mediation of demons and of magical Chaldaean practices as a road to the Good, a mediation which is perverse and with which Porphyry himself did not appear to have been satisfied.[49] The only true mediator, whom Porphyry refused to recognize, is Christ. We might add that Augustine's account of the Neoplatonic use of religion for the salvation of souls fits very well also the theory of religious mediation of Porphyry's opponent and respondent, Iamblichus, as described in *On Mysteries*, a theory which had been given political application by Julian.[50]

But what of a Christian Emperor acting as God's intermediary, bringing back to God a world now subject to his Christian imperial rule, as advocated by Eusebius? Augustine appreciates the advantages represented by a Christian emperor,[51] and makes use of political power, now Christian, in the conflict with pagans and heretical Christians. A well-regulated state can provide conditions favourable to the pilgrimage of the members of the city of God towards the ultimate goal, in particular the condition of peace (XIX, 17). However, even such a state cannot be free of the miseries of the mortal condition, injustice, and conflict, and the goods it can provide are not true goods for the citizen of the city of God. This citizen must therefore remain somewhat detached from such a state, being entirely directed to a community of love oriented to God. Even less can worldly states be images or foreshadowings of the city of God to the extent that they are made up, as

[47] *City of God* XIX, 3 and 5; XV, 3.

[48] XIX, 21; XXII, 30. These characteristics of the city of God (justice, harmony, unity) are of course those of the ideal Platonic city.

[49] See X, 27 and 32; Fuhrer (1997: 102–8).

[50] Above, Ch. 10, 2–3.

[51] See his praise of Constantine and of Theodosius (V, 24–6), where however the *personal* Christian virtue of the emperors is singled out; cf. Duval (1966: 174–5).

is indeed the institutional Church, of citizens both of the city of God and of the city of Satan, intermingled and to be separated only at the final judgement, when the city of God, already in existence in heaven, will be fully realized and the adherents of the opposed city will find their predestined damnation.[52] Thus no political community on earth, pagan or Christian, can represent a preliminary stage or image of the city of God, nor can its ruler, even a Christian one, act as the saving mediator between God and humanity. In short, Augustine replaces the hierarchical structure, whereby political life (in Neoplatonism and in Eusebius' theocracy) represents a stage leading to a higher existence, with a dualism of opposed cities traversing the history of all political structures and even of the Church, which might seem to come near to being, but is not, the city of God.[53]

In conclusion, one might recall the fundamental political importance of religion, of the gods, and of piety in the city of Plato's *Laws* and in Neoplatonic philosophy.[54] Eusebius replaced the pagan gods with the Christian god and the philosopher-king with the Christian Emperor. Yet he retains the hierarchical structure of assimilation whereby political life, reformed by a Christian philosopher-king, assists the return of the soul to God. The fundamental importance of religious orientation remains, of course, in Augustine. However, he evolved in his thinking from an early interest in the Neoplatonic approach towards a view similar to Eusebius' rejection of pagan gods and Christian application of the philosophers' hierarchical integration of political life, a view which he also came later to reject. The rejection was comprehensive as regards Neoplatonic political philosophy, both in its religious content (its polytheism) and in its structure (hierarchical assimilation).[55] Following Eusebius' example in the former respect, Augustine did not accept the latter aspect (a structure of hierarchical assimilation) even if given a Christian application in a Eusebian theocracy.

Eusebius and Augustine may be considered in this way as providing two different and very influential cases of reaction to Neoplatonic political philosophy in the fourth and early fifth centuries: partial acceptance in

---

[52] I, 35; XV, 1; cf. Markus (1970: 59–63).

[53] See J. O'Meara (1961: 52–3). On the relation between the Church and the city of God, see also Ladner (1967: 270–82).

[54] Above, Ch. 10, 2–4.

[55] Scholars are generally agreed on this anti-Neoplatonic direction of Augustine's theory of two cities; see van Oort (1991); Neschke (1999a: 234–42). For a critique of an earlier attempt to see Augustine's theory as Neoplatonic, see Cranz (1950), who also traces (1954) Augustine's evolution from Neoplatonism to a dualistic position. Parma's revival (1968) of a Plotinian reading of the Augustinian theory of two cities is not based on an adequate study of the *City of God*.

Eusebius; complete rejection, after a long evolution from the opposite position, in Augustine. If it is the case that Eusebius and Augustine need not be reacting exclusively to philosophical opponents, the fact remains that Neoplatonic political philosophy of the fourth century provides some background throwing light on the character and relevance of their respective positions.

Ideals of Church and State 13
in the Sixth Century

In the Eastern Roman Empire of the sixth century two authors, both anonymous, developed elaborate frameworks, one for an ideal Church, the other for an ideal state. Both authors were at home in later Neoplatonic philosophy, in particular that of Proclus and his school. The first, known generally as (Pseudo-)Dionysius the Areopagite, transformed Neoplatonic political ideas, as I will attempt to show, into a Christian ecclesiology. The second, probably a high official in the court of the Emperor Justinian (527–65), composed a dialogue *On Political Science* in which a project for political reform is proposed along lines inspired, I will also argue, by later Neoplatonism. Between these contrasting ideals of Church and State, whose puzzling interrelationship will require some notice, we will also consider, more briefly, a 'Mirror of Princes' written by Agapetus for Justinian on his accession to power, a third possible instance of Neoplatonic influence on political thought in the sixth century.

1. The Neoplatonic Ecclesiology of the Pseudo-Dionysius

(i) The Date and Neoplatonic Sources of the Pseudo-Dionysius

A set of writings known collectively as the 'Dionysian corpus' (*Divine Names, Mystical Theology, Celestial Hierarchy, Ecclesiastical Hierarchy, Letters*) gives the reader the impression that its author is the Dionysius whom St Paul converted on the Areopagus at Athens (*Acts* 17, 34). This suggestion had the effect in the Middle Ages of conferring on the Dionysian corpus a quasi-apostolic authority. Such authority would be further strengthened by the identification of Dionysius the Areopagite with St Denis, a bishop held to have converted Gaul to Christianity. The Byzantine emperor therefore could have hardly made a more appropriate gesture when his ambassadors presented to the Frankish king in 827 a manuscript of the Dionysian corpus, a manuscript which can still be read today in Paris.[1] Intensified by such nationalistic associations, the apostolic claim of the Dionysian corpus presented, however, certain serious problems. For example, the corpus is cited by no Christian writer before the sixth century. Furthermore, in its language and content, the corpus seems remarkably close to later Neoplatonic texts such as those of Proclus. Early doubts about the authenticity of the corpus were nevertheless quickly argued away. It was claimed, for instance, that the intellectual proximity to Proclus meant that Proclus must have used the Dionysian corpus (just as it was once claimed, by Jewish and Christian authors, that Greek philosophers had been inspired by the Bible). However it has now been established beyond any doubt that the relationship goes the other way, that the Pseudo-Dionysius made use of specific works of Proclus.[2] Deprived of his apostolic disguise, the author of the Dionysian corpus remains an enigmatic figure whose precise identity still escapes us,[3] but whose date must be put somewhere between the mature years of Proclus, in the second half of the fifth century, and the 530s, when the Dionysian corpus was defended in its claims to authenticity and explained by John of Scythopolis.[4]

Interesting comparisons have been made between the Pseudo-Dionysius' theory of the Church and Plato's political ideas and it has been suggested that the Pseudo-Dionysius takes up Plato's political ambitions.[5] However, it has also been pointed out that significant structural differences separate the Dionysian Church from Plato's ideal city[6] and that comparisons can be made in this regard with a philosopher much closer to the

---

[1] A page is reproduced in de Andia (1997: pl. I).

[2] Saffrey (1998); Steel (1997) provides a precise philological comparison of the texts of Proclus and the Pseudo-Dionysius on evil which provided the proof by Stiglmayr and Koch in 1895 of the dependence of the Pseudo-Dionysius on Proclus.

[3] See Hathaway (1969b), 31–5 for a list of the very many conjectures that have been made concerning the Pseudo-Dionysius' true identity.

[4] On John of Scythopolis (who was also very well read in Plotinus and Proclus), see Beierwaltes (1972), Saffrey (1998); Rorem and Lamoreaux (1998: pt. i, ch. 5). Of course the Neoplatonists (and in particular Iamblichus) had promoted their own (pseudo-) ancient authorities, Pythagorean, Orphic, Egyptian, and Chaldaean.

[5] Roques (1954: 81–3, 89 (a section titled 'République platonicienne et cité dionysienne' in the Table of Contents)); (1962: 122). Roques's comparisons will be noted below.

[6] Goltz (1970: 70–1); see below n. 45.

Pseudo-Dionysius, Proclus.[7] In what follows I propose to explore these suggestions, in the light of what has been brought together in the earlier parts of this book, with a view to showing in detail that Dionysian ecclesiology is a transposition of the later Neoplatonic interpretation of Plato's political philosophy. As will become evident, Dionysius' Church is not the real Church of his time as he might have described it,[8] but the 'true' Church, i.e. an ideal Church as he would have wished it to be.

(ii) The Church as a Structure of Divinization[9]

The reader of the Dionysian corpus cannot but notice that its overall purpose is the same as that of Neoplatonic philosophy, the assimilation of man to God, or divinization (ὁμοίωσις θεῷ). This assimilation is realized within a structure consisting of an ecclesiastical hierarchy linked, through a celestial hierarchy, to God. The close relation between these hierarchical structures and divine assimilation can be seen, for example, in the Pseudo-Dionysius' definition of 'hierarchy', a term which he himself coined, it appears:

In my opinion a hierarchy is a sacred order, a state of understanding and an activity approximating as closely as possible to the divine. And it is uplifted to the imitation of God in proportion to the enlightenments divinely given to it.   (trans. Luibheid)[10]

The assimilatory or divinizing function of the ecclesiastical hierarchy in particular is often emphasized.[11]

The ecclesiastical and celestial hierarchies constitute together a scale of divine assimilation comparable to the scale of virtues, sciences, and texts whereby divine assimilation is achieved in Neoplatonism. Composed of embodied intelligences (humans, making up the ecclesiastical hierarchy) and of pure intelligences (the ranks of angels in the celestial hierarchy), the Dionysian structure acts as a scale of divine assimilation to the extent that the lower ranks in the scale imitate and assimilate themselves to the higher ranks, which are indispensable intermediates communicating divinizing power to the lower ranks.

---

[7] Hathaway (1969b: 38): 'The external features of [the Pseudo-Dionysius'] ranks of men and angels are patterned on Proclus' theory of the celestial *politeia* of which all earthly *politeiai* are images'; see also 45, 102.

[8] See Roques (1954: 198–9, 287).

[9] In this and in the following two sections I summarize, with some additions, my article (1997: 77–86).   [10] *CH* III, 1, 164D.

[11] *EH* I, 369A–372B, pp. 63, 3–64,14; 376A, p. 66, 12–19; II, 392A, p. 68, 16–17; III, 424C, p. 79, 7–12; 441C–444B, pp. 92, 2–93, 10.

The total structure of divine assimilation through levels of mediation might be represented from top to bottom as follows:

Celestial Hierarchy:

1st triad	1.1. Seraphim
	1.2. Cherubim
	1.3. Thrones
2nd triad	2.1. Dominations
	2.2. Virtues
	2.3. Powers
3rd triad	3.1. Principalities
	3.2. Archangels
	3.3. Angels

Ecclesiastical Hierarchy:

Sacraments	1.
Initiators	2.1. Bishops
	2.2. Priests
	2.3. Deacons
Initiated	3.1. Monks
	3.2. The purified admitted to the sacraments
	3.3. The purified not admitted to the sacraments.

Starting from the bottom of the scale, we will examine first some general characteristics of the two lower triads of the ecclesiastical hierarchy, those of the 'initiated' and of the 'initiators'.

To become members of the Church, the 'initiated' must receive instruction in the 'divine way of life' (ἡ ἔνθεος πολιτεία) so as to live this life, purifying themselves of the life of vice (ἡ ἐν κακίᾳ πολιτεία).[12] They thus require teaching and a moral reform, followed by purification which leads to a contemplative mode of life exemplified at its highest level, in the order of the 'initiated', by the rank of monks.[13] These steps in divine assimilation can be compared to levels in divinization as described by later Neoplatonic philosophers. Moral reform, for example, is expressed by the Pseudo-Dionysius in terms of the definitions given of the four cardinal virtues in Plato's *Republic*,[14] i.e. the virtues described as 'political' by the

---

[12] *EH* II, 396A, p. 71, 10–16; II, 397B, pp. 73, 15–74, 2. On the Dionysian meaning of πολιτεία, cf. Roques (1954: 82).

[13] *EH* III, 428B, pp. 81, 19–82, 4; Roques (1954: 261–2); (1962: 207–9).

[14] Cf. *Ep*. VIII, 3, 1093A–B, pp. 182, 3–183, 4; noted by Roques (1954: 89).

Neoplatonists.[15] This 'political' mode (πολιτικῶς) in theology is subordinated by Dionysius to a 'purificatory' mode (καθαρτικῶς),[16] just as the Neoplatonists distinguished a 'political' level of assimilation from the 'purificatory' level to which it leads. In Neoplatonism, purification gives access in turn to a yet higher form of life, a life of knowledge. So also in the Pseudo-Dionysius do moral ('political') reform and purification lead the initiated to the highest rank in their order, the 'theoretical' or contemplative, i.e. monastic, life.

The order of the initiated is subordinated in the Dionysian ecclesiastical hierarchy to the order of the 'initiators' made up of deacons, priests, and bishops. The order of initiators represents, like that of the initiated, a path to divine assimilation, each rank reaching towards a higher, more divine life. Each rank is divinized by the rank superior to it, the highest rank, that of bishops, being subordinated to the celestial hierarchy. There is, however, together of course with a difference in ranking, a factor which distinguishes the order of the initiators as a whole from that of the initiated: if both orders show the same movement of *ascent* to God, only the order of initiators acts as a mediator of divinizing power *descending* on what is lower; even the highest rank of the order of the initiated, that of the monks, does not have this power of transmitting what can divinize to lower ranks.[17]

The following general characteristics of the order of initiators might also be noted. The Pseudo-Dionysius insists, for example, on the importance of the transmission of divinization through intermediary levels: this rule of mediation is essential, not only for the order of ecclesiastical initiators, but also for the orders of the celestial hierarchy, for it is a law instituted, he claims, by God himself. Thus violation of rank-ordering cannot be tolerated in the ecclesiastical hierarchy.[18] This principle has been compared with the law of mean terms formulated by Proclus.[19] The Pseudo-Dionysius also insists on the rule that the members of each rank of the ecclesiastical order must carry out their proper function and none other. In this rule we can recognize the principle of justice of Plato's *Republic* (433b4): to each his

---

[15] Above, Ch. 4.

[16] *Ep.* IX, 2, 1108B, p. 199, 2–6 (with apparatus fontium). Hathaway (1969b: 87, 99), emphasizes the 'political' vocabulary of *Ep.* VIII, which he contrasts with the 'contemplative' language of *Ep.* IX, arguing also (79) for the use of Plato's *Gorgias* (a 'political' dialogue according to the Neoplatonists, above Ch. 6, 2–3), in *Ep.* VIII.

[17] See Roques (1954: 286); (1962: 210–12).

[18] *CH* IV, 3, 180D–181A, p. 22, 11–17; *EH* V, 504C, p. 106, 24–5; *Ep.* VIII, 1, 1088C, pp. 175,14–176, 3.

[19] See Proclus, *El. Theol.* 132.

proper task (τὰ αὑτοῦ πράττειν).[20] Plato's principle of justice is also found of course in Neoplatonic texts, for example in Proclus.[21] Perhaps, as a further general trait of the order of initiators, we might note the essential relation Dionysius sees between an ecclesiastical function and the moral and spiritual quality of the soul of the person who exercises this function.[22] This notion, not characteristic of Western Latin ecclesiology, reminds one[23] of the Platonic idea that the quality of moral and political action depends on the moral quality of the soul of the person who acts: in the political sphere, in particular, philosopher-kings must be morally perfect. If we examine in more detail the highest rank of the order of 'initiators', that represented by bishops, we can develop this point further by comparing Dionysian bishops with Platonic philosopher-kings.

(iii) Bishops as Philosopher-kings

The order of bishops in the ecclesiastical hierarchy was anticipated, according to the Pseudo-Dionysius, by Moses, founder of the 'legal hierarchy', i.e. the sacred order of the Old Testament which prepares the Christian ecclesiastical hierarchy.[24] Moses indeed reached a high degree of assimilation to God, in Dionyius' view: he became divine-like, modelling himself by imitating God.[25] This closeness and resemblance to God is connected to Moses' function as founder and legislator of the legal hierarchy:

The guides were those whom Moses, himself the foremost initiator and leader among the hierarchs of the Law, had initiated into the holy tabernacle. It was Moses who, for the edification of others, depicted in this holy tabernacle the institutions of the hierarchy of law. He described all the sacred actions of the law as images of what was revealed to him on Mount Sinai.[26]

Moses thus legislated in function of, in the image (εἰκόνα) of, his vision on Mount Sinai: his legislation is in the image of a divine revelation. We may compare this with Plato's philosopher-kings who act by imitating, as if painters, a transcendent model (*Rep.* 500d–e). This idea of political action

---

[20] *Ep.* VIII, 4, 1093c, pp. 183, 11–184, 1; noted by Roques (1954: 89); (1962: 122 n., 215).

[21] See Hathaway (1969b: 45, 102).

[22] *EH* III, 445A–B, pp. 93, 26–94, 10.

[23] As Roques (1954: 182–3, 297) suggests.

[24] See Roques (1954: 69 n., 171 ff); Harl (1984). Melchisidech, like Moses, is a forerunner of the Christian high priest (*CH* IX, 3; cf. Dagron 1996: 184–7).

[25] *Ep.* VIII, 1, 1085B, pp. 172, 4–173, 5.

[26] *EH* V, 501c.

as imitation of a transcendent model is found in Plotinus' interpretation of the figure of Minos as a legislator inspired by Zeus (above, Ch. 7, 1) and Plato's comparison of philosopher-kings with painters imitating transcendent models is taken up again in detail by Iamblichus and Hierocles.[27]

The influence of the Platonic comparison with painters is particularly evident in a passage where Dionysius is describing those whose rank is anticipated by Moses, Christian bishops:

It is thus with those artists who love beauty in the mind. They make an image of it within their minds. The concentration and the persistence of their contemplation of this fragrant, secret beauty enables them to produce an exact likeness of God. And so these divine artists never cease to shape the power of their minds along the lines of a loveliness which is conceptual, transcendent, and fragrant, and if they practise the virtues called for by imitation of God it is not to be seen by men, as scripture puts it. Rather, they sacredly behold those infinitely sacred things of the Church disguised in the rite of the ointment, as in an image. That is why they too sacredly disguise whatever is sacred and virtuously godlike in their mind, imitating and depicting God. They gaze solely on conceptual originals. Not only do they not look at dissimilar things, but they refuse to be dragged down towards the sight of them. And as one would expect of such people, they yearn only for what is truly Beautiful and Just and not for empty appearances. They do not gaze after that glory so stupidly praised by the mob. Imitating God, as they do, they can tell the difference between real beauty and real evil. They are the truly divine images of that infinitely divine fragrance.[28]

Comparing these episcopal 'painters' with the 'painting' philosopher-kings of Plato and the later Neoplatonists, we notice that Dionysius has modified the Platonic image in various ways. In particular, the Platonic and Neoplatonic philosopher-king who models both his soul and the state after a transcendent paradigm becomes, in Dionysius, the holy man who models his soul after this paradigm. Stress is placed on the inner, 'secret' reform of the soul. This interiorization, this hiddenness means, however, a further emphasis on the moral and spiritual quality of the holy man which is the source of his beneficial action, his communication of the good to lower

---

[27] Above, Ch. 8, 1. It is true that Exodus mentions a model (25, 8: παράδειγμα; cf. 26, 30: τό εἶδος, 25, 40: τὸν τύπον) which God shows Moses and which Moses must imitate in the construction of the sanctuary. However, Dionysius interprets this model as the archetype of which all priestly institutions are an image. The interpretation of Moses as legislator in the light of Plato's *Rep.* can already be found in Philo of Alexandria (*De vita Mosis* II, 2, quoting *Rep.* 473d), Eusebius (*Praep. Ev.* XII, 19, quoting *Rep.* 500c–501c) and Gregory of Nyssa (*De vita Moysis* 26). The interpretations of Moses in Philo, Gregory of Nyssa, and the Pseudo-Dionysius are compared in detail by de Andia (1996: ch. 14).

[28] *EH* IV, 473c–476A.

ranks. The communicative secrecy of the bishop is thus in the image of the double movement of transcendent independence and outgoing communication of the good that characterizes the divinity.[29] In effect, then, Dionysius has pushed to its limits the paradox of the Neoplatonic philosopher-king, who is both detached from the world in reaching union with the divine, and transmits to the world an image of this union.[30] The secrecy of the Dionysian bishop expresses the Neoplatonic principle that the outgoing strength of virtue depends on its inward concentration.

The Dionysian bishop, withdrawn in secrecy as he is, is active indeed in the Church. He is the source of the knowledge and actions on which lower ranks depend so as to be brought closer and assimilated to God. In referring to this outgoing, beneficial function of the bishop, Dionysius speaks of his 'philanthropy', a term which is common enough in Patristic ecclesiological language and a banality in monarchic ideology. However, Dionysius uses the term, as do the later Neoplatonists, in connection with the goodness, the generosity without envy (ἄφθονος) of the first cause, of which the bishop is an image.[31] As such, the Dionysian bishop can also be described as 'providential': in communicating divinizing power to humanity he recalls the providential care for the lower shown by a divinity which remains transcendent.[32] The political 'providence' of the divine-like philosopher-king had also been compared by the later Neoplatonists with the providence of the highest cause.[33] 'Philanthropy' and 'providence' thus express the same idea: be one Neoplatonist philosopher or Dionysian bishop, one's action, political or ecclesiastical, is a reflection of one's divinization.

(iv) Three Structural Anomalies

The comparison between Neoplatonic political ideas and Pseudo-Dionysius' ecclesiology may be extended further so as to explain certain difficulties and puzzles that arise in the study of this ecclesiology. I take up three of these problems here.

(*a*) Dionysius describes the ecclesiastical hierarchy as an imitation of the celestial hierarchy, i.e. the hierarchy of angels which links it to God.[34]

---

[29] See *EH* II, 400B, p. 75, 3–9; III, 428D–429B, pp. 82, 13–83, 10; 437D–440A, p. 89, 11–21.

[30] The idea is well formulated by Rouche (1996: 158–9): 'cette dialectique du mépris du monde qui permet, ensuite, d'être renvoyé au monde pour mieux le transformer'.

[31] See *EH* II, 400B, p. 75, 4–7; III, 429B, p. 83, 3–10; Roques (1954: 283n., 316); above, Ch. 7, 1.

[32] See *Ep.* IX, 3, 1109C–D, p. 203, 1–5; *Ep.* VIII, 3, 1093A, p. 182, 3–5.

[33] Above, Ch. 7, 1.

[34] *CH* I, 3, 121C–124A, pp. 8, 14–9, 15; *EH* VI, 536D, p. 119, 12–15; Roques (1954: 173).

However, this does not quite seem to be the case, as can be seen from the diagram (above, sec. (ii)): the celestial hierarchy is made up of three orders of angels (pure intelligences), each subdivided into three ranks, whereas the ecclesiastical hierarchy includes three orders of which the lowest and the middle orders, also subdivided each into three ranks, are subordinated to a highest order made up, not of *intelligences*, but of *rites* or *sacraments*.[35] As a structure of intelligences, the Dionysian Church thus appears to be dyadic, not triadic, although its model, the celestial hierarchy, is through and through triadic. How is this structural anomaly to be explained?[36] The following explanation has been offered.[37] Dionysius structured the world of angels on the model of a Proclean system of three sets of triads and sought to structure the Church on the same lines, given that it should be an image of the higher hierarchy. However, the realities of church organization prevented this, since the Church was divided (dyadically) into the consecrated orders and the laity. By adding the order of sacraments to this dyadic structure, Dionysius sought a compromise between actual church organization and the requirements derived from his Proclean vision of the angelic world. A weakness in this explanation is that Dionysius does not seem much constrained by the concrete ecclesiastical facts of his time[38] and that he could easily have imagined his Church as truly triadic, a true image of the celestial hierarchy.[39]

(*b*) Another structural anomaly may be found in the exceptional importance given to the rank of bishops in the order of the 'initiators', an importance which seems to go beyond what one would expect in a structure of graduated continuous mediation such as that exemplified in the celestial hierarchy.[40] Might this be another case of a compromise between given realities and theoretical requirements? This suggestion must meet the same objection as that met by the proposed explanation of the first anomaly.

(*c*) A third difficulty might be felt in the fact that Dionysius scarcely treats of the relationships between the ranks of the order of the 'initiated',[41]

---

[35] See *EH* V, 501A, p. 104, 11–15; 501D, p. 105, 21–4; Roques (1954: 175, 196).

[36] Dionysius seems himself to be sensitive to the difficulty, since he insists on the ritual aspect (τελετή) of the activity of highest order of angels, an aspect that anticipates the highest order of the ecclesiastical hierarchy (*EH* V, 501A, p. 104, 15–18). However, the latter order consists of rites or sacraments, not of intelligences performing these rites.

[37] Roques (1954: 175, 196); (1962: 126).   [38] Above n. 8.

[39] Duby (1980: 114ff.), noting the dyadic structure of the Dionysian Church, discusses an attempt in the medieval Latin West to transform it into a trifunctional structure; a similar effort can be found in the Byzantine East (Wenger 1957: 307–8).

[40] See Roques et al. (1970: 160 n. 1); Roques (1954: 183, 197–8).

[41] Roques (1954: 197–8).

although the theory of continuous graduated mediation of divinization would seem to call for such treatment. No mediation between these ranks seems to be envisaged. The monks, for example, the highest rank of the 'initiated', do not appear to have a mediatory function in relation to lower ranks. The continuity of Dionysian hierarchy is again somewhat disturbed. And here again, one might wonder, for example, if some reference (perhaps implicitly critical) to the realities of monastic politics might be at issue.

Whatever the concrete situations that Dionysius may have had in mind, descriptively or prescriptively, some light can be thrown on these structural anomalies if we take it that his ecclesiology is a transposition of Platonic political philosophy. For these anomalies can already be found in this philosophy. Beginning with the first difficulty (*a*), we might note that the ideal city in Plato's *Republic*, if commonly described as tripartite in structure (guardians, auxiliaries, producers), is fundamentally dyadic in conception. In founding this city, Plato distinguishes between two functions, that of the guardians and that of the producers. It is only later in the text (412b–c, 414b) that he distinguishes, *within* the group of guardians, between guardians and auxiliaries. The auxiliaries, however, remain guardians, incomplete guardians, so to speak, as compared to the 'complete' guardians (φύλακες παντελεῖς) who will be the philosopher-kings.[42] This essentially dyadic division of the city is found again in Plato's summary of the theory of the ideal city in the *Timaeus* (17c–d), in Aristotle's references to the *Republic*,[43] and it is taken up again by Proclus.[44]

The relation, within Plato's group of guardians, between 'complete' and incomplete guardians (philosopher-kings and auxiliaries) may also throw some light on the second structural anomaly (*b*) in Dionysius, if Dionysian bishops are seen as corresponding to Platonic philosopher-kings. As the philosopher-kings represent, so to speak, the essence of the group of guardians, of which the others (the auxiliaries) are imperfect and ancillary members, so are the Dionysian bishops the essence of the order of 'initiators', the other ranks being inferior and ancillary.

Finally, as regards the third anomaly (*c*), if we compare the 'initiator'/'initiated' distinction of orders in Dionysius with the Platonic distinction between the functions of 'guardians' and 'producers', we might note that Plato neglects the relationships between producers just as does Dionysius the relationships between the 'initiated'. In Plato, the fundamental

---

[42] *Rep.* 414b1–2; cf. 428d7: τελέους φύλακας.
[43] *Politics* II, 5, 1264a25–9, 1264b20–4.
[44] *In Tim.* I, pp. 34, 27–35, 9; *In Remp.* II, p. 77, 20–1.

distinction between functions is that between those who govern and those who are governed. What is at issue is the best way of govern*ing*. Thus the relationships among the govern*ed* remain undiscussed. Similarly, the equivalent distinction in Dionysius is that between the functions of 'initiators' and 'initiated' and thus the relationships between the 'initiated', not relating to the fundamental function of initiating, remain somewhat obscure.

Whatever the concrete implications of Dionysius' ecclesiastical hierarchy, it seems then that it involves structural peculiarities which disturb somewhat its status as an image of the celestial hierarchy, but which correspond to characteristics of the ideal city of Plato's *Republic*. If, furthermore, the Dionysian ecclesiastical hierarchy forms part of a larger system of divinization which corresponds in general and in many details to the later Neoplatonic structure of divinization through political life, purification, and knowledge, and if, in particular, Dionysian bishops come very close to the Neoplatonic interpretation of Plato's philosopher-kings, then it would seem that Dionysius is inspired, not by a direct reading of Plato, but by a Neoplatonic interpretation of the political philosophy of the *Republic*.[45] We may conclude thus that Dionysius' Church is a Christian transposition of a Neoplatonic version of the ideal city of the *Republic*.

To reach some idea of what this Neoplatonic version transposed by Dionysius might have been like, we need only reverse the transposition while keeping the same functional structures. We may thus replace angels by the divinities of later Neoplatonic metaphysics, bishops by philosopher-kings, priests and deacons by auxiliaries, the order of the initiated by producers, and sacraments by rites such as those that Julian the Emperor had tried to revive. What remains is a structure of political life that is based on the Platonic principle of justice, as expressed in a dyadic order governed by philosopher-kings inspired by transcendent models, as integrated in a larger scale of divinization leading beyond political life to higher levels of divine-like existence.

A final suggestion might be made on the basis of these comparisons

---

[45] Thus Goltz (1970: 70–1), distinguishing between the social paradigm represented by the Dionysian hierarchy and Plato's ideal city, describes the latter as the coordination of a number of different functions and forms of knowledge, whereas the former is a structure of vertical dependence in which functions are carried out and communicated at degrees of decreasing intensity. This distinction describes, I suggest, the difference between Plato's city and a later Neoplatonic version of Plato's city. It thus brings the Pseudo-Dionysius closer to later Neoplatonic political philosophy than to Plato.

between Dionysian ecclesiology and later Neoplatonic political philosophy. If this ecclesiology is approached from a Neoplatonic point of view, it would seem to follow that the prominence of the paradigm represented by (a Neoplatonic version of) the ideal city of the *Republic*, in Dionysius, suggests that, in the scale of levels of political reform envisaged by the Neoplatonists (above, Ch. 8, 2), the Dionysian Church represents the highest, most ambitious level of reform, a level of perfection well beyond the more human project of the *Laws* or projects of lesser ambition.

(v) Concluding Questions

Seen from outside, the Pseudo-Dionysius' Church raises questions for which no clear and direct answer is provided by the Dionysian corpus. For example, in relation to western papal claims, one might wonder if the Dionysian hierarchy is ruled at its highest level by one or by a number of patriarchs or bishops, in other words, whether the Church, in political terms, should be a monarchy or an aristocracy. No clear-cut, strong view on this issue emerges from Dionysius' works:[46] it would seem that each bishop is considered to be absolutely first in his church and that the bishops, on the whole, are, in relation to each other, of equal rank. In philosophical terms, we might recall Plato's position that, as regards the philosopher-kings, what matters is not their number, one or more, but their moral and intellectual perfection.[47]

Another open question concerns the relation between the Dionysian Church and the State. If the Dionysian Church takes over in effect the function of divinization which the State should assume according to later Neoplatonists, what function remains for the State and how does it relate to the Church? If the Pseudo-Dionysius does not develop this matter in any detail (he seems exclusively concerned with an ideal spiritual community), some indications given in a chapter of the *Celestial Hierarchy* (IX, 4) might be felt to point to his position. In this chapter he interprets the Bible as describing the rulers of the Egyptians and Babylonians as inspired by angels, i.e. members of the celestial hierarchy. This does not mean, however, that these rulers, as if equals of the princes of the Church, derived their knowledge and power directly from the celestial hierarchy. These rulers, to comprehend their angelic inspiration, required interpreters who were 'servants of the true God', members at that time of the Jewish legal hierarchy and who

---

[46] Cf. the discussion in Roques (1954: 179–82), whose conclusions I summarize here.
[47] Above, Ch. 8, 5.

now would be part of the Christian ecclesiastical hierarchy. It would seem that, at least as regards pagan rulers, the State is subordinated to the mediation of divinization provided by the ecclesiastical hierarchy. The State would seem thus to be subordinate to the Church. The Christian ruler of a Christian state may be superior to the pagan rulers to whom Dionysius refers. However, it seems unlikely that a Christian state and Christian ruler could somehow represent a structure of divinization parallel to that provided by the Church, both subordinated to the celestial hierarchy. One suspects that even the most Christian of emperors must depend in some way on the mediation provided by the ecclesiastical hierarchy, even if this matter remains obscure in the Pseudo-Dionysius.

2. The Anonymous Dialogue *On Political Science*

Sometime following his accession to power in 527, the Emperor Justinian was presented with a 'Mirror of Princes', the *Ekthesis* compiled by Agapetus, deacon it seems of the church of St Sophia in Constantinople (not long after to be burnt down in the Nika riots and replaced by Justinian's Great Church). The *Ekthesis* is made up of seventy-two admonitions on ideal rulership, many of which derive from the stock-in-trade of the literature of 'Mirrors of Princes' going back through the Roman imperial period to Hellenistic times and eventually to Isocrates. These conventional ideas are adapted and controlled in Agapetus' compilation by Christian values.[48] As such, this work would not be of particular interest in relation to the theme of this chapter, were it not the case that Neoplatonic philosophy has been claimed to form a part of the intellectual background of the *Ekthesis*.[49]

The comparisons that have been made between Agapetus and Neoplatonic texts are not, however, very compelling,[50] certainly not strong

---

[48] On the immense popularity of various versions of and extracts from the *Ekthesis* in the Latin West, in Byzantium, and in Slavic lands, cf. Dvornik (1966: i. 714–15); Ševčenko (1978). Dvornik also provides (1966: 712–14) a brief summary of the *Ekthesis* and Barker (1957) a selection of chapters in translation. Cf. also Henry (1967).

[49] Frohne (1985: 193–4), who relates chapters in Agapetus to passages in Hierocles, *In carm. aur.*, while also discussing other sources, including Isocrates (238) and the Pseudo-Pythagorean kingship texts (176).

[50] See Frohne (1985: 194), for example, on the theme of εὐζωΐα in Agapetus and Hierocles; but see also the text in Eusebius to which she next refers (195). Eusebius' *Praise of Constantine* seems to be an important source for Agapetus, whose first chapter could be said to be the *Praise of Constantine* in a nutshell.

enough to argue for any significant specific impact of Neoplatonism on Agapetus' imperial ideology. In general Agapetus stays within the conventional framework: the Emperor is chosen by God, called to imitate God in his rule, displaying in his actions generosity (in particular to the poor) and justice, cultivating personal virtues to a high degree. An example of Agapetus' Christian use of these commonplaces of the tradition of mirrors of princes is provided by a chapter (17) which takes up the Platonic theme of the philosopher-king:

> In our time the period of a life which is good has been shown to us, foretold as coming by one of the ancients, when philosophers would be kings or kings would philosophize. For in philosophizing you were deemed worthy of kingship, and in being king you have not left philosophy. For if the love of wisdom makes philosophy, and the beginning of wisdom is the fear of God [*Proverbs* 1: 7], which you cherish throughout in your heart, then what I say is clearly true.

What Agapetus understands by 'philosophy' seems to reduce to Christian piety. Little real philosophical content is included in Justinian's 'wisdom', as Agapetus describes it, and his imitation of God does not appear to require any particular metaphysical or mathematical knowledge. The Neoplatonists themselves in Athens would soon learn Justinian's 'philosophy', when, in his vigorous campaign against pagans, his legislation of 529 led to the closing of their school and their exile in Persia.[51]

In contrast to Agapetus, the importance of later Neoplatonism as a source of inspiration for another document associated with Justinian's court, an anonymous dialogue *On Political Science* (Περὶ πολιτικῆς ἐπιστήμης), is quite evident. It would certainly have been most illuminating for our purposes to have been able to read this text, had it survived. As it is, we must work with a number of poorly preserved fragments of it that have been discovered in a palimpsest manuscript. However, these fragments are informative enough to yield some very interesting insights into what a later Neoplatonic text of political philosophy might contain. The debt of the anonymous dialogue to later Neoplatonism was demonstrated over a century ago,[52] by means of comparisons betweens details in ideas and terminology. However, an overall comparison of the dialogue's conception of political science with Neoplatonic political philosophy has not

---

[51] Above, Ch. 2, 3.   [52] Praechter (1900).

been undertaken,[53] a task which the earlier parts of this book will make possible, as I hope to show in what follows.[54]

(i) Date and Contents of the Anonymous Dialogue

The discoverer of the fragments of the dialogue, Angelo Mai, identified their author as Peter the Patrician, a high official in the court of Justinian. Although this identification is purely speculative, there is at least agreement that the anonymous dialogue must date to the Justinianic period. The most recent editor of the text thinks that it was written in the earlier part of the Justinianic reign, before 535, and that it derives from the higher circles of Justinian's administration.[55] But it has also been suggested that the dialogue should be placed towards the end of Justinian's reign (565) and that it voices the interests of a senatorial elite.[56] The later dating seems more plausible, since, as will be seen in a moment, the two speakers in the dialogue correspond to high officials active in Justinian's administration in 529 and it seems unlikely that the dialogue, in portraying them, would have been written close to the time of their activity.[57]

The fragments of the dialogue have also been identified by Mai (here there is no good reason to doubt the identification) with a dialogue of the same title on which Photius reports in his *Bibliotheca* (cod. 37). The dialogue *On Political Science* read by Photius involved, according to his report, two speakers, the patrician Menas and the referendarius Thomas. No referendarius of this name is known for the period, but an identification has been suggested with the quaestor Thomas who, as a pagan, was purged in 529,[58] the year of Justinian's anti-pagan legislation. Menas is likely to have been the Praetorian Prefect of the Orient of that name for 528–9.[59] Photius tells us that the dialogue was made up of six books (λόγοι) and that it introduced a type of constitution different from earlier constitutions. This constitution

---

[53] Presumably for the simple reason that Neoplatonism has been thought not to have political theories; cf. Valdenberg (1925: 56).

[54] A longer version of the following sections, with discussion of some difficulties, can be found in O'Meara (2002a).

[55] Anonymous, *Dialogue on Political Science*, p. xiii (C. Mazzucchi).

[56] Cameron (1985: 250–1).

[57] I owe this point to discussion with J. Duffy.

[58] Cameron (1985: 249).

[59] Rashed (2000) has recently discovered an epigram in honour of a Menas, Platonist and lawgiver, whom he identifies as the praetorian prefect who played an important part in the production of the Justinianic Code, as the interlocutor of the anonymous dialogue, and even as the author of the dialogue.

was called 'dicaearchic' and consisted of a mix of the best of royal, aristo-cratic, and democratic constitutions and thus was itself the best of consti-tutional types. Photius also tells us that the dialogue 'rightly found fault (ἐπιμέμφεται . . . δικαίως)' with Plato's (ideal) republic or constitution (πολιτεία).

Turning to the fragments of the dialogue that have survived in the palimpsest manuscript, we find that only a small part of Book IV and some-what more of Book V are extant. The speakers of the dialogue are named Menodorus and Thaumasius, no doubt Platonizing versions of Menas and Thomas, names which Photius may have been able to read in his manu-script. The fiction of a Platonic dialogue is pushed very far in the fragments: the atmosphere and life of the conversation between Menodorus and Thaumasius remind us very much of a Platonic dialogue such as the *Republic*: Thaumasius closely follows Menodorus' speculations, asking for clarifications; Menodorus sometimes formulates general principles, which then require explanation and exemplification. The fragments from Book IV have to do with military science and virtue. Menodorus and Thaumasius discuss the conduct of military exercises, the importance of infantry, a mil-itary moral code, and the relations between the military and civilians. A list of the contents of Book V survives in the fragments. According to this list (p. 15, 2–19), Book V dealt, among other things, with kingship (βασιλεία) and kingly science (βασιλικὴ ἐπιστήμη); how this science relates to other sciences; its laws, doctrines, and practices; how the king imitates God, knows the divine, and rules accordingly. These points are covered to some degree by the remaining fragments. In the following sections I discuss in particular what the fragments from Book V tell us about the purpose of political science, the relation between political and kingly science, and the way in which kingly science is an imitation of the divine.

(ii) The Purpose of Political Science

Political science arises, according to a fragment from Book V (pp. 46, 11–47, 12), as a consequence of the human condition, the predicament in which we find ourselves, mid-way between the rational and the irrational, between the divine life of pure intellect (νοῦς) and nature (φύσις). If both transcendent intellect and nature know peace, being unmixed with each other, humanity, being torn between them, lives in turmoil and conflict, striving both up towards the divine life of intellect and down towards nature. In its goodness, however, divine providence supplied human reason with two most excellent remedies for its condition, 'dialectical science', which relates to the incorporeal, and 'political science', which relates to the corporeal and concerns political action.

A little later (p. 49, 15–22), we are told that God devised political science as a divine method for the use of men in their exile here below, so that they may attain good order, through which to return to the transcendent metropolis, the dignity of the immortal city. Political knowledge therefore prepares the way and is subordinate to a higher union with the divine; political knowledge, relating to the body, produces good order in our terrestrial lives, which in turn provides the condition for a return to the divine homeland, that of divine intellect from which we are exiled here below. If the purpose then of political science is to achieve well-being, in accord with justice, for the salvation of humans,[60] this is in view of a divine life above terrestrial existence.

We have found above[61] the same interpretation of the functions and gradation of political and dialectical science in later Neoplatonism: political philosophy encompasses the practical sciences which are subordinate to the theoretical sciences of which 'theology' (also called 'dialectic' in later Neoplatonism) is the highest. The practical and theoretical sciences are understood as constituting a scale aiming at progressive divinization, or assimilation to the divine. Political philosophy, as a practical science, has to do with soul related to the body, soul using body as an instrument. Its objective is to bring 'political' virtue, i.e. good order, to the incorporated life of soul. This good order makes possible the access to higher knowledge and virtue, the theoretical sciences and virtues of which 'theology' (or 'dialectic') is the summit, where soul, as intellect, attains the life of the divine.

The anonymous dialogue presents this theory of the hierarchy and divinizing function of political science and dialectic as part of a quasi-mythical or cosmogonic account of the human condition. One is reminded of the combination of opposed constituents that go to make up human nature in Plato's *Timaeus* and of the turmoil, moral and epistemic, that follows soul's union with the body (43b–44a). What can serve to check this turmoil, according to the *Timaeus*, is the greatest gift of the gods to mortals, i.e. philosophy (47b). But what philosophy? The *Timaeus* passage speaks of the observation of the orderly movements of the heavens which will bring order to the movements of our soul. The theme of a divine gift to humanity in perdition also occurs in the myth of Plato's *Protagoras* (322c–d), where

---

[60] p. 19, 20–4; cf. p. 47, 22–4.   [61] Ch.5.

Zeus, through Hermes, supplies us with the means, i.e. justice and shame, whereby we may live together without destroying each other. Zeus' divine gift reappears in Julian the Emperor's vision, in which, following a Platonic ascent to the highest levels of the divine, Julian receives instruction, on Zeus' orders, on how to rule, i.e. he is taught the political knowledge that will guide him as Emperor.[62] Here again we are very near to the ideas of the anonymous dialogue. Since, for the later Neoplatonists, philosophical knowledge in general is a divine gift to humanity, mediated by superior souls such as those of Pythagoras and Plato,[63] we can include political philosophy as part of this gift. Indeed Iamblichus claims that Pythagoras, as well as revealing other sciences, bestowed 'political science' on his followers, a science also revealed, for the later Neoplatonist, by Plato in the *Gorgias*, the *Republic*, and the *Laws*.[64]

Finally the metaphor of exile and return to a mother city above, whereby the anonymous dialogue describes human existence, also has a good Platonic and Neoplatonic pedigree, not only in the heavenly city of Plato's *Republic* and in Proclus' intelligible city,[65] but also in Plotinus' interpretation of Odysseus' return to his homeland as the return of the soul to the One.[66] Julian, too, describes our condition as that of an exile from which we seek to return.[67]

The broad context and specific function of political science, as described by the anonymous dialogue, are clearly Neoplatonic in inspiration. But what of the *content* of this science? It includes, in view of its purpose of the salvation of humanity, laws, doctrines, and practices. Among the laws are five fundamental provisions concerning the election of kings, the constitution of an elite (senatorial) body, the choice of church authorities and of the high officers of state, and the protection of the laws (pp. 19, 27–20, 10). Expressed in this legislation, 'political science' is said to be identical to kingship or 'kingly science', which in turn is described as an imitation of God (p. 18, 5–7). In the following I would like to examine these two points further.

(iii) Political Science as Kingly Science

The identity that is established between political and kingly science seems puzzling, if we assume that kingly science is simply a part of political

---

[62] Above, Ch. 7, 1.
[64] Above, Ch. 8, 4; Ch. 6, 2.
[66] Plotinus, *Enn.* I 6, 8.
[63] See *PR* 36–9, 149–51.
[65] Above, Ch. 8, 3.
[67] Julian, *Or.* III, 30, 90b; VIII, 9, 169b–c.

science, which would also include, for example, the military science explored in Book IV of the dialogue.[68] Military science, we would expect, has its own specific concerns, as distinct from the concerns of kingship discussed in Book V of the dialogue. It is true that in some places, Plato identified political and kingly science.[69] But how does the author of the anonymous dialogue understand this identity?

A fragment of the dialogue allows us to see how kingship can be both a part of, and identical to, political science. Kingship is the fountain of political light which is communicated, by a scientific method, to the ranks subordinated to it in the state, rank after rank, so that each rank shares in the knowledge possessed by the rank above it that rules it.[70] Thus, we may infer, if kingship communicates political knowledge to the lower orders of the state, then the other parts of political knowledge derive from kingship as if from a source. The language of this fragment is close to that of the Pseudo-Dionysius, particularly at the beginning of the *Celestial Hierarchy*. Both authors express a fundamental principle of Neoplatonic metaphysics, the principle that the first member of a series pre-contains and produces the subsequent members of the series.[71] As applying in the anonymous dialogue, this principle means that kingship or kingly science is both a part of, and identical to, political science: it is *part* of political science, because there are other parts, such as military science; it *is* political science, because it pre-contains, as the highest part and source of all political knowledge, the other parts.[72]

To see how this would work out in practice, we could try to see if the military science described in Book IV of the anonymous dialogue can be derived from the kingly science of Book V, account being taken of the lower ranks that are concerned. I believe this can, in fact, be done, but would like at present to look rather into the notion that kingly science is an imitation of God.

---

[68] Plato (*Prot.* 322b5) describes military science as part of political knowledge. Judicial and military science, with rhetoric, are subordinated to political science in Plato, *Statesman* 304c–305c.

[69] *Euthyd.* 291c4–5, *Statesman* 259c–d.

[70] p. 27, 7–15. The question of the relation between kingly science and other sciences is listed in the table of contents of Book V (p. 15, 3–4).

[71] See Lloyd (1990: 76–8).

[72] See Proclus, *In Parm.*, p. 814, 23–36. This may be seen as a Neoplatonic interpretation of the subordination of other arts and skills to political or kingly science in Plato's *Statesman* (above, n. 68).

(iv) Kingly Science as Imitation of God

It is asserted, both in the list of contents and in the fragments of Book V, that kingly science is an imitation of God, or assimilation to God (pp. 16, 6–7; 18, 6–7; 37, 14–15). A banality in the literature of monarchy of the Hellenistic and Roman imperial periods, we have also found this idea, for example, in Eusebius' *Praise of Constantine* and in the *Ekthesis* of Agapetus. The later Neoplatonists provided their own particular interpretation of the theme of kingship as imitation of the divine. Relating it to their view of philosophy as an assimilation of man to the divine, they specified what this divinization might mean. Two aspects of the divine, of god, were distinguished, knowledge, or perfect thought (θεωρία), and providence, or care of what is lower. If the life of the divine has these two aspects, then the philosopher who is assimilated to the divine, or imitates it, will exhibit these two sorts of activity: theoretical activity, or knowledge, and providential activity, i.e. political rule.[73]

To describe kingship as imitation of divine providential rule is not to explain *how*, in particular, kingship imitates the divine. This question already arises for the reader of Plato's *Republic* who asks how precisely the philosopher-kings model their city according to a divine paradigm (500e): do they copy the Platonic Forms in the exercise of their rule, and what does this mean? For the Neoplatonists, we have seen (Ch. 8, 3), these questions cannot but have become more difficult. Plotinus, for example, speaks in *Enn.* VI 9, 7 of the legendary legislator Minos making laws in the image of his communion with Zeus, i.e. the One. But if the One is beyond knowledge and determinate being, how can it be the paradigm of laws made in its image?

The leading speaker of the anonymous dialogue, Menodorus, shows awareness of the problem and addresses himself directly to the question of how, if God is unknown, he may function as an archetype for kingly science (pp. 16, 13–17, 8). Menodorus distinguishes what may be discovered *scientifically* by reason and what is found by mere correct *opinion* guided by divine creation (p. 17, 21–4). This scale of knowledge reappears later in the fragments, where an ascent of the intellect is described, going from opinion and reasoning (διάνοια) using hypotheses, up to science, a vision of the light, of truth stamped in the resemblance of the Form of the Good (pp. 35, 16–36, 4). This is the world of Plato's *Republic*, the ascent of the future

---

[73] Above, Ch. 7, 1.

philosopher-king from the cave to the light of the sun, from hypotheses to the Form of the Good. In an interior dialogue (pp. 36, 6–37, 2), the ascended intellect of our anonymous text affirms the first cause of all beings, a cause beyond (ἐπέκεινα) all things. This cause does not go out of itself, but contains within itself the λόγοι of all things. It is like the centre of a circle from which progress radii, that is to say, an intelligible sun and intelligible world, a rank of intellectual beings, the visible sun and world, all ordered, down to the elements, in a hierarchy of rule which includes humans, themselves ordered in a monarchic structure. Intellect thus discovers a Neoplatonic metaphysical structure, dominated by a supra-intelligible hidden first cause from which derives an elaborate gradation of intelligible, intellectual, and visible being. But what does the metaphysical knowledge thus attained signify for political philosophy?

Three political principles may be inferred, it seems, from this metaphysical knowledge: (a) political order is monarchic in structure (cf. p. 37, 3–8); (b) the monarch, the political 'first cause', is transcendent; and (c) power is exercised through a system of mediating ranks. The first two principles are subject to some restrictions, to be considered in the next section. As for the third principle, we can find its application in the dialogue's insistence that the king choose and deal *only* with the highest officers of the state administration and of the Church (pp. 26, 23–27, 6; 28, 6–13). If the king rules correctly as regards the highest rank subordinate to him, then this rank will function correspondingly as regards the rank subordinate to it, and so on. The same principle, the later Neoplatonic law of mean terms, inspires the hierarchical system of the Pseudo-Dionysius (above, s. 1, ii).

Returning to the anonymous dialogue, the question of how rulership is an imitation of God is raised again a little later in the fragments (p. 38, 13 ff.). Here, various divine attributes are picked out (goodness, wisdom, power, justice), attributes which are one in God, but which can only be conceived by us as distinct, and still less adequately expressed.[74] Regarding *goodness*, this means that the ruler, as imitator of God, must be good in terms of his moral integrity, a veritable paradigm of virtue for his subjects, and in terms of providential care for his subjects, ruling for *their* good and not his own.[75] As for divine *wisdom*, this means, for the ruler, respecting the third principle (c), that of mediated rule, for it is a wisdom manifest in God's creation. Thus the ruler will deal only with his immediate subordinates and they, in turn, will

---

[74] Cf. Elias, *In Is.*, pp. 16, 19–17, 21; David, *Prol.*, pp. 35, 20–36, 34.

[75] pp. 38, 19–39, 8; cf. p. 25, 10–11 (the reference to Plato seems to concern *Rep.* 342e).

transmit his providential rule, creating thereby a harmonious political structure (p. 39, 8–22). As regards divine *power*, this means, for the ruler, moral excellence and other practical qualities such as courage, practical sense, daring, benevolence (pp. 39, 22–40, 2). Finally, divine *justice* involves for the ruler both internal justice of the soul, such as that described by Plato in the *Republic*, and an external justice which assigns to each rank its due (p. 40, 2–7). This we might describe as a fourth principle (d), 'to each its due', i.e. the principle of geometrical proportion that underlies Plato's ideal city and that is also exemplified in the metaphysical structure of reality.[76]

Summarizing, we can say that the anonymous dialogue, in providing an answer to the question as to how political knowledge may be modelled on a transcendent paradigm, refers to a scientific knowledge of intelligible principles and to the lower level of correct opinion concerning visible creation.[77] This corresponds to the later Neoplatonists' answer to the same question, when they refer to the different levels of metaphysical, mathematical, and cosmic order as divine paradigms for political imitation (above, Ch. 8, 3). On both of the levels distinguished in the anonymous dialogue, that of scientific knowledge and that of correct opinion, the paradigm is the structure of reality deriving from a supra-intelligible first cause: the complete metaphysical structure in the case of scientific knowledge, the cosmic structure in the case of correct opinion. This structure manifests the first cause and, in its organizational principles (monarchic order, transcendence of the first cause, mediated transmission, ranked distribution), provides the principles of kingly science. It is in this way that kingly science imitates the divine.

If the idea that the king imitates the cosmic order in his rule is found already in Stoicism and in the Pseudo-Pythagorean treatises on kingship, for example,[78] this idea is extended in the anonymous dialogue to include the various levels of a metaphysical structure of Neoplatonic inspiration, levels also distinguished by the later Neoplatonists as paradigms of political rule.

(v) Law

The application of principles (a) and (b) is subject to restrictions in the anonymous dialogue in the sense that the access of the monarch to rule and the exercise of this rule are subject to *law*. The author of the dialogue is of

[76] Above, Ch. 8, 5.   [77] See Plato, *Statesman* 301a10–b2.
[78] Above, Ch. 8, 3.

the opinion that the source of political evils, of the disease of the state, is the absence of the requisite political knowledge among rulers who seek rule, not in the interest of others, but in their own interest, reaching it by illegitimate means, by the use of force, money, flattery.[79] A method has to be found, therefore, whereby Plato's dream of the union of philosophy and kingship may be realized (cf. pp. 52, 23–53, 4), that is, a method allowing for the lawful selection of rulers among those best equipped, morally and intellectually, for a rule which they do not, of themselves, desire. The method proposed by the dialogue involves a complicated legislation regulating the identification of the best possible candidates for kingship, nomination of them by the heads of all groups of the state, and a divine sanction through a religiously conducted drawing of lots.[80] The legitimacy of the ruler depends therefore on his intrinsic moral and intellectual qualities, on his designation by the subjects in whose interest he is to rule, and on the divine sanction to which he is subordinate in the cosmic order. The ruler is furthermore expected to preserve the law (p. 38, 23), as stipulated in the fifth fundamental provision (p. 20, 8–10). Another legal restriction on monarchic absolutism mentioned in the fragments concerns the age of retirement of the monarch (p. 44, 1 ff.).

This stress on law as governing the election and conduct of rulers reminds us more of the level of reform sought in Plato's *Laws* than that described in Plato's *Republic*, as these dialogues were interpreted as representing different levels of reform by the later Neoplatonists (above, Ch. 8, 2). A further indication in this direction is Photius' report that the anonymous dialogue proposed a *mixed* constitution, including monarchic, aristocratic, and democratic elements. In the fragments we find elements corresponding to this: the monarch is chosen by divine sanction from candidates proposed by representatives of all orders of society and thus entrusted with the common good; he rules in conjunction with an important senatorial body. The second-best city of the *Laws* also involves a mixed constitution, as compared with the absolute monarchy/aristocracy of the *Republic*.[81] The second-best city of the *Laws* is developed in abstraction from the particular circumstances that might concern the founding of a specific state (745e–746c). The anonymous dialogue also claims to be abstract

---

[79] pp. 54, 17–55, 8; 24, 24–25, 4 (referring to tyranny).

[80] pp. 19, 27–21, 10; cf. 25, 20–26, 7. For drawing by lot, see above p. 119 n. 11; Morrow (1960: 161, 181).

[81] See above, Ch. 8, 5 on mixed constitutions in Pseudo-Pythagorean texts read by Neoplatonists.

in this sense: it does not discuss the particulars of a specific state (p. 27, 18–21).

If the anonymous dialogue describes a project comparable to the second-best city of Plato's *Laws*, then the criticism in the dialogue of Plato's 'communism', the abolition in the *Republic* of private family life among the elite (p. 22, 22–5), should be read, not as an attack on Plato himself, but as a rejection of this hallmark of the highest, divine, and indeed impossible city for humans in which all is held in common, a hallmark also rejected in the city of the *Laws*. I do not therefore think that we should conclude that the author of the dialogue, in rejecting this feature of the *Republic*, despite an obvious Neoplatonic inspiration, was not a Neoplatonist.[82] Nor should we be too influenced by the negative tone of Photius' report on the dialogue's criticism of Plato: Photius was no friend of Plato's *Republic*,[83] and the list of contents of Book V preserved in the fragments suggests a more restricted critique.[84] A further argument against the author of the anonymous dialogue being a Neoplatonist has been found in the dialogue's rejection of divination.[85] But here also the point at issue is much too limited to yield such a conclusion. The dialogue rejects divination as a basis for political decisions, which should derive rather from political knowledge (cf. p. 41, 24–6). This does not in principle preclude the use of divination in other contexts.

(vi) Concluding Remarks: the Anonymous Dialogue and the Pseudo-Dionysius

The anonymous dialogue *On Political Science* can thus be related closely to Neoplatonic political philosophy, as regards its conception of the structure and functions of the parts of philosophy; the place of political philosophy in this structure; its nature as an imitation of the divine; the divine as expressed in a metaphysical order. Although he leaves aside the particulars of a specific state, like Plato in the *Laws*, the author of the dialogue is very much aware of the political problems of the time, of which his philosophical predecessors, Plato, Aristotle, and Cicero, were ignorant, problems posed by factions in Constantinople, by large numbers of unemployed,

---

[82] As claimed by Praechter (1900: 629).

[83] See Photius, *Ep.* 187, 168–71.

[84] p. 15, 17 mentions 'objections to some things said in Plato', referring perhaps to the rejection of communal life in p. 22, 22–5, also possibly the passage to which Photius is alluding.

[85] Praechter (1900: 629).

unoccupied people and of unworthy monks.[86] It is in part with an eye to these problems, but mostly in relation to the fundamental question of the appropriate selection, lawful election, and proclamation of the monarch, that the author of the dialogue proposes a new constitutional order. This proposal for reform describes, not a divine utopia such as that of Plato's *Republic*, but a less ambitious model such as that of the *Laws*, in which law is paramount and specifies a mixed constitution. If this general approach is not new, the particular dispositions proposed do seem to constitute a new framework for reconciling a number of claims: that of the importance of political science and of the sovereignty of law expressing this science; that of the moral and intellectual superiority required of the ruler who will conform to this science and law; that of the citizens in whose interest rule is to be exercised; and that of the divine to which human political order is subordinate.

Was the author of the anonymous dialogue a Christian? One reference to man as image of God (p. 37, 5–6) might possibly suggest Christianity, but it is an isolated and rather weak indication.[87] The situation reminds one of Boethius, whose Christianity is not exactly evident in the *Consolation of Philosophy*. Boethius, a contemporary of or earlier than the author of our dialogue, was his peer in the court of the Gothic king Theoderic. Like our anonymous, Boethius was trained in Neoplatonic philosophy, at home both in Greek and Latin culture, fascinated by Plato's call for the union of philosophy and politics, while finding himself at the higher levels of an imperial administration.[88] The author of the anonymous dialogue may well have been Christian. But it is intriguing that one of the interlocutors in the dialogue, Thaumasius, may commemorate a pagan purged from Justinian's court in 529.

Sharing a common philosophical background in later Neoplatonism, the anonymous author of the dialogue *On Political Science* reminds us, not only of Boethius, but also very much of the Pseudo-Dionysius.[89] The Pseudo-Dionysius appears to be earlier, perhaps several generations earlier if the later dating of the anonymous dialogue is correct. Dionysius is concerned exclusively, it seems, with spiritual salvation, whereas the anonymous dialogue responds to specific political problems. Furthermore, Dionysius, in his ecclesiological transposition of Neoplatonic political philosophy, describes a

---

[86]   pp. 28, 15–20; 29, 4 and 9–12; 33, 7–26.
[87]   As Praechter suggested (1900: 631). See above p. 78 n. 19.
[88]   Above, Ch. 7, 1.
[89]   See Praechter (1900).

reform of the ambition of Plato's *Republic*, whereas the anonymous dialogue appears to propose a reform of lesser ambition comparable to that of the *Laws*. Notwithstanding these differences, it is tempting to compare the two projects. In the Pseudo-Dionysius, the divinization of humanity is achieved through celestial and ecclesiastical hierarchies. Curiously, no divinizing function is left to the political order, to the State, and it may be the case, as suggested above (sec. 1, v), that Dionysius would have considered the political order as subordinate to the Church. In the anonymous dialogue, however, the divinization of humans is achieved on the level of incorporated life in the political order, as it is in later Neoplatonic philosophy. The Church is integrated in constitutional legislation and in the political order (as religion is in Plato's *Laws*) and is part of the monarch's responsibility (pp. 27, 31–28, 13). It would thus seem that the author of the anonymous dialogue has a different view of the relation between Church and State than that implicit in the Pseudo-Dionysius, a view closer to the point of view of a later Neoplatonist.

Platonopolis in Islam: 14
Al-Farabi's Perfect State

Together with the examples explored in Chapters 12 and 13 of the presence
of Neoplatonic political ideas in the work of some influential thinkers in
the Latin West and in the Greek and Byzantine world, I propose taking in
this chapter a final example which derives from the Islamic East. The example is provided by al-Farabi in his book *Principles of the Views of the Citizens of
the Best State*,[1] a book which he wrote towards the end of his life, beginning
its composition according to some sources at the end of his period in
Baghdad (941) and finishing it in Aleppo in 942/3.[2]

   This example, of course, is not in any way intended to stand in general
for medieval Islamic political philosophy. Nor do I attempt to reach a view
of al-Farabi's political philosophy as a whole, an attempt which would
involve a full discussion of his other works and their relation to the *Best
State*.[3] However, the example chosen is not without significance. Al-Farabi
is commonly described as the 'founder' of political philosophy in Islam and
his *Best State* was an important and influential work.[4] In this chapter I
would like to show that the *Best State* expresses, in an Islamic context,
Neoplatonic views of the ideal state as reconstructed in the first two parts of
this book.

---

[1] To which I will refer as '*Best State*'. I am very much indebted to the translation (which I cite)
and excellent commentary by Walzer which accompany his edition of the Arabic text, published
posthumously. His commentary will be referred to as 'W.'.
   [2] On the date of the *Best State*, cf. Galston (1990: 3 n. 1); on al-Farabi's biography cf. W. 2–5.
   [3] For an interesting and sensitive discussion of difficulties in reconciling views al-Farabi
expresses in his various works, difficulties whose discovery seems however sometimes somewhat
programmatic, cf. Galston (1990). I will come back to some of these difficulties below, n. 40. If not
attempting to reach a complete view of al-Farabi's political philosophy, I will refer sometimes to
works of his other than the *Best State* (cited without his name and by an abbreviated title, e.g.
Aphorisms = al-Farabi, *Aphorisms of the Statesman*) when they confirm or elaborate ideas expressed
in the *Best State*.
   [4] See W. 19–22; Butterworth (1992: *passim*).

The Arab conquests of the eastern parts of the Roman Empire in the 630s and 640s not only concerned the cities in Egypt and Syria where Neoplatonists had managed to survive despite measures taken against them such as those of Justinian. It also meant a certain protection, integration and expansion of their teaching within Islamic culture. Syriac Christians collaborated with Muslims in an impressive programme to translate Greek texts into Arabic, directly or through Syriac or Persian versions, a programme which was largely carried out in Baghdad (founded in 762) between the eight and tenth centuries and which included a considerable part of Greek philosophical literature.[5] We can observe in particular that the curriculum typical of later Greek Neoplatonic schools such as that of Alexandria was known in Baghdad, as was its rationale: the definitions of philosophy given by Ammonius and his pupils, the hierarchy of the virtues and of the sciences, the combination of works of Aristotle and Plato as representing these sciences and as expressing a world-view of Neoplatonic inspiration.[6] Arabic translations and summaries of works of Plato and Aristotle were read together with Neoplatonic texts such as the *Theology of Aristotle* (a version of Plotinus, *Enneads* IV–VI), the *Liber de causis* (a version of parts of Proclus' *Elements of Theology*)—both works produced it seems for al-Kindi in Baghdad in the ninth century[7]—and other Neoplatonic texts, by Porphyry, Simplicius, Philoponus, and others, some of which indeed have survived only in Arabic translation.[8]

If a strong continuity can thus be observed between the practice of the later Greek Neoplatonic schools of the fifth, sixth, and early seventh centuries and the development of philosophy in Baghdad in the ninth and tenth centuries, there is one important respect in which early Islamic philosophy, it is commonly thought, *departs* from later Greek Neoplatonism: its interest in political philosophy. Al-Farabi had a deep knowledge of Plato's *Republic* and produced a summary of the *Laws*.[9] He also wrote much on political philosophy, as did his school and later Islamic philosophers, in particular Averroes who commented on the *Republic*.[10]

---

[5] See Gutas (1998).   [6] See Hein (1985), a detailed and very useful study.

[7] See Endress (1987: 428) (with references to further literature).

[8] See Nicolaus' treatise on ethics (above, Ch. 4, 2), the Arabic commentaries on the *Golden Verses* attributed to Iamblichus and Proclus, and below n. 40, to name only those texts I use in this book.

[9] On ninth-century Arabic versions of the *Republic* and *Laws*, cf. W. 426. On the *Statesman*, see below, n. 39.

[10] *Faute de mieux*: Averroes would have preferred to use Aristotle's *Politics*, but no Arabic translation seems to have been made of the *Politics*; cf. Brague (1993).

Although specific conditions and reasons contributed no doubt to this emphasis on political philosophy in the Islamic world, the reconstruction of Neoplatonic political philosophy that I propose in this book suggests that there is greater continuity in this field between later Greek Neoplatonism and early Islamic philosophy than has hitherto been supposed, a supposition influenced by the conventional view that Greek Neoplatonists had no interest in political philosophy.

Al-Farabi's *Best State* provides, I will argue, an illustration of this continuity. In all likelihood al-Farabi is inspired by Greek sources. Yet if we assume that Neoplatonists did not share in the political interests of Plato and Aristotle, if we suppose that philosophers such as Plotinus and Proclus disliked 'political Platonism', then we are obliged to conclude that al-Farabi's Greek source, if dating to the period of Late Antiquity, does not belong to the mainstream of late antique Neoplatonism.[11] However, these assumptions, it should be clear, are unsound and it will be seen in what follows that the political ideas of al-Farabi come very near to what has been found in later Greek Neoplatonism in the first two parts of this book.

1. The Metaphysical Background

Al-Farabi's *Best State* begins with an elaborate explanation of the structure of reality going from the first principle (God), through various levels of being emanating from the first principle, down to the elements of the physical world and to human nature (chs. 1–14). In a rigorous argument reminiscent of Proclus' *Elements of Theology*, al-Farabi first demonstrates (ch. 1) that the first cause of things must be absolutely perfect, deficient in no respect, posterior to nothing, immaterial, indivisible, unique, an intellect in act that thinks itself (1, 6). All else emanates from this first principle in a sequence of immaterial and material levels. This emanation reflects the nature of the first principle in various ways, of which the following four deserve emphasis (2, 2):

(i) The emanation of things from the first principle is a function of the *generosity* of the first principle: generosity is its substance, a perfection which is the reason for the emanation of things from it;[12]

---

[11] This is W.'s conjecture (8, 10, 12–13): he refers to an explanation of Plato's *Republic* of the period of the Roman Empire (sixth century?); see below, sec. 5 for W.'s specific arguments.

[12] 1, 1. W. 359–60 refers to the corresponding texts in Plato's *Timaeus* (29e) and in Proclus. This generosity is the Good's self-diffusiveness in Neoplatonism; see above, Ch. 7, 1.

(ii) What emanates from the first principle is arranged in *hierarchical* order,[13] as is stressed in the following passage:

But the substance of the First is also such that all the existents, when they emanate from it, are arranged in an order of rank, and that every existent gets its allotted share and rank of existence from it. It starts with the most perfect existent and is followed by something a little less perfect than it. Afterwards it is followed successively by more and more deficient existents until the final stage of being is reached.

The text does not make explicit what it is in the substance of the first principle that entails that its production be arranged in a hierarchy, but one may suppose that such is the perfection of the First that its expression in (necessarily) imperfect being requires a range of degrees of imperfect being.

(iii) The hierarchical order, as the passage quoted above indicates, is also an expression of *justice*:

Inasmuch as all the existents receive their order of rank from it, and each existent receives from the First its allotted share of existence in accordance with its rank, the First is just, and its justice is in its substance.

This is, as has been pointed out,[14] the Platonic principle of geometrical equality (or proportion): to each its appropriate rank or function.[15] It applies for al-Farabi throughout the metaphysical, physical, and political realms. There is even a 'natural justice' observed in the transformation of the four basic elements into each other: each constituent has its 'rights' and receives in turn its just due in an elaborate process of compensatory chemical transformation.[16]

(iv) Finally, the emanated things are *connected* to each other to form wholes (2, 3). The example given is that of the love (or friendship) that brings humans together.[17] This connectedness or community of emanated things is also rooted in the perfection (unity) of the first principle.

Al-Farabi then presents in descending order the various ranks of emanated immaterial beings, ten angels which are intellects and to which correspond celestial bodies (ch. 3), the tenth being the Agent Intellect

---

[13] W. 8–9 emphasizes the importance of hierarchical order.

[14] W. 358–9.

[15] See above, Ch. 8, 5. Al-Farabi summarizes the passage on geometrical proportion in Plato's *Laws* (757a–b) in his *Compendium Legum Platonis*, p. 24.

[16] See 6, 1–2; 9, 1–2 and 6–7; 15, 6.

[17] Cf. the important passage in *Aphorisms*, 57 (a text which must go back to a Greek account of political φιλία).

which is the transcendent efficient cause of human thought.[18] The material sublunary world is then described, first natural beings (the elements, minerals, plants, animals: chs. 4–9) and then 'voluntary' being, i.e. man (chs. 10–14).

Man is represented as constituted by a hierarchy of faculties of the soul, each faculty subordinate to and at the service of higher faculties,[19] the ruler of all in man being the rational faculty (10, 1–5 and 9). This natural order in human nature means that the finality of this nature is the finality of its ruling part, reason. Within reason, practical reason's finality is subordinate to that of the higher aspect of reason, theoretical reason (cf. 13, 7). The finality of theoretical reason is described as follows:

Felicity means that the human soul reaches a degree of perfection in (its) existence where it is in no need of matter for its support, since it becomes one of the incorporeal things and of the immaterial substances and remains in that state continuously for ever. But its rank is beneath the rank of the Active (Agent) Intellect. (13, 5)

Man's goal is thus the life of pure intellect (as it was for the Greek Neoplatonists),[20] a life which comes as near as possible to that enjoyed by a transcendent immaterial intellect.[21] In this sense the human goal can be described as 'assimilation to the divine', a concept transmitted by the later Neoplatonic commentaries to philosophers in Islam and very familiar to them.[22]

2. The Best State as a Means for Reaching the Human Goal

Human finality is achieved through the practice of virtuous actions (13, 6) which take place in a social framework. Thus political organization is required, not only for human survival and self-preservation, but also as a

---

[18] Cf. 13, 2. The 'Agent Intellect' is the efficient cause of intellection mentioned rather enigmatically in Aristotle's *De anima* (III, 5) and which in Late Antiquity was taken by some commentators as being a transcendent divine intellect.

[19] The lower faculties of the soul are each composed of three functions constituting a tripartite system of government (ruling/auxiliary/subordinate): the political image is omnipresent in chs. 11–12.

[20] Above, Ch. 4, 1.

[21] Cf. also *Aphorisms* 76 (*in fine*); *Philosophy of Aristotle* 93, 98: man's finality is the perfection of theoretical intellect, coming close to the Agent Intellect which is man's example. Compare Hierocles as cited above, Ch. 3 n. 30.

[22] See Altmann and Stern (1958: 16 n., 29, 197); Hein (1985: 116–17); Druart (1993: 336–7).

means for reaching the highest perfection (15, 1). Political order may serve then as a method of moral edification,[23] a structure for progress in virtue leading to felicity (16, 2) both as regards what is shared in common by citizens and as regards what is specific to each group, a felicity in an immaterial afterlife which is also both collective (16, 3–4) and differentiated in being attained to different degrees (16, 5). Human felicity manifests therefore the three metaphysical principles (mentioned above) of connectedness or community (iv), justice (iii) and hierarchy (ii), which also apply to the political context of virtuous actions through which felicity is sought.[24] To reach the highest virtue and the highest felicity, the best political structure as the means to this is required.[25] Al-Farabi therefore distinguishes between societies which seek minimal goals (survival, self-preservation) and those excellent societies which are organized so as to lead to felicity in the afterlife.[26]

In speaking of excellent or perfect societies, al-Farabi distinguishes between complete and incomplete societies. Incomplete societies are social groupings such as households and villages which are mere parts of a complete political whole which may be a city-state (*medina*: *polis*), a nation, or a universal state.[27] Among complete states, what distinguishes perfect from evil states is their finality: the finality which defines perfect states is the goal of felicity as this is described by al-Farabi, whereas imperfect, evil states are based on other goals, such as money, pleasure, or power.[28]

The perfect or best state is further characterized by its hierarchical structure. It is compared to an organism in which different parts and organs perform their appropriate functions in a system of coordination subordinated to a ruling part (15, 4). In the best state the different functions are performed voluntarily by citizens in relation to their appropriate capacities. Thus Plato's principle of geometrical equality obtains.[29]

---

[23] See also *Attainment* 38 on the edificatory role of the ruler (in teaching and in action).

[24] On the collective aspect see also *Aphorisms* 22 (on the good of the parts being reached through the good of the whole); Iamblichus and Proclus as discussed above, Ch. 8, 1.

[25] See *Aphorisms* 84.

[26] *Aphorisms* 25 and 84. Reports in later authors suggest that al-Farabi, in his (lost) commentary on the *Nicomachean Ethics*, denied individual immortality (cf. Galston 1990: 59–60; Endress 1992: 41–2, with further references) and thus felicity in an afterlife. Al-Farabi may have thought that only a few attain a sufficient level of immaterial intellective being; he also allowed for a variety of degrees in felicity in a scale leading up to the highest degree.

[27] *Best State* 15, 2; see also *Regime*, p. 32.

[28] *Best State* 18–19; 15, 15–19. W. 484 refers to Plato's *Laws* (625e ff.), *Gorgias* and *Rep.* Cf. *Best State* 18, 2–5 where the notion of war as a political goal is connected to the view of nature as a war of all against all, where might is right. See also *Regime*, pp. 42–53.

[29] As pointed out by W. 434. See also *Aphorisms* 58, 61.

In his *Aphorisms of the Statesman* (53), al-Farabi provides the following list of the ranks making up the state:

The wise
Priests, orators, poets[30]
Mathematicians
Soldiers
Wealth-producers.

The top three ranks might be compared with the group of guardians in Plato's *Republic*, which would give us then the tripartite structure (guardians, auxiliaries, producers) of Plato's ideal city.[31]

In the *Best State* al-Farabi stresses the hierarchical, monarchical structure of the state[32] as found already in the metaphysical structure of reality,[33] of which the best state is an imitation. In this state the citizens imitate in their various ranks their ruler, just as the ranks of reality imitate at their appropriate level the first principle (15, 6). This monarchical structure does not entail, however, that there be only one ruler *in number* in the state: there may be several kings in a best state, if they remain one as if a single soul.[34] One might wonder, in the light of Plato's *Republic* (above, Ch. 7, 3), if the group of rulers might include women. If al-Farabi does not discuss this possibility in the *Best State*, it does not seem ruled out in principle, given his claim for equal cognitive capacities in men and women: 'But in the case of the faculty of sense, the faculty of representation, and the faculty of reason male and female do not differ' (12, 8).

3. The Ruler(s) of the Best State

The ruler of the best state must be the best of its citizens (15, 5), endowed to the highest degree with natural, moral, and intellectual qualities,[35] an object of imitation for other citizens, a perfect philosopher who has become intellect in act (15, 8). As such the ruler has reached a high degree of human

[30] This group is described in the *Attainment* 42–8 as assisting the ruler in the task of political persuasion (as distinct from the use of coercion).
[31] For this comparison see W. 436–8.
[32] Vertical transmission downwards through the ranks is indicated in *Regime*, p. 39. Cf. Galston (1990: 129), and above, Ch. 13, 1 (ii).
[33] 15, 6, and in the structure of the world (*Attainment* 20).
[34] 16, 1; cf. *Regime*, p. 37; above, Ch. 8, 5.
[35] 15, 11–12; W. 445–6 notes how al-Farabi follows Plato's *Rep.* here.

happiness or felicity, a proximity to the life of the transcendent Agent Intellect which we can compare to the 'assimilation to the divine' sought by the Neoplatonic philosopher. Becoming divine-like means, for the later Neoplatonist, imitating the divine, not only by leading a life of theoretical wisdom, but also by exercising a providential (i.e. political) role, since the divine not only enjoys perfect intellection, but also confers benefit (providence) on what is lower.[36] The same interpretation of divine assimilation as both theoretical and providential is found in early Islamic philosophy[37] and can be found in al-Farabi's perfect ruler, who possesses not only perfect theoretical wisdom, but also the capacity to use this wisdom for the benefit of others.[38]

We should distinguish at this point between the perfect ruler's capacity for providential, political rule and the actual use of this capacity. Following Plato's *Statesman* very closely, al-Farabi describes the ruler as king, whether or not this rule is exercised, since it is the kingly science (and not its application) that makes the king a king.[39] This claim allows us to conclude that the personal happiness (or felicity) of the perfect ruler will include both theoretical and practical wisdom, whether or not this practical wisdom finds occasion for political application.[40] In corrupt societies, where the philosopher cannot act, withdrawal in the form of emigration is suggested.[41]

---

[36] Above, Ch. 7, 1.

[37] Cf. Altmann and Stern (1958: 16): 'philosophy is likeness to God. . .according to man's capacity, through the knowledge of truth and the doing of good' (Ibn at-Tayyib); for al-Kindi cf. Druart (1993: 337, 344). Berman (1961) restricts imitation of the divine to political action. However, this restriction applies neither to the later Greek Neoplatonists, nor to the Islamic philosophers just cited, nor to al-Farabi.

[38] See *Attainment* 54; Galston (1990: 82–3).

[39] *Aphorisms* 29, using Plato, *Statesman* 259b. See also *Attainment* 54, 57, 62.

[40] This may resolve difficulties Galston (1990: 59–68) finds in al-Farabi's theory of happiness. She finds passages in al-Farabi where an 'exclusive' concept of happiness (i.e. happiness as theoretical) is put forward, whereas other passages suggest rather a 'comprehensive' view (i.e. happiness as including both theoretical and practical components; the categories 'exclusive'/'comprehensive' are derived from modern discussions of Aristotle's views on happiness in the final chapters of the *Nicomachean Ethics*). A solution to this difficulty may run as follows. The happiness of the philosopher will include both theoretical (*primary*) and practical (*secondary*) wisdom, even if the latter finds no appropriate occasion for expression. Thus the philosopher's happiness is not dependent on actual rule, but includes (secondarily) the capacity to rule. See above, Ch. 7, 2 and the Greek text on the *Virtues of the Soul* in Arabic translation in Miskawayh (Pines 1986: 13–16; see above, Ch. 7, 1 n. 20): having reached, in a hierarchy of virtues, the highest degree, man acts corresponding to the act of the first principle; the first principle's providential action does not have an external finality, but is an act secondary to the divine self-act; helping others in imitating the divine means then, for man, an action secondary to the primary intellective act (see above, Ch. 7, 1).

[41] *Aphorisms* 88; cf. *Philosophy of Plato* 30. For this theme in later Neoplatonism, see above, Ch. 8, 2, and, for its elaboration in Ibn Bajjah's advocacy of the solitary life for the philosopher, see Harvey (1992).

Let us look in more detail at the theoretical and practical wisdom possessed by the perfect philosopher-king. The theoretical aspect involves metaphysical knowledge such as that summarized above in section 1, a wisdom which includes knowledge of the goal of human nature. Becoming intellect in act through the agency of the transcendent Agent Intellect, the perfect ruler receives knowledge transmitted or inspired by the Agent Intellect (15, 8). As receptive of this transcendent knowledge, the philosopher-king is also described as prophet, Imam, lawgiver.[42] This means that the philosopher-king also possesses practical wisdom (15, 10), a wisdom which concerns the means whereby the human goal may be reached,[43] a wisdom which involves legislative ability, the capacity to formulate laws instrumental in reaching felicity. Laws thus form part of practical wisdom, which takes account of material accidents, of time and of place, in relation to the immaterial goal (felicity), to the realization of which it contributes.[44]

Such a perfect ruler is obviously rare.[45] However, one such ruler had existed for al-Farabi, the prophet and lawgiver of Islam, Muhammad.[46] But there may also be rulers of the second rank, rulers who follow the laws and customs laid down by earlier rulers and are able to deduce new laws from principles given by the first Imams (15, 13). Yet lower approximations to the perfect ruler are also considered, in which the various qualities of rulership are represented by a body of rulers.[47] We are reminded in this scale of more or less perfect rulers of the contrast between the perfect philosopher-kings of Plato's *Republic* and the constitutional arrangement of the second-best city of the *Laws*.

[42] Cf also *Attainment* 54, 57–9. W. 441–2 discusses the identity of the Imam and suggests that al-Farabi is alluding to Muhammad as prophet and lawgiver who transmitted his knowledge and legislation in the Koran. With Muhammad as philosopher-king we can compare the Jewish and Christian Moses as philosopher-king (above, Ch. 13, 1 (iii)) and the Greek Neoplatonist's Minos as philosopher-king (above, Ch. 7, 1).

[43] See *Aphorisms* 49 and 89; *Enumeration*, pp. 24–5.

[44] See *Attainment* 56. See above, Ch. 11, 1–2.

[45] *Best State* 15, 13 (cf. W. 447, who refers to Plato, *Rep.* 491a).

[46] See W. 447.

[47] See *Regime*, p. 37 and *Aphorisms* 54 (with Dunlop's commentary, 86–8), where a more developed scheme is given. The idea of a distribution of rulership qualities among a body of citizens is of Aristotelian inspiration and is used by Proclus (above, Ch. 11, at n. 26).

4. Religion in the Best State

All of the preceding, as set out in the *Best State*, represents truths that should be known by the citizens of the perfect state (17, 1). However these truths are known in different ways (17, 2). The philosopher-rulers and their close followers, the leading group of the state, know these truths as such, whereas the other, lower groups of society know the same truths in the form of symbolic representations which vary, depending on national differences and differences in intellectual capacity. These symbolic representations of metaphysical truths correspond to religion. As false metaphysical views find expression in false religious views,[48] so correct religious views express true metaphysics and are consequently rejected by adherents of false views of the world (18, 12). Religion is thus an image, an imaginative representation of philosophical truths, which may be used by the rulers of the state as a means of political persuasion in relation to citizens incapable of understanding fully these truths.[49]

The political use made of religion by al-Farabi in his perfect state is very similar to the political function given to religion by Plato in the *Laws*, a function which reappears in later Neoplatonism, for example in the work of Julian the Emperor (above, Ch. 10). Religious myths such as those found in Plato's *Gorgias*, *Symposium*, and *Protagoras* are indeed considered by Proclus as symbolic representations of metaphysical truths, a lower level of communication of these truths which are known at a higher level and more directly by 'dialectical' science, i.e. by the highest philosophical science.[50] The political importance of such religious myths as symbolic representations of reality appropriate for the moral edification of citizens of a lesser, even 'infantile', intellectual capacity is made clear by Julian (above, Ch. 10, 3). As there are politically corrupting myths for Plato, which must be corrected so as to express true philosophical views, so, in al-Farabi, are there false religious views expressing false metaphysics and correct religious views symbolizing the philosophical truths on which the perfect state, as the means to human felicity, is founded.

---

[48] 19, 7.

[49] *Attainment* 55; cf. *Regime*, pp. 40–1.

[50] Proclus, *Plat. Theol.* I, 4, pp. 18, 25–19, 5; 20, 6–25; 21, 3–22, 7; cf. *In Remp.* I, pp. 84, 21–5; 85, 12–15 on the educational function of myths. See O'Meara (2002b) for a more detailed comparison with al-Farabi.

5. Conclusion

Al-Farabi's project of a perfect state obviously has a bearing on the Islamic world of his time, on questions concerning the Imam, the Prophet, and the interpretation and political expression of the Prophet's legacy. Al-Farabi's metaphysical views also reflect the development of Islamic philosophy, in particular an Aristotelianizing of the Neoplatonic scheme of the emanation of reality in which the first principle is identified as a divine Intellect which thinks itself, whereas in Greek Neoplatonism the transcendence of the first principle, as beyond all forms of intellection, is very much stressed. Nevertheless, in all major respects, al-Farabi's political project corresponds to later Greek Neoplatonic political philosophy as reconstructed in this book and as exemplified by the anonymous dialogue *On Political Science* and by Pseudo-Dionysius' Christian ecclesiological transposition (above, Ch. 13). The main points of convergence may be summarized as follows:

(i) Political structure (at its best) reflects on the human level the structural principles of reality, metaphysical and physical, of which it is an imitation. The metaphysical principles of generosity (the self-diffusiveness of the Good), hierarchy, justice (geometrical equality), and community operate throughout, in al-Farabi as in Greek Neoplatonism. Al-Farabi's *Best State* formulates with particular clarity what Proclus and other Greek Neoplatonists had held (above, Ch. 8, 3), that the metaphysical and physical worlds, in their organization, are paradigms of the best political order.

(ii) Political order should function as a means for reaching a transcendent goal, a life of intellect which represents the highest degree of human felicity, which approximates to divine life and thus constitutes an 'assimilation to the divine'. This goal is reached through a virtuous life lived in a political order which allows and promotes virtuous action. Al-Farabi's emphasis on the importance of this function of the political order and on the scale of degrees through which ever higher levels of approximation to felicity are reached reminds us more of the gradualistic approach of Iamblichus and of other later Greek Neoplatonists than of Plotinus, who gives less emphasis than they do to political life as a stage in human perfection (above, Ch. 4, 1–3).

(iii) Al-Farabi's philosopher-king is inspired, as are the Greek Neoplatonist philosopher-kings (above, Ch. 8, 1), by a transcendent intellect, an inspiration expressing itself in legislation. This inspiration is received by philosophers who have reached the highest level of knowledge, who live the degree of felicity which this represents, and who are moved to political action, circumstances allowing, in imitation of the providential action of the divine. Al-Farabi also distinguishes between different levels of perfection among rulers, from the (rare) perfect ruler to lower ranks of rulers subordinate to transmitted laws and sharing collectively rulership qualities. With this we can compare Neoplatonic interpretations of the cities of Plato's *Republic* and *Laws*.

(iv) Finally, the political function given to religious views by al-Farabi again reminds us, not only of Plato, but also of later Greek Neoplatonic interpretations of the nature and political function of religious myths.

Other, more detailed comparisons have been noted in the preceding pages. But perhaps the points just summarized suffice to support the claim that al-Farabi's *Best State* is an admirably clear exposition of later Greek Neoplatonic political philosophy, adapted to the Islamic world. Yet it has been thought that, if al-Farabi is following a late antique Greek source, this source does not belong to the mainstream of later Greek Neoplatonism. The principal reasons given for this are the following:[51] al-Farabi (a) presents no negative theology: his first principle is Mind, not the ineffable Neoplatonic One; (b) prefers Ptolemy's astronomy to the outdated Aristotelian astronomy of Proclus; (c) rejects the extreme otherworldliness and contempt for the body of Neoplatonism; and (d) rejects Neoplatonic mystical unification with the divine, subordinating the visionary power of the soul to reason.

However, none of these arguments is compelling. (a) The identification of the first principle as Mind (or intellect) and not as the One does not affect the political theory.[52] The same metaphysical principles govern the ideal state (the Good as self-diffusive, hierarchy, justice, community), whether the first principle is Mind or the One. The second argument (b) does not really touch the question of al-Farabi's source for political philosophy.[53] The rejection of Neoplatonic otherworldliness (c) applies more to earlier Neoplatonists, such as Plotinus and Porphyry, than to later Greek Neoplatonists, who took more seriously soul's connection with the body and gave more importance to the material (and therefore political) conditions that govern soul's return to an immaterial felicity.[54] Al-Farabi's

---

[51] W. 12–13.

[52] However, some Platonists in Late Antiquity identified the first principle as mind; cf. Proclus, *Theol. Plato*, II, 4.

[53] Yet it should be noted that Ptolemy provided standard textbooks for astronomy in the later Greek Neoplatonic schools and was commented on by Proclus, for example.

[54] Above, Ch. 4, 3.

polemic (cf. *Best State* 19, 4 and 6) with otherworldliness fits certain tendencies in Neoplatonism (in particular in Porphyry) better than others. The last argument (d) does not quite suffice either. It concerns epistemological matters of limited importance for the question of the source of al-Farabi's political ideas and suggests contrasts which might be relativized: Neoplatonic mystical unification finds its place far beyond the framework of political divinization and reason is superior to symbolic representation in Neoplatonism also.[55]

As regards these arguments we might say in general that we should not expect every detail of the *Best State* to correspond to a hypothetical single Greek source. We must expect that al-Farabi interpreted and adapted his Greek source(s) in relation to his place in the history of Islamic philosophy and in the Islamic world of his time. Perhaps the strongest argument against supposing that al-Farabi's *Best State* is an adaptation of this kind of later Greek Neoplatonic political philosophy is the belief that no such philosophy ever existed. This belief, I suggest, must be abandoned.

[55] See above n. 50.

Conclusion

Wenn Tugend und Gerechtigkeit
Der Großen Pfad mit Ruhm bestreut,
Dann ist die Erd'ein Himmelreich,
Und Sterbliche den Göttern gleich.
(*The Magic Flute*)

It may be useful to bring together here the main parts of the argument of this book. The purpose of the argument has been to determine more clearly the particular place and function of political philosophy within Neoplatonic thought. This has involved a reconstruction of Neoplatonic political philosophy, or rather a sketch of its main outlines, its principal articulations, and major themes. Such a sketch has not yet been attempted and I realize that what is proposed here requires further development. The main difficulty has been to see how Neoplatonic political philosophy might be structured and this in turn has involved reaching a better understanding of how Neoplatonists saw political theory in the context of their philosophy as a whole. Although this book has been concerned with the reconstruction of a *theory*, this theory was elaborated in particular historical circumstances which I have sometimes noted. However, my purpose has not been to make claims about the concrete impact (or lack of impact) of the theory thus reconstructed. Having summarized the main points of the argument, I will then suggest further possibilities in the study of the influence of Neoplatonic political philosophy on later political thought and conclude with comments on some criticisms of this philosophy.

A reconstruction of Neoplatonic political philosophy has been proposed as part of an argument suggesting a revision of the common view in modern studies that no such political philosophy can or does exist. This view infers that the otherworldly orientation of Neoplatonism must exclude interest in political matters. I have argued that this inference is unsound and that a more exact view of the relation between divinization (as the goal of

198

Neoplatonism) and political life leads to other results. If in general in Greek philosophy, the human good, the goal of philosophy, can be described in some sense as divinization (Ch. 3), this goal usually involved a collectivity. As Augustine rightly remarked,[1] the philosophers saw human felicity as 'social'. In this regard, if we follow the common view, Neoplatonists would have been exceptional in excluding political life from divinization. However, it has been shown that it is the case rather that political life, as the context in which 'political' virtues may be developed, can have an important function as a preparatory and necessary stage for the transition of the human soul to a higher, transcendent divine life. The context in which the soul may acquire the 'political' virtues requires reform, a divinization brought about by philosophers who have already reached divine life. These philosophers bring to bear a political science for the development of political structures allowing and promoting the 'political' virtues other souls should acquire in order to reach the Good. I have thus distinguished two aspects of the relation between political life and divinization in Neoplatonism: the divinization of soul by means of the 'political' virtues (Chs. 3–6) and the divinization of the state through political science as a means of promoting 'political' virtue (Chs. 7–11).

The divinization of soul through the 'political' virtues concerns the soul as related to the body, using the body as instrument, according to a definition of man Neoplatonists found in Plato. The 'political' virtues are thus human virtues and involve the rational organization of desires and of whatever relates to the bodily condition. Once bodily affairs are put in order, reason is free to develop its own potentiality by attaining higher virtues ('purificatory', 'theoretical') which lead it from human goodness to the divine Good. In speaking of 'political' virtues, Plotinus had in mind the inner republic of the soul. However, later Neoplatonists, Porphyry, Macrobius, Damascius, for example, related them also to the political sphere where such virtues could and ought to be exercised.[2] However, in many cases, we can assume, these virtues were cultivated primarily in the domestic world of the philosophical school, where the inner rational order

---

[1] Above, p. 155.

[2] Indeed Iamblichus makes a strong claim (above, Ch. 8, 1) that the individual good must be reached through the common (political) good. This concerns the good represented by 'political' virtues. Once possessing this good, does the soul then ascend, *by itself*, to higher levels of divine life? Iamblichus' claim seems more far-reaching and one can suppose (cf. Ch. 8, n. 15) that soul joins collectivities over and beyond the political (i.e. body-related) community (cf. also Proclus, *In Remp.* II, p. 325, 22–5). However the study of such transcendent collectivities lies beyond the scope of this book.

of the soul (as related to the body) could show itself in relations with others. The school provided the best social context in which the 'political' virtues could be developed, not only by promoting appropriate moral habituation,[3] but also by providing instruction in practical philosophy, the wisdom required by reason in 'political' virtue. This practical philosophy included ethics, 'economics' (what we might call domestic ethics), and politics. Since, however, these three branches of practical philosophy merely applied the same practical wisdom on three scales (the soul, the household, and the state), the Neoplatonists preferred to distinguish between legislative and judicial branches. 'Political' virtue and wisdom, they felt, were taught primarily in Plato's dialogues, the *Gorgias*, *Republic*, and *Laws*, and it is consequently mainly by using their commentaries on these dialogues that we can reconstruct their political philosophy. However, they also found this philosophy in other texts, Pseudo-Pythagorean and Aristotelian.

Having reached higher, more divine levels of life through the purificatory and theoretical virtues, the philosopher may wish to return to the political level to contribute to reforms which promote a life of 'political' virtue for other souls. The return of the philosopher to political life can be approached in the light of Neoplatonic discussions of questions concerning the philosopher-kings of Plato's *Republic*. The return of the philosopher, for Neoplatonists, arises from participation in the transcendent Good. This Good is communicative of itself, as will be the philosopher who shares in it, who will seek to give political expression to the transcendent Good, in the form for example of legislation. More simply, the point is made that assimilation to god means not only attaining knowledge but also exercising a 'providential', i.e. political function. This function does not in principle affect the higher perfection of life, the happiness attained by the philosopher. Plato's conception of philosopher-queens is taken seriously and defended by Neoplatonists, a position which corresponds to the important place of women in their schools. However, in terms of what is humanly possible in political reform, Proclus took a weaker position, justified also, he thought, by indications in Plato.

The philosopher who returns to political affairs, the 'political philosopher' described by Hermias,[4] will bring to bear 'political science'. Political science, revealed, according to Iamblichus by Pythagoras to his followers, is defined by Olympiodorus as a ruling (architectonic) science concerned with moral improvement in actions (πρακτά) in a consenting human community,

---

[3] Above, p. 60.   [4] Above, p. 77 n. 14.

a science depending on practical wisdom (φρόνησις) and seeking to achieve communal harmony and unity.[5] The political goal is also defined elsewhere by Olympiodorus as 'political happiness',[6] itself subordinated to a higher good, i.e. higher levels of divinization. The political goal is therefore that of a community organized for the purpose of a moral improvement (in the 'political' virtues), which provides the conditions for the further divinization of human souls. Different levels could be conceived in the political reform to be attempted, levels going from the city of Plato's *Republic* to the second-best project of the *Laws* and to yet lower degrees of ambition. The project of the *Republic* was taken to be the city of gods to which Plato refers in the *Laws*, hardly therefore a realistic ambition for political science which, for Proclus, aims at the advantageous *and* the possible.[7] The project of the *Laws* was thus more relevant, as were less ambitious ideals of reform. A consequence of this was a greater stress on the importance of law, as the expression of political science. The doubtful prospect of rulers being philosophers perfect in morals and knowledge meant that rulers such as Julian, advised by philosophers, should be guardians of laws which serve to express moral values and develop the 'political' virtues of citizens.

The political science of the philosopher (as ruler or adviser) depends on practical wisdom. This wisdom, as Iamblichus describes it, is inspired by divine sources. What this means, in the primary, legislative branch of political science, is that models of constitutional order are found in the order of the cosmos, in mathematical principles, or in the divine orders responsible for the making of the universe. These models show hierarchical structures in which the principle of geometrical equality applies, i.e. rank and function are determined by corresponding capacities. In political terms, this means a 'monarchic' or 'aristocratic' constitution, as understood in Platonic terms, i.e. the rule of those with the requisite moral and intellectual qualities. The *Laws* suggest, however, a less utopian structure for realizing geometrical equality, a mixed constitution of which we have found examples, in particular in the anonymous dialogue *On Political Science*.

The judicial branch of political science concerns the correction of transgression of the law and restitution of lawful order. Using Plato's eschatological myths as expressions of judicial science, Neoplatonists interpreted the myths as representing punishment as being therapeutic and reformative, not as retributive: punishment should seek the moral reform of those

---

[5] Above, p. 55.   [6] Above, p. 90.   [7] Above, Ch. 8, 1.

who transgress. Sopatros' letter to Himerius suggests a flexible approach in the administration of human justice, an approach that takes account of individual characters. His letter is also an interesting document concerning the way in which an authority might seek the moral good of citizens while protecting them from the immoral requirements of an autocratic ruler to whom he is subject.

We have also seen that religion has an important political function for Neoplatonists, as it had in Plato's *Laws*. Public cult develops the relation with transcendent divinities; it represents and consolidates the moral values of political life as a form of divinization. The importance both of political life and of public cult in the divinization of human nature emerged more clearly when, with Iamblichus, the relevance of soul's relation to body in the divinization of soul was emphasized, in criticism of Plotinus' relative neglect of the material aspects of the human condition.[8] In Julian, I have suggested, we find an example of a later Neoplatonic use of religion as part of a political reform.

Finally, the sketch of Neoplatonic political philosophy has shown that it included reflection on aspects of the practical reasoning involved in political decisions, the deficiencies this reasoning entails, the heteronomy of actions that are undertaken, and the reasons for failure.

In Chapters 12–14 I have suggested that various thinkers, Christian and Islamic, were influenced by Neoplatonic philosophy and reacted to it in different ways. Eusebius' theocratic ideology might be described as a Christian appropriation: the philosopher-king and the pagan divine hierarchy are replaced by Constantine and the Christian Trinity, but the state remains a school of virtue preparatory, under the Emperor's rule and teaching, to a higher existence. Augustine seems to have been impressed at first by Neoplatonic political ideas, but he eventually completely rejected them: the state (even a Christian state) was not a stage in a scale for the divinization of man. Such a scale of divinization was to be found later in the (ideal) Church of the Pseudo-Dionysius, another example, I have argued, of Christian appropriation of Neoplatonic political philosophy. In the fragments of the anonymous dialogue *On Political Science* of the Justinianic period, we read, I suggest, an important expression of Neoplatonic political thought.

---

[8] Ehrhardt (1953) observes that Neoplatonists became more and more interested in political philosophy, an observation which this book confirms. However, he explains this interest as a reaction to Christianity, whereas I would suggest that it has to do (at first at least) with Iamblichus' anti-Plotinian emphasis on the importance of soul's embodied condition for its divinization, an emphasis made at a time when Christianity was not yet politically dominant.

Finally, al-Farabi's *Best State* corresponds in many respects to the ideas of the later Greek Neoplatonists traced in this book, ideas which find in him an Islamic adaptation. This example suggests more broadly that political philosophy in the medieval Islamic world, contrary to what is often supposed, has roots in the philosophy of Late Antiquity.

Perhaps one might mention briefly here two more examples in the history of political thought where the possibility of a Neoplatonic influence might be investigated. The first is that of George Gemistos Plethon (*c*.1360–1452), 'the last of the Hellenes',[9] who died the year before Constantinople fell to the Ottoman Turks. Established at Mistra, near Sparta, Plethon was a Platonic philosopher who saw in political reform the last hope for saving Hellenic culture from destruction. In two memoirs (addressed to Theodore despot of the Morea and to the Byzantine Emperor Manuel Palaeologus), he proposed a reform inspired by Plato's *Republic*: a division of social functions, full-time professional soldiers and rulers, public possession of land.[10] Plethon also indicates the political importance of correct views concerning the divinity and implicitly criticizes the Christian Church. The significance of this religious dimension becomes clear in Plethon's *Book on Laws*, a major and extraordinary work which, after Plethon's death, came into the possession of his opponent Scholarios, now Gennadios, patriarch of Constantinople, who had it destroyed. Even if some indications of the content of the book and some extracts survive,[11] it is very difficult at present to reach an idea of the whole and of the significance of the surviving extracts for the whole. We might note that in Chapter 2, Plethon lists as guides to the truth a series of ancient wise men and legislators culminating with Pythagoras, Plato, and the Neoplatonists Plotinus, Porphyry, and Iamblichus.[12] Following these guides, Plethon elaborates a pagan polytheistic theology which expresses Neoplatonic metaphysical principles. The political importance of this emerges in the extracts from hymns and prayers,[13] the daily recitation of which promotes piety, virtue, and assimilation to the divine through correct grasp of the order and nature of the gods. It seems thus that (as in al-Farabi's *Best State*), correct metaphysics and philosophical theology

---

[9] See Woodhouse (1986).

[10] Extracts and paraphrases of these texts can be found in Barker (1957: 198–212); see also Woodhouse (1986: ch. vi).

[11] See the edition and Woodhouse (1986: ch. xvii).

[12] Proclus is not mentioned in the list, but seems to have been an important source for Plethon, as were other later Neoplatonists; see Woodhouse (1986: 68, 73–7).

[13] See e.g. III, 34.

provide the model of political reform in the sense of moral improvement aimed at divinization. It is possible then that the reconstruction of Neoplatonic political philosophy attempted in this book may throw some light on the political project of Plethon's *Book on Laws*, a last, badly damaged Greek image of this philosophy.[14]

Plethon, while participating in the Council of Florence in 1439, much impressed Italian humanists and in particular Cosimo de' Medici. It is because of this meeting, Marsilio Ficino believed, that Cosimo came to his idea of a Florentine 'Academy', sponsoring in particular Ficino's work in making available in Latin, through translations and commentaries, the texts of Plato, Plotinus, and other Neoplatonists. Preliminary studies of Ficino's comments on Plato's *Republic* and *Laws* suggest, here also, that political life is seen as the context of moral reform leading to a higher more divine life and that a Neoplatonic metaphysical theology functions as the model of political reform.[15] However, further research is required in order to establish to what extent and in what ways Ficino may have transmitted aspects of Neoplatonic political thought to Renaissance humanists.

In conclusion, I would like to return to the critique of Neoplatonic political theorists offered by one of the very few scholars to have paid attention to the subject, Arnold Ehrhardt.[16] Ehrhardt attributes a 'complete failure' to Neoplatonism 'in the political field'. He does not specify if the failure was in theory or in political praxis, but means probably the latter. The reason for the failure, he claims, was that Neoplatonism found no 'valid relation between its metaphysical and its practical philosophy'. The Neoplatonists (erroneously) believed

that pure reason had the supremacy over any ethical decisions. They held that the starting point was the study of the pure, unchanging and eternal law which was the centre of the utopian hope for a Golden Age . . . the error lay in the assumption that there was an eternal law which was intelligible, and that it would influence human actions, if it was rightly understood.   (Ehrhardt 1953: 476–7)

Whatever the failure in real politics, it finds its roots, therefore, according to Ehrhardt, in theoretical errors. He mentions a number of points relating to

---

[14] See also Plethon's treatise *On Virtues*, in particular II, 11. The editor of this text, Tambrun-Krasker, contrasts Plethon's political Platonism with Neoplatonism (39) in a way that requires qualification in view of the reconstruction of Neoplatonic political philosophy I have proposed. She also usefully compares (107–8) aspects of the religious programme of Plato's *Laws* with that of Plethon's *Books of Laws*.

[15] Cf. Neschke (1999b: 227–30); (2000); (forthcoming).   [16] Ehrhardt (1953: 476–7).

such theoretical error, which I would like to distinguish and assess. Some of these points, as I will also suggest, relate specifically to Neoplatonism, but others apply more broadly to Greek political philosophy in general.

Ehrhardt's denial of any 'valid relation' between Neoplatonist metaphysics and political philosophy may be understood in various ways. (1) It may be thought that no transfer or derivation of laws and structures from the metaphysical to the political domains is actually made. This, however, is not the case.[17] (2) It may be thought that such a derivation, if indeed it is made, is not 'valid'. It may not be valid because (i) there *is* no eternal, intelligible, metaphysical law from which such a derivation could be made. However, this is a criticism which applies also to Plato and the Stoics. It involves a rejection of particular metaphysical positions. We might feel that the hierarchical transcendent metaphysics of Neoplatonism is antithetical to the flat reductionist physicalism of today. (ii) Or it may be felt that there *can* be no deduction of ethical/political norms (what ought to be done) from physical/metaphysical fact (what is the case). This is also a question which concerns Plato and Stoicism. (iii) Or perhaps, as Ehrhardt suggests, (theoretical) reason should not be assumed to be translatable directly into ethical and political decisions and actions. This assumption, the Socratic belief that 'virtue is knowledge', is not made by Neoplatonists: referring to texts in Plato (and influenced by Aristotle), they noted the importance of habituation[18] and integrated in political philosophy (again under Aristotelian influence) the concepts of practical wisdom and deliberation.[19] They also took seriously the problem of the possible, had differentiated views on what might be attempted, and were not utopian dreamers.[20]

Perhaps the major disagreements that remain concern the particular metaphysical theory which the Neoplatonists used as a paradigm for political philosophy and their use of this theory as a normative foundation for political theory. Such disagreements also arise with regard to other ancient philosophers, in particular Plato and the Stoics. Modern views of political philosophy will also tend to exclude essentially moralistic views of political life such as those of the ancient Neoplatonists, views of political life as a school of virtue through which humans attain their good.[21] But here also the difficulty is more general, applying in this case, beyond the Neoplatonic schools, to ancient philosophy in general. It is a difficulty which shows the distance between ancient and modern positions.

[17] See above, Chs. 8, 13, 14. [18] See above, p. 60.
[19] See above, Ch. 11. [20] See above, p. 93.
[21] See above, Ch. 1, 2.

APPENDIX 1
THEMISTIUS AND NEOPLATONIC POLITICAL PHILOSOPHY

A major political writer and politician of the fourth century AD, Themistius has not been included among the sources used in this book for the purpose of reconstructing Neoplatonic political philosophy. Themistius is not usually regarded by modern scholars as a representative of Neoplatonic philosophy. However, this opinion has also been challenged.[1] In view of this debate, it has seemed more prudent, for reasons of method, not to make use of Themistius' works in developing an outline of Neoplatonic political thought. However, once this outline is elaborated, the question of Themistius' position can again be raised: should Themistius be regarded as fitting into our reconstruction of Neoplatonic political philosophy, or should he be seen rather as independent of it, as offering a different political approach? Some elements of an answer to these questions are proposed in the following. Whatever Themistius' position, it can be assumed that he was aware, not only of the work of Plotinus and of Porphyry, but also of the thought of Iamblichus and of the Iamblichean schools visited by Julian the Emperor.[2]

Throughout his rhetorical works, Themistius advocates a political theory which remains constant and which can be summarized as follows. The king (or Roman Emperor) is an emanation of god and god's delegate on earth, a living law granted men by god. The king is called to imitate god, to assimilate himself as far as possible to god, in particular through his virtue. The royal virtue of philanthropy is stressed: it is the primary virtue whereby the king may imitate divine rule. The king should try to make his reign to be in the image of the cosmic rule of god, a rule characterized by order, peace, and goodness.[3] Themistius regards the successive Roman Emperors praised in his speeches as promoting such a divine cosmic order,[4] of which a focus for him is Constantinople, his *kallipolis*,[5] whose political, economic, and cultural interests he never tires of promoting.

---

[1] Cf. Balériaux (1994), who argues in particular against the position taken by Blumenthal.

[2] Cf. Balériaux (1994); Guldentops (2001a: 110–11, 114).

[3] *Or.* I, pp. 11, 26–12, 9; p. 13, 14–24; *Or.* V, pp. 93, 19–94, 11; *Or.* VI, pp. 116, 19–117, 9; *Or.* IX, p. 191, 17–23; *Or.* XI, p. 217, 17–28; *Or.* XV, p. 273, 2–3 and 14–15; *Or.* XVIII, p. 315, 17–19; cf. *Or.* XXXIV, p. 215, 17–21 (referring to Plato), p. 232, 11–21 (referring to Themistius himself as assuming office); Dvornik (1966: 623–6); Dagron (1968: 85–6, 135, 138); de Romilly (1979: 322–3).

[4] See *Or.* VI, pp. 108, 12–109, 3 (denying that Minos in Crete or Lycurgus in Sparta achieved this).

[5] See Guldentops (2001b: 131–2): this is not Plato's *kallipolis*, the utopia of *Rep.* 527c2.

With the exception of the theme of Constantinople, this political theory corresponds to the ideologies of monarchy of the Hellenistic and early Roman imperial periods, as expressed for example in the Pseudo-Pythagorean texts on kingship and in the speeches of Dio Chrysostom and (in a Christian adaptation) of Eusebius.[6] It is as if Themistius found in the kingship theory of earlier periods of the Roman Empire a pattern for the resolution of the problems of his time, the external and internal wars and religious conflicts of the fourth century. As far as I can tell, there is no clear presence in Themistius' theory of specifically Neoplatonic interpretations of political themes, as these interpretations have been described in earlier parts of this book. One has rather the impression that Themistius implicitly rejects positions taken by Neoplatonic philosophers of his time and that his evocation of the ideology of an earlier period in the history of the Roman Empire relates to a divergence in approach to the situation at hand. A reaction of this kind is suggested by the following positions that he takes.

Themistius emphasizes the priority of political action as a form of imitation of the divine. This action can be most fully carried out by the ruler who has power and thus the means for achieving more fully an imitation of god. The philosopher has the same aim, but lacks the necessary power; in comparison to the ruler he 'limps'.[7] The superiority claimed by Themistius for political action in relation to the philosophical life became a subject of dissension with Julian who, responding to advice offered by Themistius, insists on the priority of the life of knowledge (contemplation) and points out that action includes, not only the execution of tasks, but also legislation and political thought as forms of action inspired by knowledge.[8] Julian, contradicting Themistius, thus insists on the Neoplatonic subordination of the political life to the life of knowledge. Imitation of the divine can be achieved in political action, but it is inferior to and dependent on the imitation of the divine constituted by the life of knowledge.

In his advice to Julian, Themistius suggested that he quit his chambered philosophy for a philosophy in the open.[9] This contrast corresponds to a difference Themistius saw between the attitude of Neoplatonic philosophers of his time and his own view of the role of the philosopher. Elsewhere he refers to the descendants of Socrates, Platonists, who withdraw from public life, hiding themselves as if behind a wall.[10] The reference has been plausibly taken to be to Neoplatonists such as those who had trained Julian.[11] Against this attitude of withdrawal, Themistius argues that conditions are not as dangerous as those that obtained at Athens in the time of Socrates, that there are well-disposed rulers open to listening to philosophy, that the philosopher should produce

[6] See above, Ch. 12, 1–2; on Themistius' use of Dio Chrysostom, cf. Colpi (1987: 149–63).

[7] *Or.* I, p. 13, 14–22; *Or.* II, p. 46, 12–14.

[8] Julian, *Or.* VI, 8–10, 262a–264c; see above, Ch. 8, 2. Vanderspoel (1995: 244–9), argues that the *Epistula de republica gerenda*, a text preserved in Arabic (cf. the edition of Themistius, III, pp. 83–119), is by Themistius and is addressed to Julian.

[9] Julian, *Or.* VI, 9, 262d.

[10] Themistius, *Or.* XXVI, pp. 139, 2–15; 143, 6–14; *Or.* XXVIII, pp. 170, 17–171, 24; cf. *Or.* VIII, pp. 158, 12–159, 7. On the image of the wall, see above p. 93.

[11] See Dagron (1968: 43).

himself in public, combining rhetoric and philosophy in seeking to influence events by his advice, advice such as that which Themistius offered to a succession of Emperors concerning a virtuous rule in the image of the divine order of the universe.[12]

The conclusion that we might draw is that Themistius shares with the Neoplatonic philosophers of his time neither their metaphysical and political theory, nor their attitude to the involvement of the philosopher in political life. Themistius appeals to a monarchic ideology of a traditional kind such as that advocated by Dio Chrysostom in the second century AD. Themistius' view of the political vocation of the philosopher appears to be more sanguine, optimistic, if not disingenuous, than that of the Neoplatonist. His subordination of the philosopher to the king, of knowledge to action, is certainly a reversal of the Neoplatonic scale of values.

---

[12] See *Or.* VIII, pp. 162, 20–163, 1. On Themistius' non-Platonic metaphysics, see Guldentops (2001a).

APPENDIX II
NOTES ON A PLATONIST RHETOR: SOPATROS 3

To Iamblichus' pupil ('Sopatros 1') and his son, author of the letter to Himerius ('Sopatros 2'), we might add a third Sopatros ('Sopatros 3'),[1] a 'fourth century Athenian rhetorician working in Neoplatonic circles' and perhaps a grandson of Sopatros 1,[2] pupil, it seems, of the prominent rhetor Himerius.[3] This third Sopatros appears to be the author of a number of rhetorical texts, in particular a series of comments on Hermogenes,[4] which show sympathy with Platonism, and some *Prolegomena* to and glosses on Aristides. The work on Aristides is of particular interest in the context of the study of Platonic political thought in Late Antiquity since it deals with the relation between political science and rhetoric in connection with the interpretation of Plato's *Gorgias* and *Statesman*. As this material is hardly ever noticed, and its use of Plato's *Statesman* not recognized, some notes concerning it may be of interest.

Rhetoric and philosophy were often combined in the education and careers of Neoplatonists. Philosophers such as Porphyry, Iamblichus, and Syrianus were skilled rhetoricians and wrote on rhetorical questions.[5] Although Plato had attacked rhetoric in the *Gorgias*, Neoplatonists found in the same dialogue a distinction between bad or false rhetoric, whose objective was pleasure, and a true rhetoric compatible with, and serving the same goal as, philosophy: the good.[6]

For in general the philosopher, whenever he is turned towards intelligible being and the knowledge of intelligibles and of god, having the eye of reason turned upwards, he is the first [i.e. theoretical] philosopher; but when he turns from this knowledge to the care of the city and orders it according to that knowledge, then he becomes a political philosopher; but whenever he addresses words to the community, persuading the people to act as they should, then he is a true rhetor, for knowing the truth from that knowledge, he persuades them to do what is true and fitting for them.[7]

---

[1] *PLRE* II, 1020 (= 'Sopater 2').

[2] Kennedy (1983: 104–5).

[3] Not to be confused with Himerius the brother of 'Sopatros 2'. On the connections of the rhetor Himerius with Platonists cf. Schamp in *DPA* iii. 721–2.

[4] Walz (1832–6: v. 1–211).

[5] There is here a large body of material, printed in Walz (1832–6), that has never been fully examined.

[6] See *Gorg.* 503a; Olympiodorus, *In Gorg.*, p. 14, 4–7; p. 73, 1–4. See also Plato, *Phaedr.* 259e–260a; 'Sopatros 2' (letter to Himerius) in Stobaeus, *Anth.* IV, p. 215, 2–10 (on the distinction between good and bad rhetoric).

[7] Hermias, *In Phaedr.*, p. 221, 11–24; cf. p. 219, 3–9.

In Plato's *Statesman* (304c–305e), rhetoric appears as one of the arts subordinate to and in the service of the commanding art or skill, political science.

Plato's attack on rhetoric in the *Gorgias* found a response on behalf of rhetoric in a group of works by the second-century rhetorician Aristides, including a discourse *In Defence of the Four*, i.e. the four Athenian politicians (Themistocles, Cimon, Miltiades, and Pericles) criticized in the *Gorgias*. Porphyry responded in turn to Aristides in a lost work and Sopatros 3 takes up the debate again in his *Prolegomena* to Aristides' discourse, presenting and comparing the positions of Plato and of Aristides.

As a preliminary to this comparison, Sopatros proposes a description of the true 'political [man]' (πολιτικός), a description taken in many of its details from Plato's *Statesman*. The true political man possesses political science,[8] has knowledge of all that concerns ordering the city, ordering others but not acting himself, being a king in his royal providence (πρόνοια).[9] His science is legislative and architectonic: to its finality are subordinated the goals of other arts and skills, including the judicial art.[10] As identified with his royal science, the true political man is the finality of the city and represents perfect virtue and happiness, the goal of all other arts and skills.[11]

Following this account of the true statesman, Sopatros quotes extensively from Plato's description in the *Gorgias* of rhetoric as a form of flattery and explains the arguments of Plato and of Aristides as corresponding to a difference in method, Plato arguing from demonstrative necessity, Aristides using arguments of persuasion taken from particulars, an approach which is compared to the moralizing advice given in Isocrates.[12]

These pages of Sopatros' *Prolegomena* provide an example of the use of Plato's *Statesman* in conjunction with the *Gorgias* in the teaching of an Athenian rhetorician of the fourth century. They show how a rhetorician with Platonic sympathies saw the relation between philosophy, in particular political philosophy, and other arts and skills, including rhetoric.

Another interesting insight into this milieu is provided by one of Sopatros' glosses on Aristides, which is one of the earliest reports claiming that the entrance to Plato's Academy bore the inscription 'No one shall enter who is no geometer'.[13] Sopatros explains that not being a geometer means 'being unequal and unjust. For geometry seeks equality and justice'.[14] It has been observed that Sopatros is referring to geometrical equality (or proportion), as introduced in Plato's *Gorgias* and as associated in Plato and by later Platonists with justice.[15] What was thus required, according to Sopatros, on

---

[8] Sopatros, *Prol.*, p. 128, 5–6; Plato, *Statesman* 259d.

[9] *Prol.* p. 127, 9–11; cf. p. 130, 5–7; *Statesman* 258e, 260c.

[10] Cf. *Prol.*, p. 128, 1–2, *Statesman* 304d–305e.

[11] *Prol.*, p. 128, 14–15; cf. p. 129, 13–14.

[12] See pp. 127, 2–5; 139, 4–12; 140, 1–141, 2. On Isocrates see above, Ch. 6, 3.

[13] This gloss has been discussed by Saffrey (1968: 72–4), who also presents other reports of this inscription, including another of the earliest reports, in Julian the Emperor.

[14] Aristides III, p. 464, 11–15.

[15] Saffrey (1968: 74); cf. above, Ch. 8, 5.

entry to Plato's Academy was a moral character, the virtue of justice. This interpretation may be an echo of a debate about how the legendary inscription of the Academy was to be related to the question of what the appropriate starting-point of philosophy might be, moral education or mathematics.[16]

It is not clear what connection there might be between Sopatros 3 and a Sopatros 'sophist', whose collection of excerpts in twelve books is described by Photius.[17] This collection, Photius reports, included, in Book XII, excerpts from Aristotle's *Constitutions* concerning the constitutions of five cities and of those cities discussed in Aristotle's *Politics*.

---

[16] Cf. Saffrey (1968: 77–84) and above, Ch. 5, 3.

[17] *Bibliotheca* 161, II, pp. 123–8.

Bibliography

1. Ancient Authors

AGAPETUS, *Ekthesis*, in Migne, *Patrologia graeca*, lxxxvi, 1164–85 (trans.: Frohne 1985).

ALBINUS, *Prologue*, ed. C. Hermann, *Platonis opera*, vi (Leipzig, 1853).

ALCINOUS, *Didaskalikos*, ed. and trans. J. Whittaker and P. Louis, *Alkinoos: Enseignement des doctrines de Platon* (Paris, 1990; trans.: Dillon 1993).

AL-FARABI, *The Attainment of Happiness*, trans. M. Mahdi, *Alfarabi's Philosophy of Plato and Aristotle* (Ithaca, 1969), 13–15.

—— *Compendium Legum Platonis*, ed. F. Gabrieli (London, 1952).

—— *The Enumeration of the Sciences*, trans. F. Najjar, in R. Lerner and M. Mahdi (eds.), *Medieval Political Philosophy* (Ithaca, 1963), 24–30.

—— *The Fusal al-Madani. Aphorisms of the Statesman*, ed. and trans. D. M. Dunlop (Cambridge, 1961).

—— *On the Perfect State*, ed., trans. R. Walzer (Oxford, 1985).

—— *The Philosophy of Aristotle*, trans. M. Mahdi, *Alfarabi's Philosophy of Plato and Aristotle* (Ithaca, 1969), 71–130.

—— *The Philosophy of Plato*, trans. M. Mahdi, *Alfarabi's Philosophy of Plato and Aristotle* (Ithaca, 1969), 53–67.

—— *The Political Regime*, trans. F. Najjar, in R. Lerner and M. Mahdi (eds.), *Medieval Political Philosophy* (Ithaca, 1963), 32–56.

AMMIANUS MARCELLINUS, *Res gestae*, ed. W. Seyfarth (Leipzig, 1970–1).

AMMONIUS, *In Porphyrii Isagogen*, ed. A. Busse (*CAG* IV 3; Berlin, 1891).

—— *In Aristotelis Categorias commentarius*, ed. A. Busse (*CAG* IV 4; Berlin, 1895).

—— *In de interpretatione*, ed. A. Busse (*CAG* IV 5; Berlin, 1897).

ANONYMOUS, *On Political Science*, ed. and trans. C. Mazzucchi, *Menae patricii cum Thoma referendario de scientia politica dialogus* (Milan, 1982).

—— *Prolegomena to Platonic Philosophy*, ed. and trans. L. G. Westerink, J. Trouillard, and A. Segonds, *Prolégomènes à la philosophie de Platon* (Paris, 1990).

ARISTIDES, *Orationes*, ed. W. Dindorf (Leipzig, 1829).

AUGUSTINE, *The City of God*, ed. B. Dombart and A. Kalb (Turnhout ,1955).

—— *Confessions*, ed. and trans. P. de Labriolle (Paris, 1950).

—— *Contra Academicos*, ed. and trans. R. Jolivet, *Œuvres de saint Augustin* 4/1 (Paris, 1939).

213

Bibliography

AUGUSTINE, *De ordine*, ed. and trans. J. Doignon, *Œuvres de saint Augustin* 4/2 (Paris, 1997).

—— *Retractationes*, ed. and trans. G. Bardy, *Œuvres de saint Augustin* 12 (Paris, 1950).

BOETHIUS, *The Consolation of Philosophy*, ed. and trans. H. Stewart, E. Rand, and S. Tester (Cambridge, Mass., 1973).

CALCIDIUS, *Commentarium in Timaeum*, ed. J. H. Waszink (London and Leiden, 1975).

DAMASCIUS, *Commentary on Plato's Phaedo*, ed. and trans. L. G. Westerink, *The Greek Commentaries on Plato's Phaedo*, ii (Amsterdam, 1977).

—— *In Philebum*, ed. and trans. L. G. Westerink (Amsterdam, 1959).

—— *On First Principles*, ed. and trans. L. G. Westerink, J. Combès, *Damascius Traité des premiers principes* (Paris, 1986–91).

—— *Vitae Isidori reliquiae*, ed. C. Zintzen (Hildesheim, 1967; trans.: Athanassiadi 1999).

DAVID, *Prolegomena*, ed. A. Busse (*CAG* XVIII 2; Berlin, 1904).

DIO CHRYSOSTOM, *Orations*, ed. and trans. J. Cohoon (Cambridge, Mass., 1932).

DIOGENES OF OINOANDA, *Fragments*, ed. and trans. M. F. Smith, *Diogenes of Oinoanda the Epicurean Inscription* (Naples, 1993).

(PSEUDO-)DIONYSIUS, *Corpus Dionysiacum*, ed. G. Heil and A. Ritter (Berlin, 1991; trans.: Luibheid 1987).

ELIAS, *In Porphyrii Isagogen et Aristotelis Categorias commentaria*, ed. A. Busse (*CAG* XVIII; Berlin, 1900).

—— *Prolegomena*, ed. A. Busse (*CAG* XVIII 1; Berlin, 1900).

PSEUDO-ELIAS (Pseudo-David), *Lectures on Porphyry's Isagoge*, ed. L. G. Westerink (Amsterdam, 1967).

EUNAPIUS, *Lives of the Philosophers and Sophists*, ed. and trans. W. C. Wright, *Philostratus and Eunapius, The Lives of the Sophists* (Cambridge, Mass., 1921).

EUSEBIUS, *Praise of Constantine*, ed. I. Heikel (Leipzig ,1902; trans.: Drake 1976).

—— *Life of Constantine*, ed. F. Winkelmann (Berlin, 1975; trans.: Cameron and Hall 1999).

—— *Praeparatio evangelica*, ed. K. Mras (Berlin, 1954–6).

HERMIAS, *In Platonis Phaedrum Scholia*, ed. P. Couvreur (Paris, 1901; repr. with additions by C. Zintzen, Hildesheim, 1971; trans.: Bernard 1997).

HIEROCLES, *In Aureum Pythagoreorum carmen commentarius*, ed. F. Köhler (Stuttgart,1974; trans.: Köhler 1983, Schibli 2002).

IAMBLICHUS, [?] *Commentary on the Pythagorean Golden Verses*: see Daiber (1995).

—— *De mysteriis*, ed. G. Parthey (Berlin, 1857; repr. Amsterdam, 1965; trans.: des Places 1966).

—— *Fragments*: *Commentaries on Plato*: cf. Dillon (1973); *Commentaries on Aristotle*: cf. Larsen (1972); *De anima*: cf. Stobaeus; *Letters*: cf. Stobaeus.

—— *On Pythagoreanism*:

Book I. *De Vita Pythagorica*, ed. L. Deubner (Leipzig, 1937, repr. Stuttgart, 1975; trans.: Clark 1989, Brisson and Segonds 1996).

Book II. *Protrepticus*, ed. L. Pistelli, Leipzig (1888), repr. Stuttgart, 1967 (trans.: des Places 1989).

Book III. *De communi mathematica scientia*, ed. N. Festa (Leipzig, 1891; repr. Stuttgart, 1975).

Book IV. *In Nicomachi Arithmeticam introductionem*, ed. H. Pistelli (Leipzig, 1894, repr. Stuttgart, 1975).

Books V–VII. *Fragments*, ed., trans. O'Meara, *PR* 218–29 (*Phys. arith.*, *Eth. arith.*, *Theol. arith.*).

ISOCRATES, *Ad Nicoclem, Nicocles, Ad Demonicum*, ed. and trans. G. Mathieu and E. Brémond, *Isocrate Discours*, i–ii (Paris, 1929).

JEROME, *Epistula adversus Rufinum*, ed. P. Lardet, *S. Hieronymi...Opera* III 1 (Turnhout, 1982).

JULIAN THE EMPEROR, *Opera*, ed. and trans. J. Bidez et al., *L'Empereur Julien Œuvres complètes* (4 vols.) (Paris, 1924–64).

—— *Contra Christianos*, ed. C. Neumann (Leipzig, 1880).

LYDUS, *De mensibus*, ed. R. Wünsch (Leipzig, 1898).

MACROBIUS, *Commentarii in somnium Scipionis*, ed. J. Willis (Leipzig, 1970).

MARINUS, *Proclus, ou sur le Bonheur (Vita Procli)*, ed. and trans. H.-D. Saffrey and A. Segonds (Paris, 2001; Engl. trans.: Edwards 2000).

OLYMPIODORUS, *Commentary on Plato's Phaedo*, ed., trans. L. G. Westerink, *The Greek Commentaries on Plato's Phaedo*, i. (Amsterdam, 1976).

—— *In Alcibiadem*, ed. L. G. Westerink (Amsterdam, 1982).

—— *In Platonis Gorgiam commentaria*, ed. L. G. Westerink (Leipzig, 1970; trans.: Jackson, Lykos, and Tarrant 1998).

—— *Prolegomena*, ed. A. Busse (*CAG* XII 1; Berlin, 1902).

PHILOPONUS, *De aeternitate mundi*, ed. H. Rabe (Leipzig, 1899).

—— *In Aristotelis Categorias commentarium*, ed. A. Busse (*CAG* XIII 1; Berlin, 1898).

PHOTIUS, *Epistulae*, ed. B. Laourdas and L. G. Westerink (Leipzig, 1983–5).

—— *Bibliotheca*, ed., trans. R. Henry (Paris, 1959–77).

PLETHON, *Traité des lois*, ed. and trans. C. Alexandre 2nd edn. (Paris, 1982).

—— *Traité des vertus*, ed. and trans. B. Tambrun-Krasker (Athens, 1987).

PLOTINUS, *Enneads*, ed. P. Henry and H.-R. Schwyzer (Brusselles, Paris, and Leiden, 1951–73; revised study edn., Oxford, 1964–82; trans.: Armstrong 1966–88).

PORPHYRY, *De abstinentia*, ed. and trans. J. Bouffartigue, M. Patillon, A. Segonds, L. Brisson, 3 vols. (Paris, 1977–95).

—— *Fragments*, ed. A. Smith (Stuttgart and Leipzig, 1993).

—— *Opuscula Selecta*, ed. A. Nauck (Leipzig, 1886; repr. Hildesheim, 1963).

—— *Sentences*, ed. F. Lamberz (Leipzig, 1975).

—— *Vita Plotini*, edited at head of Plotinus' *Enneads*.

PROCLUS, *Commentaria in Parmenidem*, in Proclus, *Opera inedita*, ed. V. Cousin (Paris, 1864; trans.: Morrow and Dillon 1987).

—— *Commentary on the First Alcibiades of Plato*, ed. L. G. Westerink (Amsterdam, 1954; trans.: O'Neill 1965, Segonds 1985).

Bibliography

PROCLUS [?] *Commentary on the Pythagorean Golden Verses* (Extracts made by Ibn at-Tayyib), ed. and trans. N. Linley (Buffalo, 1984).

—— *The Elements of Theology*, ed. and trans. E. R. Dodds, 2nd edn. (Oxford, 1963).

—— *In Platonis Cratylum commentaria*, ed. G. Pasquali (Leipzig, 1908).

—— *In Platonis Rempublicam*, ed. W. Kroll (Leipzig, 1899; trans.: Festugière 1970).

—— *In Platonis Timaeum*, ed. E. Diehl (Leipzig, 1903; trans.: Festugière 1966–8).

—— *In Primum Euclidis Elementorum librum commentarii*, ed. G. Friedlein (Leipzig, 1873, repr. 1967; trans.: Morrow 1970).

—— *Théologie Platonicienne*, ed. and trans. H.-D. Saffrey and L. G. Westerink (Paris, 1968–97).

—— *Tria opuscula* (=*X dub.*, *De prov.*, *De mal.*), ed. H. Boese (Berlin, 1960).

MICHAEL PSELLUS, *Philosophica minora*, ed. J. M. Duffy and D. J. O'Meara; vol. ii, ed. D. J. O'Meara (Leipzig, 1989).

—— *De omnifaria doctrina*, ed. L. G. Westerink (Utrecht, 1948).

SALLUSTIUS, *De dis et de mundo*, ed., trans. A. Nock (Cambridge, 1926).

SIMPLICIUS, *Commentaire sur le Manuel d'Epictète, ch. I à XXIX*, ed. and trans. I. Hadot (Paris, 2001).

—— *In De anima*, ed. M. Hayduck (*CAG* XI; Berlin, 1882).

—— *In De caelo*, ed. I. Heiberg (*CAG* VII; Berlin, 1894).

—— *In Aristotelis Categorias commentarium*, ed. C. Kalbfleisch (*CAG* VIII; Berlin, 1907). (partial trans.: I. Hadot et al. 1990 and in P. Hoffmann et al. 2001).

—— *In Aristotelis Physicorum libros*, ed. H. Diels (*CAG* IX–X; Berlin, 1882–95).

—— *In Epictetum*, ed. I. Hadot (Leiden, 1996).

SOCRATES SCHOLASTICUS, *Historia ecclesiastica*, ed. G. C. Hansen (Berlin, 1995).

SOPATROS, *Prolegomena*, ed. F. Lenz, *The Aristeides Prolegomena* (Leiden, 1959), 127–51.

STOBAEUS, *Anthologium*, ed. C. Wachsmuth and O. Hense, 4 vols. (Berlin, 1884–1912).

Stoicorum veterum fragmenta, ed. H. von Arnim, 4 vols. (Leipzig, 1905–24; repr. Stuttgart, 1978).

SYNESIUS, *Opuscula*, ed. N. Terzaghi (Rome, 1944).

SYRIANUS, *In Metaphysica commentaria*, ed. W. Kroll (*CAG* VI; Berlin, 1902).

THEMISTIUS, *Orationes* ed. H. Schenkl and G. Downey (Leipzig, 1965–70).

2. Modern Authors

AALDERS, G. (1968), *Die Theorie der gemischten Verfassung im Altertum*, Amsterdam.

—— (1969), 'ΝΟΜΟΣ ΕΜΨΥΧΟΣ', in Steinmetz (1969: 315–29).

ABBATE, M. (1995), *Proclo. Commento alla Repubblica Dissertazioni I, III, IV, V* (Pavia).

—— (1998), *Proclo. Commento alla Republica Dissertazioni VII, VIII, IX, X* (Pavia).

—— (1999), 'Gli aspetti etico-politici della Repubblica nel Commento di Proclo (dissertazioni VII/VIII e XI)', in Vegetti and Abbate (1999: 207–18).

ALEKNIENE, T. (1999), 'Kosmios kai theios. La justice divine de l'âme selon Platon', *Freiburger Zeitschrift für Philosophie und Theologie* 46: 369–87.

ALTANER, B. (1967), *Kleine Patristische Schriften* (Berlin).

ALTMANN, A. and STERN, S. (1958), *Isaac Israeli. A Neoplatonic Philosopher of the Early Tenth Century* (Oxford).

ANDIA, Y. DE (1996), *Henosis. L'union à Dieu chez Denys l'Aréopagite* (Leiden).

—— (1997) (ed.), *Denys l'Aréopagite et sa postérité en orient et en occident* (Paris).

ANNAS, J. (1992), *Hellenistic Philosophy of Mind* (Berkeley).

—— (1999), *Platonic Ethics, Old and New* (Ithaca).

ARMSTRONG, A. H. (1966–88), *Plotinus*, Cambridge, Mass. (trans.)

ATHANASSIADI-FOWDEN, P. (1981), *Julian and Hellenism. An Intellectual Biography* (Oxford).

—— (1999), *Damascius: The Philosophical History. Text with Translation and Notes* (Athens).

BALAUDÉ, J.-F. (1990), 'Communauté divine et au-delà : les fins du dépassement selon Plotin', *Philosophie* 26: 73–94.

BALLÉRIAUX, O. (1994), 'Thémistius et le néoplatonisme. Le Νοῦς παθητικός et l'immortalité de l'âme', *Revue de philosophie ancienne* 12: 171–200.

BARKER, E. (1957), *Social and Political Thought in Byzantium* (Oxford).

—— (1959), *The Political Thought of Plato and Aristotle* (New York).

BARNES, T. (1981), *Constantine and Eusebius* (Cambridge, Mass).

BAYNES, N. (1934), 'Eusebius and the Christian Empire', *Annuaire de l'Institut de philologie et d'histoire orientales*, 2 = *Mélanges Bidez* 1, 13–18, repr. in Baynes, *Byzantine Studies and other Essays* (London, 1955).

BEIERWALTES, W. (1972), 'Johannes von Skythopolis und Plotin', *Studia patristica* 11.2 (Berlin), 3–7.

—— (1979), *Proklos Grundzüge seiner Metaphysik*, 2nd rev. edn. (Frankfurt).

—— (1985), *Denken des Einen* (Frankfurt).

BERETTA, G. (1993), *Ipazia d'Alessandria* (Rome).

BERMAN, L. (1961), 'The Political Interpretation of the Maxim: The Purpose of Philosophy is the Imitation of God', *Studia Islamica* 15: 53–61.

BERNARD, H. (1997), *Hermeias von Alexandrien. Übersetzung seines Kommentars zu Platons "Phaidros"* (Tübingen). (trans.)

BIDEZ, J. (1913), *Vie de Porphyre* (Ghent; repr. Hildesheim, 1980).

—— (1919), 'Le philosophe Jamblique et son école,' *Revue des études greques* 32: 29–40.

BLUMENTHAL, H. (1978), '529 and its sequel: What happened to the Academy', *Byzantion* 48: 369–85 (= Blumenthal 1993: Essay XVIII).

—— (1984). 'Marinus' Life of Proclus: Neoplatonist Biography', *Byzantion* 54: 469–94 (=Blumenthal 1993: Essay XIII).

—— (1993), *Soul and Intellect. Studies in Plotinus and Later Neoplatonism* (Aldershot).

—— (1996), *Aristotle and Neoplatonism in Late Antiquity. Interpretations of the De anima* (London).

BONNER, G. (1986), 'Augustine's Conception of Deification', *Journal of Theological Studies* 37: 369–86.

Bibliography

BORDES, J. (1982), *Politeia dans la pensée grecque jusqu'à Aristote* (Paris).

BOUFFARTIGUE, J. (1992), *L'Empereur Julien et la culture de son temps* (Paris).

BRAGUE, R. (1993), 'Note sur la traduction arabe de la *Politique* d'Aristote: derechef, qu'elle n'existe pas', in P. Aubenque (ed.), *Aristote Politique* (Paris), 423–33.

BRAUN, R. and RICHER, J. (1978) (ed.), *L'Empereur Julien. De l'histoire à la légende (331–1715)* (Paris).

BRISSON, L. (1974), *Le même et l'autre dans la structure ontologique du Timée de Platon* (Paris).

—— (1987), 'Proclus et l'Orphisme', in J. Pépin and H.-D. Saffrey (eds.), *Proclus lecteur et interprète des anciens* (Paris), 43–104.

—— (2000), 'La place des oracles chaldaïques dans la théologie platonicienne', in Segonds and Steel (2000: 109–62).

—— et al. (1982–92), *Porphyre: La vie de Plotin*, 2 vols. (Paris).

BRISSON, L. and SEGONDS, A. (1996), *Jamblique Vie de Pythagore* (Paris). (trans.)

BRÖCKER, W. (1966), *Platonismus ohne Sokrates* (Frankfurt).

BROWN, P. (1978), *The Philosopher and Society in Late Antiquity*. Center for Hermeneutical Studies Colloquy (Berkeley).

BROWNING, R. (1976), *The Emperor Julian* (Berkeley).

BRUNNER, F. (1992), 'L'idée de Kairos chez Proclus', *Méthexis* (*Mélanges E. Moutsopoulos*) (Athens), 173–81 = Brunner (1997: Essay XXI).

—— (1993), 'De l'action humaine selon Proclus (*De providentia* VI)', in Y. Gauthier (ed.), *Le dialogue humaniste* (*Mélanges V. Cauchy*) (Montréal), 3–11 = Brunner (1997: Essay XXII).

—— (1997), *Métaphysique d'Ibn Gabirol et de la tradition platonicienne* (Aldershot).

BRUNT, P. (1993), *Studies in Greek History and Thought* (Oxford).

BURNYEAT, M. (1999), 'Culture and Society in Plato's *Republic*', *The Tanner Lectures on Human Values* 20: 215–324.

—— (2000), 'Utopia and Fantasy: the Practicability of Plato's Ideally Just City', in Fine (2000: 779–90).

BURKERT, W. (1987), *Ancient Mystery Cults* (Cambridge, Mass).

BUTTERWORTH, C. (1992) (ed.), *The Political Aspects of Islamic Philosophy. Essays in Honor of Muhsin S. Mahdi* (Cambridge, Mass.).

CALDERONE, S. (1973), 'Teologia politica, successione dinastica e consecratio in età costantina', *Le culte des souverains dans l'empire romain* (Entretiens Hardt 19, Vandœuvres-Genève), 213–61.

CAMERON, A. (1969–70), 'Agathias on the Sassanians', *Dumbarton Oaks Papers* 23–4: 69–183.

—— (1985), *Procopius and the Sixth Century* (London).

CAMERON, A. and LONG, J. (1993), *Barbarians and Politics at the Court of Arcadius* (Berkeley).

CAMERON, A. and HALL, G. (1999), *Eusebius* Life of Constantine. *Introduction, Translation and Commentary* (Oxford).

CANDAU MORÓN, J. (1986), 'La filosophia politica de Juliano', *Habis* 17: 87–96.

CHESTNUT, G. (1979), 'The Ruler and the Logos in Neopythagorean, Middle Platonic and Later Stoic Political Philosophy', *ANRW* II, 16.2: 1310–33.

CHUVIN, P. (1990), *Chronique des derniers païens* (Paris). [Engl. trans. (chs. I–X), *A Chronicle of the last Pagans* (Cambridge, Mass., 1990).]

CLARK, G. (1989), *Iamblichus: On the Pythagorean Life* (Liverpool). (trans.)

CLARKE, E. (1998), 'Communication, Human and Divine: Saloustious Reconsidered', *Phronesis* 43: 326–50.

——— (2001), *Iamblichus' De mysteriis. A Manifesto of the Miraculous* (Aldershot).

CLEARY, J. (1999) (ed.), *Traditions of Platonism. Essays in Honour of John Dillon* (Aldershot).

COLPI, B. (1987), *Die παιδεία des Themistios* (Berne).

CRANZ, F. E. (1950), '*De Civitate Dei*, XV,2, and Augustine's Idea of the Christian Society', *Speculum* 25: 215–25.

——— (1952), 'Kingdom and Polity in Eusebius of Caesarea', *Harvard Theological Review* 45: 47–56.

——— (1954), 'The Development of Augustine's Ideas on Society before the Donatist Controversy', *Harvard Theological Review* 47: 255–316.

DAGRON, G. (1968), 'L'Empire romain d'Orient au IVe siècle et les traditions politiques de l'hellénisme. Le témoignage de Thémistios', *Travaux et Mémoires* 3: 1–242.

——— (1996), *Empereur et prêtre. Etude sur le «Césaropapisme» byzantin* (Paris).

DAIBER, H. (1995), *Neuplatonische Pythagorica in arabischem Gewande. Der Kommentar des Iamblichus zu den Carmina Aurea* (Amsterdam).

DAWSON, D. (1992), *Cities of the Gods: Communist Utopias in Greek Thought* (New York).

DELATTE, A. (1915), *Etudes sur la littérature pythagoricienne* (Paris).

——— (1922), *Essai sur la politique pythagoricienne* (Liège).

DELATTE, L. M. (1942), *Les Traités de la Royauté d'Ecphante, Diotogène et Sthénidas* (Liège).

DES PLACES, E. (1966), *Jamblique: Les mystères d'Egypte* (Paris). (trans.).

——— (1981), *Etudes platoniciennes 1929–1979* (Leiden).

——— (1989), *Jamblique Protreptique* (Paris). (trans.)

DILLON, J. (1973), *Iamblichi Chalcidensis in Platonis dialogos commentariorum fragmenta* (Leiden).

——— (1983), 'Plotinus, Philo and Origen on the Grades of Virtue', in H.-D. Blume and F. Mann (eds.), *Platonismus und Christentum (Festschrift H. Dörrie)* (Münster), 92–105 = Dillon (1990: essay XVI).

——— (1990), *The Golden Chain. Studies in the Development of Platonism and Christianity* (Aldershot).

——— (1993), *Alcinous: The Handbook of Platonism* (Oxford). (trans.)

——— (1995), 'The Neoplatonic Exegesis of the *Statesman* Myth', in Rowe (1995: 364–74).

——— (1996), 'An Ethic for the Late Antique Sage', in L. Gerson (ed.), *The Cambridge Companion to Plotinus* (Cambridge), 315–35.

——— (2000), 'The Role of the Demiurge in the *Platonic Theology*', in Segonds and Steel (2000: 339–49).

Bibliography

DILLON, J. (2001), 'The Neoplatonic Reception of Plato's *Laws*', in Lisi (2001: 243–54).

DODDS, E. R. (1959), *Plato Gorgias* (Oxford).

DÖRRIE, H. and BALTES, M. (1993–6), *Der Platonismus in der Antike*, iii–iv (Stuttgart).

DRAKE, H. (1976), *In Praise of Constantine: A Historical Study and New Translation of Eusebius' Tricennial Orations* (Berkeley).

DRUART, T.-A. (1993), 'Al-Kindi's Ethics', *Review of Metaphysics* 47: 329–57.

DUBY, G. (1980), *The Three Orders: Feudal Society Imagined* (Chicago).

DUVAL, Y.-M. (1966), 'L'éloge de Théodose dans la *Cité de Dieu* (II, 26,1)', *Recherches augustiniennes* 4: 135–79.

DVORNIK, F. (1955), 'The Emperor Julian's Reactionary Ideas on Kingship', in K. Weitzmann (ed.), *Late Classical and Medieval Studies in Honor of A.M. Friend* (Princeton, 71–81).

—— (1966), *Early Christian and Byzantine Political Philosophy. Origins and Background* (Washington, D.C.).

DZIELSKA, M. (1995), *Hypatia of Alexandria* (Cambridge, Mass.).

EDWARDS, M. (1994), 'Plotinus and the Emperors', *Symbolae Osloenses* 69: 137–47.

—— (2000), *Neoplatonic Saints. The Lives of Plotinus and Proclus by their Students* (Liverpool). (trans.)

EHRHARDT, A. (1953), 'The Political Philosophy of Neo-Platonism', *Mélanges V. Arangio-Ruiz* (Naples), i. 457–82.

—— (1959), *Politische Metaphysik von Solon bis Augustin* (Tübingen).

ENDRESS, G. (1987), 'Die wissenschaftliche Literatur', in H. Gätze (ed.), *Grundriss der arabischen Philologie II* (Wiesbaden), 400–506.

—— (1992), 'Die wissenschaftliche Literatur', in W. Fischer (ed.), *Grundriss der arabischen Philologie III*, Supplement (Wiesbaden), 3–152.

ESSER, H. (1967), *Untersuchungen zu Gebet und Gottesverehrung der Neuplatoniker* (Diss. Cologne).

FARINA, R. (1966), *L'Impero e l'Imperatore cristiano in Eusebio di Cesarea* (Zurich).

FESTUGIÈRE, A. J. (1966), 'Proclus et la religion traditionnelle', *Mélanges André Piganiol* (Paris, 1581–1590) = Festugière (1971: 575–84).

—— (1966–8), *Proclus Commentaire sur le Timée* (Paris). (trans.)

—— (1969), 'L'ordre de lecture des dialogues de Platon aux V/VIe siècles', *Museum Helveticum* 26, 281–96 = Festugière (1971: 535–50).

—— (1970) *Proclus Commentaire sur la République* (Paris). (trans.)

—— (1971), *Etudes de philosophie grecque* (Paris).

FINAMORE, J. (1985), *Iamblichus and the Theory of the Vehicle of the Soul* (Chico, Calif.).

FINE, G. (2000) (ed.), *Plato* (Oxford).

FLAMANT, J. (1977), *Macrobe et le néoplatonisme latin, à la fin du IVe siècle* (Leiden).

FLINTERMAN, J. (1995), *Power, Paideia and Pythagoreanism. Greek Identity, Conceptions of the Relationship between Philosophers and Monarchs and Political Ideas in Philostratus' Life of Apollonius* (Amsterdam).

FÖLLINGER, S. (1996), *Differenz und Gleichheit. Das Geschlechterverhältnis in der Sicht griechischer Philosophen des 4. bis 1. Jahrhunderts v. Chr.* (Stuttgart).

FOLLIET, G. (1962), '"Deificari in otio." Augustin, *Epistula* 10,2', *Recherches augustiniennes* 2: 225–36.

FOWDEN, G. (1979), 'Pagan Philosophers in Late Antique Society, with Special Reference to Iamblichus and his Followers' (Oxford, unpublished D.Phil. thesis).

—— (1982), 'The Pagan Holy Man in Late Antique Society', *Journal of Hellenic Studies* 102: 33–59.

FREND, W. (1989), 'Pythagoreanism and Hermetism in Augustine's "Hidden Years"', *Studia Patristica* 22, 251–60.

FROHNE, R. (1985), *Agapetus Diaconus: Untersuchungen* (St Gallen).

FUHRER, T. (1997), 'Die Platoniker und die *civitas dei* (Buch VIII–X)', in Horn (1997: 87–108).

FUHRER, T. and ERLER, M. (1999) (eds.), *Zur Rezeption der hellenistischen Philosophie in der Spätantike* (Stuttgart).

GALSTON, M. (1990), *Politics and Excellence. The Political Philosophy of Alfarabi* (Princeton).

GHORAB, A. (1972), 'The Greek Commentators on Aristotle quoted in Al-'Amirī's "As-Sa'āda wa'l-Is'ād"', in S. Stern et al. (eds.), *Islamic Philosophy and the Classical Tradition (Festschrift R. Walzer)* (Oxford), 77–88.

GLUCKER, J. (1978), *Antiochus and the Late Academy* (Göttingen).

GOLTZ, H. (1970), *HIERA MESITEIA. Zur Theorie der hierarchischen Sozietät im Corpus areopagiticum* (Erlangen).

GOODENOUGH, E. (1928), 'The Political Philosophy of Hellenistic Kingship', *Yale Classical Studies* 1: 55–102.

GOULET-CAZÉ, M.-O. (1982), 'L'Arrière-plan scolaire de la *Vie de Plotin*', in Brisson et al. (1982–92: i. 231–327).

GRIFFIN, M. and BARNES, J. (1989) (eds.), *Philosophia Togata I. Essays on Philosophy and Roman Society* (Oxford).

GRUBE, G. M. A. (1974), *Plato: The Republic* (Indianapolis). (trans.)

GULDENTOPS, G. (2001a), 'La science suprême selon Thémistius', *Revue de philosophie ancienne* 19: 99–120.

—— (2001b), 'Themistios' καλλίπολις between Myth and Reality', in K. Demoen (ed.), *The Greek City from Antiquity to the Present* (Louvain), 127–40.

GUTAS, D. (1998), *Greek Thought, Arabic Culture. The Graeco-Arabic Translation Movement in Bagdad and Early 'Abbāsid Society (2nd–4th / 8th–10th Centuries)* (London and New York).

HADOT, I. (1978), *Le Problème du néoplatonisme alexandrin. Hiérocles et Simplicius* (Paris).

—— (1984), *Arts libéraux et philosophie dans la pensée antique* (Paris).

—— (1987), 'La vie et l'œuvre de Simplicius d'après des sources grecques et arabes', in I. Hadot (ed.), *Simplicius sa vie, son œuvre, sa survie* (Berlin), 3–39.

HADOT, I. et al. (1990), *Simplicius commentaire sur les catégories*, fasc. i, iii; Leiden.

Bibliography

HADOT, P. (1972), 'Fürstenspiegel', *Reallexikon für Antike und Christentum* 8: 555–632.

—— (1979), 'Les Divisions des parties de la philosophie dans l'antiquité', *Museum Helveticum* 36, 201–23 = P. Hadot, *Etudes de philosophie ancienne* (Paris, 1998), ch. 8.

—— (1981), 'Ouranos, Kronos and Zeus in Plotinus' Treatise Against the Gnostics', in H. Blumenthal and R. Markus (eds.), *Neoplatonism and Early Christian Thought (Essays in Honour of A. H. Armstrong)* (London), 124–37.

—— (1987a), *Plotin Traité 38* (Paris).

—— (1987b), *Exercices spirituels et philosophie antique*, 2nd edn. (Paris).

—— (1995), *Qu'est-ce que la philosophie antique?* (Paris).

—— (1997), *Plotin ou la simplicité du regard* (Paris).

HARDER, R. (1960), *Kleine Schriften* (Munich).

HARL, K. (1990), 'Sacrifice and Pagan Belief in Fifth and Sixth Century Byzantium', *Past and Present* 128: 7–27.

HARL, M. (1984), 'Moïse figure de l'évêque dans l'éloge de Basile de Grégoire de Nysse (381). Un plaidoyer pour l'autorité épiscopale', in A. Spira (ed.), *The Biographical Works of Gregory of Nyssa* (Cambridge, Mass.), 71–119.

HARVEY, F. (1965), 'Two Kinds of Equality', *Classica et Medievalia* 262: 101–46.

HARVEY, S. (1992), 'The Place of the Philosopher in the City according to Ibn Bājjah', in Butterworth (1992: 199–233).

HATHAWAY, R. (1969a), 'The Neoplatonist Interpretation of Plato: Remarks on its Decisive Characteristics', *Journal of the History of Philosophy* 7: 19–26.

—— (1969b), *Hierarchy and the Definition of Order in the Letters of Pseudo-Dionysius* (The Hague).

HEIN, C. (1985), *Definition und Einteilung der Philosophie. Von der spätantiken Einteilungsliteratur zur arabischen Enzyklopädie* (Frankfurt, Bern, and New York).

HENRY, PAUL (1935), *Recherches sur la "Préparation Evangélique" d'Eusèbe* (Paris).

HENRY, PATRICK (1967), 'A Mirror for Justinian: The *Ekthesis* of Agapetus Diaconus', *Greek Roman and Byzantine Studies* 8: 281–308.

HOFFMANN, P. (1998), 'La fonction des prologues exégétiques dans la pensée péda-gogique néoplatonicienne', in J.-D. Dubois and B. Roussel (eds.), *Entrer en matière. Les prologues* (Paris), 209–45.

—— (2000), 'Bibliothèques et formes du livre à la fin de l'antiquité. Le témoignage de la littérature néoplatonicienne des Ve et VIe siècles', in G. Prato (ed.), *I manoscritti greci tra riflessione e dibattito* (Florence), 601–32.

—— et al. (2001), *Simplicius Commentaire sur les Catégories d'Aristote Chapitres 2–4*, Paris (continuation of I. Hadot et al. 1990).

HORN, C. (1997) (ed.), *Augustinus: De civitate dei* (Berlin).

IRWIN, T. (1979), *Plato* Gorgias (Oxford). (trans.)

JACKSON, R., LYKOS, K. and TARRANT, H. (1998), *Olympiodorus' Commentary on Plato's Gorgias* (Leiden). (trans.)

JERPHAGNON, L. (1981), 'Platonopolis ou Plotin entre le siècle et le rêve', *Cahiers de Fontenay* 19–22 (Mélanges Trouillard), 215–29.

222

KALLIGAS, P. (2001), 'Traces of Longinus' Library in Eusebius' Praeparatio Evangelica', *Classical Quarterly* 51: 584–98.

KENNEDY, G. (1983), *Greek Rhetoric under Christian Emperors* (Princeton).

KLOFT, H. (1970), *Liberalitas principis: Herkunft und Bedeutung. Studien zur Prinzipatsideologie* (Vienna).

KLOSKO, G. (1986), *The Development of Plato's Political Theory* (New York and London).

KÖHLER, F. (1983), *Hierokles Kommentar zum Pythagoreischen Goldenen Gedicht* (Stuttgart). (trans.)

KRAUT, R. (1989), *Aristotle on the Human Good* (Princeton).

KREMER, K. (1987), 'Bonum est diffusivum sui', *ANRW* II, 36.2: 994–1032.

KUTTNER, S. (1936), 'Sur les origines du terme « droit positif »', *Revue historique de droit français et étranger* 15: 728–39.

LACOMBRADE, C. (1951a), *Le Discours sur la royauté de Synésios de Cyrène à l'empereur Arcadios* (Paris).

—— (1951b), *Synésios de Cyrène. Hellène et Chrétien* (Paris).

LADNER, G. (1967), *The Idea of Reform. Its Impact on Christian Thought and Action in the Age of the Fathers*, 2nd edn. (New York).

LAKS, A. (1990), 'Legislation and Demiurgy. On the Relationship between Plato's *Republic* and *Laws*', *Classical Antiquity* 9: 209–29.

LAMBERTON, R. (1986), *Homer the Theologian. Neoplatonist Allegorical Reading and the Growth of the Epic Tradition* (Berkeley).

LANE, M. (1995), 'A New Angle on Utopia: The Political Theory of the *Statesman*', in Rowe (1995: 276–91).

—— (1998), *Method and Politics in Plato's* Statesman (Cambridge).

LARCHET, J.C. (1996), *La Divinisation de l'homme selon saint Maxime le Confesseur* (Paris).

LARSEN, B. (1972), *Jamblique de Chalcis. Exégète et philosophe* (Aarhus).

LAURAS, A. and RONDET, H. (1953), 'Le thème des deux cités dans l'œuvre de saint Augustin', *Etudes augustiniennes*: 97–160.

LERNER, R. and MAHDI, M. (1963) (eds.), *Medieval Political Philosophy* (Ithaca and New York).

LERNOULD, A. (2001), *Physique et théologie. Lecture du* Timée *de Platon par Proclus* (Villeneuve d'Ascq).

LEYS, W. (1971), 'Was Plato Non-Political?', in G. Vlastos (ed.), *Plato. A Collection of Critical Essays*, ii (Garden City, NY), 166–73.

LEWY, H. (1978), *Chaldaean Oracles and Theurgy*, New Edition by M. Tardieu (Paris).

LIESHOUT, H. VAN (1926), *La Théorie plotinienne de la vertu* (Fribourg).

LISI, F. (1985), *Einheit und Vielheit des platonischen Nomosbegriffes* (Königstein).

—— (2001) (ed.), *Plato's* Laws *and its Historical Significance* (Sankt Augustin).

LLOYD, A. (1990), *The Anatomy of Neoplatonism* (Oxford).

LONG, A. A. and SEDLEY, D. N. (1987), *The Hellenistic Philosophers* (Cambridge).

LOT-BORODINE, M. (1970), *La Déification de l'homme selon la doctrine des Pères grecs* (Paris).

LUIBHEID, C. (1987), *Pseudo-Dionysius: The Complete Works* (London). (trans.)

Bibliography

LUNA, C. (2001), Review of Thiel (1999), *Mnemosyne* 54: 482–504.

LYONS, M. C. (1960–1), 'A Greek Ethical Treatise', *Oriens* 13–14: 35–57.

MAAS, M. (1992), *John Lydus and the Roman Past. Antiquarianism and Politics in the Age of Justinian* (London).

MACKENZIE, M. M. (1981), *Plato on Punishment* (Berkeley).

MACMULLEN, R. (1990), *Changes in the Roman Empire* (Princeton).

MADEC, G. (1996), *Saint Augustin et la philosophie* (Paris).

MAHONEY, T. (1992), 'Do Plato's Philosopher-Rulers Sacrifice Self-Interest to Justice?', *Phronesis* 37: 265–82.

MAJERCIK, R. (1989), *The Chaldaean Oracles: Text, Translation, and Commentary* (Leiden).

MARAVAL, P. (1997), 'Sur un discours d'Eusèbe de Césarée (Louanges de Constantin, XI–XVIII)', *Revue des études augustiniennes* 43: 239–46.

MARKUS, R. (1970), *Saeculum: History and Society in the Theology of St. Augustine* (Cambridge).

MATTÉI, J. F. (1982), 'La généalogie du nombre nuptial chez Platon', *Les études philosophiques*: 281–303.

MERKI, H. (1952), ʽΟΜΟΙΩΣΙΣ ΘΕΩ. *Von der platonischen Angleichung an Gott zur Gottähnlichkeit bei Gregor von Nyssa* (Fribourg).

MORAUX, P. (1984), *Der Aristotelismus bei den Griechen*, ii (Berlin).

MORROW, G. R. (1960), *Plato's Cretan City. A Historical Interpretation of the Laws* (Princeton).

—— (1970), *Proclus. A Commentary on the First Book of Euclid's Elements* (Princeton; 2nd edn. 1992). (trans.)

MORROW, G. R. and DILLON, J. (1987), *Proclus' Commentary on Plato's Parmenides* (Princeton). (trans.)

NARBONNE, J.-M. (2003), 'De l'un matière à l'un forme. La réponse de Proclus à la critique aristotélicienne de l'unité du politique dans la *République* de Platon (*In Remp.* II, 361–368', in J.-M. Narbonne and A. Reckermann (eds.), *Pensées de l'Un dans la tradition métaphysique occidentale* (Festschrift W. Beierwaltes) (Paris and Montréal).

NESCHKE-HENTSCHKE, A. (1995), *Platonisme politique et théorie du droit naturel*, i (Louvain).

—— (1999a), 'La cité n'est pas à nous. "*Res publica*" et "*civitas*" dans le *XIX*ème livre du *De civitate* d'Augustin d'Hippone', in Vegetti and Abbate (1999: 219–44).

—— (1999b), 'Hierosalem caelestis pro viribus in terris expressa. Die Auslegung der platonischen Staatsentwürfe durch Marsilius Ficinus und ihre "hermeneutischen" Grundlagen', *Würzburger Jahrbücher für die Altertumswissenschaften* 23: 223–43.

—— (2000), 'Marsile Ficin lecteur des *Lois*', *Revue philosophique*: 83–102.

—— (forthcoming), *Platonisme politique et théorie du droit naturel*, ii (Louvain).

O'BRIEN, D. (1981), ' "Pondus meum amor meus" Saint Augustin et Jamblique', *Revue de l'Histoire des Religions* 198: 423–8.

O'DALY, G. (1999), *Augustine's City of God. A Reader's Guide* (Oxford).

O'MEARA, D. (1990), 'La question de l'être et du non-être des objets mathématiques chez Plotin et Jamblique', *Revue de théologie et de philosophie* 122: 405–16 = O'Meara (1998: Essay XV).

—— (1993a), *Plotinus. An Introduction to the Enneads* (Oxford).

—— (1993b), 'Aspects of Political Philosophy in Iamblichus', in H. Blumenthal and E. Clark (eds.), *The Divine Iamblichus* (Bristol), 65–73 = O'Meara (1998: Essay XVIII).

—— (1997), 'Evêques et philosophes-rois: philosophie politique néoplatonicienne chez le Pseudo-Denys', in de Andia (1997: 75–88) = O'Meara (1998: Essay XIX).

—— (1998), *The Structure of Being and the Search for the Good. Essays on Ancient and Early Medieval Platonism* (Aldershot).

—— (1999a), *Plotin Traité 51* (Paris).

—— (1999b), 'Plato's *Republic* in the School of Iamblichus', in Vegetti and Abbate (1999: 193–205).

—— (1999c), 'Neoplatonist Conceptions of the Philosopher-King', in J. Van Ophuijsen (ed.), *Plato and Platonism* (Washington, D.C.), 278–91.

—— (2001), 'Intentional Objects in Later Neoplatonism', in D. Perler (ed.), *Ancient and Medieval Theories of Intentionality* (Leiden), 115–25.

—— (2002a), 'The Justinianic Dialogue *On Political Science* and its Neoplatonic Sources', in K. Ierodiakonou (ed.), *Byzantine Philosophy and its Ancient Sources* (Oxford), 49–62.

—— (2002b), 'Religion als Abbild der Philosophie. Zum neuplatonischen Hintergrund der Lehre al-Farabis', in M. Erler and T. Kobusch (eds.), *Metaphysik und Religion. Zur Signatur des spätantiken Denkens* (Stuttgart), 343–53.

—— (2003a), 'Neoplatonic Cosmopolitanism: Some Preliminary Notes', in P. Manganaro, M. Barbanti and G. Giardina (eds.), *Henosis kai philia. Ommagio a Francesco Romano* (Naples), 289–93.

—— (2003b), 'A Neoplatonist Ethics for High-Level Officials: Sopatros' Letter to Himerios', in Smith (2003).

O'MEARA, J. (1961), *Charter of Christendom: The Significance of the City of God* (New York), = J. O'Meara, *Understanding Augustine* (Dublin, 1997), pt. ii.

OORT, J. VAN (1991), *Jerusalem and Babylon. A Study into Augustine's City of God and the Sources of his Doctrine of the Two Cities* (Leiden).

O'NEILL, W. (1965), *Proclus: Alcibiades I* (The Hague). (trans.)

OPSOMER, J. (2000), 'Proclus on Demiurgy and Procession: a Neoplatonic Reading of the *Timaeus*', in M. R. Wright (ed.), *Reason and Necessity. Essays on Plato's Timaeus* (London), 113–43.

PARMA, C. (1968), 'Plotinische Motive in Augustins Begriff der Civitas Dei', *Vigiliae Christianae* 22: 45–8.

PENELLA, R. (1990), *Greek Philosophers and Sophists in the Fourth Century A.D. Studies in Eunapius of Sardis* (Leeds).

—— (2000), *The Private Orations of Themistius* (Berkeley). (trans.)

PERTUSI, A. (1990), *Il pensiero politico bizantino* (Bologna).

PETERSON, E. (1935), *Der Monotheismus als politisches Problem. Ein Beitrag zur Geschichte der politischen Theologie im Imperium Romanum* (Leipzig).

Bibliography

PICCIONE, R. (2002). 'Encyclopédisme et *enkyklios paideia*? A propos de Jean Stobée et de l'*Anthologion*', *Philosophie antique* 2.

PIÉRART, M. (1974), *Platon et la cité grecque: théorie et réalité dans la constitution des "Lois"* (Brussels).

PINES, S. (1986), *Studies in Arabic Versions of Greek Texts and in Medieval Science (Collected Works*, ii; Jerusalem).

PLESSNER, M. (1928), *Der OIKONOMIKOΣ des Neupythagoreers 'Bryson' und sein Einfluss auf die islamische Wissenschaft* (Heidelberg).

PRAECHTER, K. (1900), 'Zum Maischen Anonymus περὶ πολιτικῆς ἐπιστήμης', *Byzantinische Zeitschrift* 9: 621–32.

RASHED, M. (2000), 'Menas, préfet du prétoire (528–9) et philosophe: une épigramme inconnue', *Elenchos* 21: 89–98.

RAWSON, E. (1989), 'Roman Rulers and the Philosophic Adviser', in Griffin and Barnes (1989: 233–57).

REVERDIN, O. (1945), *La Religion de la cité platonicienne* (Paris).

RICKEN, F. (1967), 'Die Logoslehre des Eusebios von Caesarea und der Mittelplatonismus', *Theologie und Philosophie* 42: 341–58.

—— (1978), 'Zur Rezeption der platonischen Ontologie bei Eusebios von Kaisareia, Areios und Athanasios', *Theologie und Philosophie* 53: 321–52.

RIEDWEG, C. (1987), *Mysterienterminologie bei Platon, Philon und Klemens von Alexandrien* (Berlin).

—— (1999), 'Mit Stoa und Platon gegen die Christen: philosophische Argumentationsstrukturen in Julians *Contra Galilaeos*', in Fuhrer and Erler (1999: 55–81).

RIST, J. (1962), 'Theos and the One in some Texts of Plotinus', *Medieval Studies* 24: 169–80.

—— (1964), *Eros and Psyche. Studies in Plato, Plotinus and Origen* (Toronto).

ROLOFF, D. (1970), *Gottähnlichkeit, Vergöttlichung und Erhöhung zu seligen Leben. Untersuchung zur Herkunft der platonischen Angleichung an Gott* (Berlin).

ROMILLY, J. DE (1971), *La Loi dans la pensée grecque des origines à Aristote* (Paris).

—— (1972), 'Les différents aspects de la concorde dans l'œuvre de Platon', *Revue de Philologie* 46: 7–20.

—— (1979), *La Douceur dans la pensée grecque* (Paris).

ROQUES, R. (1954), *L'Univers dionysien. Structure hiérarchique du monde selon le Pseudo-Denys* (Paris).

—— (1962), *Structures théologiques. De la gnose à Richard de Saint-Victor*, Paris.

ROQUES, R., HEIL, G., and DE GANDILLAC, M. (1970), *Denys l'Aréopagite. La hiérarchie céleste* (Paris).

ROREM, P. and LAMOREAUX, J. (1998), *John of Scythopolis and the Dionysian Corpus* (Oxford).

ROUCHE, M. (1996), *Clovis* (Paris).

ROWE, C. (1995) (ed.), *Reading the Statesman* (Sankt Augustin).

ROWE, C. and SCHOFIELD, M. (2000) (eds.), *The Cambridge History of Greek and Roman Political Thought* (Cambridge).

SAFFREY, H. (1968). 'ΑΓΕΩΜΕΤΡΗΤΟΣ ΜΗΔΕΙΣ ΕΙΣΙΤΩ. Une inscription légendaire', *Revue des études grecques* 81: 67–87 = Saffrey (1990: 251–71).

—— (1971), 'Abamon, pseudonyme de Jamblique', in R. Palmer et al. (eds.), *Philomathes. Studies and Essays in the Humanities in Memory of Philip Merlan* (The Hague), 227–39 = Saffrey (1990: 95–107).

—— (1975), 'Allusions antichrétiennes chez Proclus le diadoque platonicien', *Revue des sciences philosophiques et théologiques* 59: 553–63 = Saffrey (1990: 201–11).

—— (1984), 'Quelques aspects de la spiritualité des philosophes néoplatoniciens de Jamblique à Proclus et Damascius', *Revue des sciences philosophiques et théologiques* 68, 169–82 = Saffrey (1990: 213–26).

—— (1990), *Recherches sur le néoplatonisme après Plotin* (Paris).

—— (1992), 'Pourquoi Porphyre a-t-il édité Plotin?', in Brisson et al. (1982–92: ii, 31–57) = Saffrey (2000b: 3–26).

—— (1998), 'Le lien le plus objectif entre le pseudo-Denys et Proclus', *Roma, magistra mundi (Mélanges... L. Boyle)* (Louvain), 791–810 = Saffrey (2000b: 239–52).

—— (2000a), 'Analyse de la réponse de Jamblique à Porphyre, connue sous le titre *De mysteriis*', *Revue des sciences philosophiques et théologiques* 84: 489–511 = Saffrey (2000b: 77–99).

—— (2000b), *Le Néoplatonisme après Plotin* (Paris).

SAUNDERS, T. (1995), 'Plato on Women in the *Laws*', in A. Powell (ed.), *The Greek World* (London), 591–609.

SCHALL, J. V. (1985), 'Plotinus and Political Philosophy', *Gregorianum* 66: 687–707.

SCHIBLI, H. (2002), *Hierocles of Alexandria* (Oxford).

SCHISSEL VON FLESCHENBERG, O. (1928), *Marinos von Neapolis und die neuplatonischen Tugendgrade* (Athens).

SCHOFIELD, M. (1991), *The Stoic Idea of the City* (Cambridge).

—— (1999), *Saving the City. Philosopher-Kings and Other Classical Paradigms* (London).

SCHÖPSDAU, K. (1991), 'Der Staatsentwurf der Nomoi zwischen Ideal und Wirklichkeit. Zu Plato leg. 739a 1–e 7 und 745 e 7–746 d 2', *Rheinisches Museum* 134: 136–52.

SCHULTE, J. M. (2001), *Speculum Regis. Studien zur Fürstenspiegel-Literatur in der griechisch-römischen Antike* (Münster).

SEDLEY, D. (2000), 'The Ideal of Godlikeness', in Fine (2000: 791–810).

SEGONDS, A. (1985), *Proclus sur le premier Alcibiade de Platon* (Paris). (trans.)

SEGONDS, A. and STEEL, C. (2000) (eds.), *Proclus et la théologie platonicienne* (Leuven and Paris).

ŠEVČENKO, I. (1978), 'Agapetus East and West', *Revue des Etudes Sud-Est Européennes* 16: 3–44 = I. Ševčenko, *Ideology, Letters and Culture in the Byzantine World* (London, 1982), essay III.

SHAW, G. (1993), 'The Geometry of Grace: A Pythagorean Approach to Theurgy', in H. Blumenthal and E. Clark (eds.), *The Divine Iamblichus* (Bristol), 116–37.

—— (1995), *Theurgy and the Soul. The Neoplatonism of Iamblichus* (University Park, Pa.).

Bibliography

SHEPPARD, A. (1980), *Studies on the 5th and 6th Essays of Proclus' Commentary on the Republic* (Göttingen).

SILVESTRE, M. L. (1996), 'Forme di governo e proporzioni matematiche: Severino Boezio e la ricerca dell'*Aequum ius*', *Elenchos* 17: 95–109.

SINCLAIR, T. (1951), *A History of Greek Political Thought* (London).

SIORVANES, L. (1996), *Proclus* (Edinburgh).

SMITH, A. (1974), *Porphyry's Place in the Neoplatonic Tradition* (The Hague).

—— (2003) (ed.), *The Philosopher and Society in Late Antiquity* (Bristol).

SMITH, R. (1995), *Julian's Gods* (London).

SORABJI, R. (1990) (ed.), *Aristotle Transformed* (London).

SPICQ, C. (1958), 'La philanthropie hellénistique, vertu divine et royale', *Studia Theologica* (Lund) 12: 169–91.

SQUILLONI, A. (1991), *Il concetto di 'regno' nel pensiero dello ps. Ecfanto. Le fonti e i trattati ΠΕΡΙ ΒΑΣΙΛΕΙΑΣ* (Florence).

STAAB, G. (2002), *Pythagoras in der Spätantike. Studien zu De Vita Pythagorica des Iamblichos von Chalkis* (Munich and Leipzig).

STALLEY, R. (1983), *An Introduction to Plato's Laws* (Indianapolis).

—— (1995), 'The Unity of the State: Plato, Aristotle and Proclus', *Polis* (Newsletter of the Society for the Study of Greek Political Thought) 14: 129–49.

—— (1999), 'Plato and Aristotle on Political Unity', in Vegetti and Abbate (1999: 29–48).

STEEL, C. (1978), *The Changing Self. A Study on the Soul in Later Neoplatonism: Iamblichus, Damascius and Priscianus* (Brussels).

—— (1997), 'Denys et Proclus: de l'existence du mal', in de Andia (1997: 89–116).

STEINMETZ, P. (1969) (ed.), *Politeia und Res publica* (Wiesbaden).

STRAUB, J. (1939), *Vom Herrscherideal in der Spätantike* (Stuttgart).

TAORMINA, D. (1999), *Jamblique critique de Plotin et de Porphyre* (Paris).

TARRANT, H. (1999), 'The *Gorgias* and the Demiurge', in Cleary (1999), 369–73.

TAYLOR, A. E. (1934), *The Laws of Plato* (London). (trans.)

THEILER, W. (1929), Review of Schissel (1928), *Gnomon* 5: 307–17.

—— (1960), 'Plotin zwischen Platon und Stoa', *Les Sources de Plotin* (Entretiens sur l'antiquité classique V; Vandœvres-Geneva), 63–103.

THÉRIAULT, G. (1996), *Le Culte d'homonoia dans les cités greques* (Lyons and Québec).

THESLEFF, H. (1961), *An Introduction to the Pythagorean Writings of the Hellenistic Period* (Åbo).

THIEL, R. (1999), *Simplikios und das Ende der neuplatonischen Schule in Athen* (Stuttgart).

TRAMPEDACH, K. (1994), *Platon, die Akademie und die zeitgenössische Politik* (Stuttgart).

TRÉDÉ, M. (1992), *Kairos. L'à-propos et l'occasion (le mot et la notion, d'Homère à la fin du IVe siècle avant J.-C.)* (Paris).

TREDENNICK, H. (1954), *Plato. The Last Days of Socrates. Euthyphro, The Apology, Crito, Phaedo* (Harmondsworth). (trans.)

TROMBLEY, F. (1993–4), *Hellenic Religion and Christianization c. 370–529*, 2 vols. (Leiden).

VALDENBERG, V. (1925), 'Les idées politiques dans les fragments attribués à Pierre le Patrice', *Byzantion* 2: 55–76.

VAN DEN BERG, B. (1999), 'Plotinus' Attitude to Traditional Cult: A Note on Porphyry VP c. 10', *Ancient Philosophy* 19: 345–60.

—— (2001), *Proclus' Hymns. Essays, Translation, Commentary* (Leiden).

—— (2003), 'Live Unnoticed! The Invisible Neoplatonic Politician', in Smith (2003).

VANDERSPOEL, J. (1995), *Themistius and the Imperial Court* (Ann Arbor).

VAN LIEFFERINGE, C. (1999), *La Théurgie. Des* Oracles Chaldaïques *à Proclus* (Liège).

VATAI, F. (1984), *Intellectuals in Politics in the Greek World. From Early Times to the Hellenistic Age* (London).

VEGETTI, M. (1999), 'L'autocritica di Platone: il *Timeo* e le *Leggi*', in Vegetti and Abbate (1999: 13–27).

VEGETTI, M. and ABBATE, M. (1999) (eds.), *La Repubblica di Platone nella tradizione antica* (Naples).

VORWERK, M. (2001), 'Plato on Virtue: Definitions of ΣΩΦΡΟΣΥΝΗ in Plato's *Charmides* and in Plotinus *Enneads* 1. 2 (19)', *American Journal of Philology* 122: 29–47.

WALZ, C. (1832–6), *Rhetores graeci*, 9 vols. (Stuttgart).

WENGER, A. (1957), 'Denys l'Aréopagite: en orient', *Dictionnaire de spiritualité*, iii (Paris), 304–9.

WESTERINK, L. G. (1981), 'The Title of Plato's *Republic*', *Illinois Classical Studies* 6: 112–15.

—— (1987), 'Proclus commentateur des *Vers d'Or*', in G. Boss and G. Seel (eds.), *Proclus et son influence* (Zurich), 61–78.

—— (1990), 'The Alexandrian Commentators and the Introduction to their Commentaries', in Sorabji (1990: 325–48).

WILHELM, F. (1917–18), 'Der Regentenspiegel des Sopatros', *Rheinisches Museum* 72: 374–402.

—— (1930), 'Zu Iamblichs Brief an Sopatros περὶ παίδων ἀγωγῆς', *Philologische Wochenzeitschrift*: 427–31.

WOODHOUSE, C. (1986), *George Gemistos Plethon* (Oxford).

ZINTZEN, C. (1969), 'Römisches und Neuplatonisches bei Macrobius (Bemerkungen zur πολιτικὴ ἀρετή im *Comm. in Somn. Scip.* I 8)', in Steinmetz (1969: 357–76).

Index of Names and Subjects

(Biographical references are included here for philosophers listed in the Index of Passages)

Index of Passages

Index of Passages

Printed in the United Kingdom
by Lightning Source UK Ltd.
106319UKS00001BB/190-213